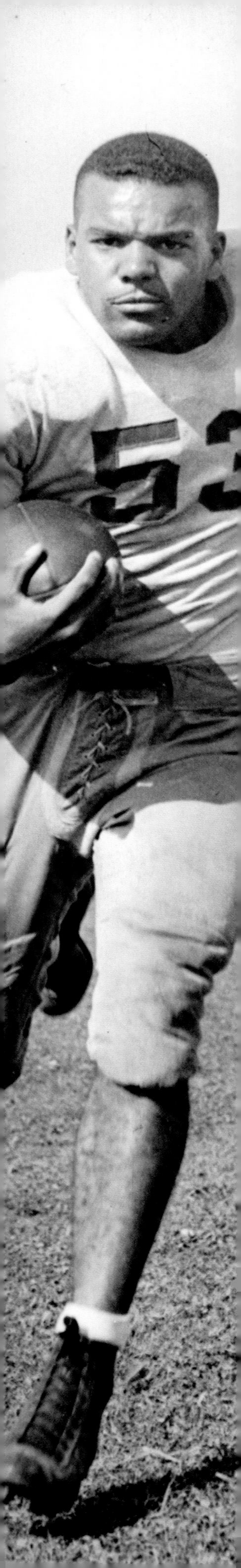

MICHAEL J. PELLOWSKI

RUTGERS FOOTBALL

A GRIDIRON TRADITION IN SCARLET

RIVERGATE BOOKS AN IMPRINT OF RUTGERS UNIVERSITY PRESS
NEW BRUNSWICK, NEW JERSEY

Visit our Web site: http://rutgerspress.rutgers.edu

Library of Congress Cataloging-in-Publication Data
Pellowski, Michael.
Rutgers football : a gridiron tradition in scarlet / Michael J. Pellowski.
p. cm.
Includes bibliographical references and index.
ISBN 978-0-8135-4283-6 (hardcover : alk. paper)
1. Rutgers University—Football—History. I. Title.
GV958.R87P45 2008
796.332'630974942—dc22 2007022096

A British Cataloging-in-Publication record for this book is available from the British Library.

Detail images:
Page ii: Henry Pryor starred as a return specialist and running back for Rutgers in 1948. (Courtesy Special Collections and University Archives, Rutgers University Libraries)
Page viii: Fans. (Courtesy Jim O'Connor/Rutgers Athletic Communications)
Page 250: A statue of an early Rutgers football player stands along the Scarlet Walk, the path players and coaches take into Rutgers Stadium before a game. (Courtesy Melanie J. Pellowski)
Page 263: Rutgers Stadium. (Courtesy Melanie J. Pellowski)

Production coordinator: Alison Hack
Edited by Nick Allison
Proofread by Barbara McGill
Designed by Jeff Wincapaw
Color separations by iocolor, Seattle
Produced by Marquand Books, Inc., Seattle
www.marquand.com
Printed in Canada by Friesens

To my oldest son, Morgan J. Pellowski, Rutgers College Class of 1995.
Only a fatal accident could deny you the degree you worked so hard to earn.

PART ONE : 1869–1949

PART TWO : 1950–1972

PART THREE : 1973–2000

PART FOUR : 2001–2006

CONTENTS

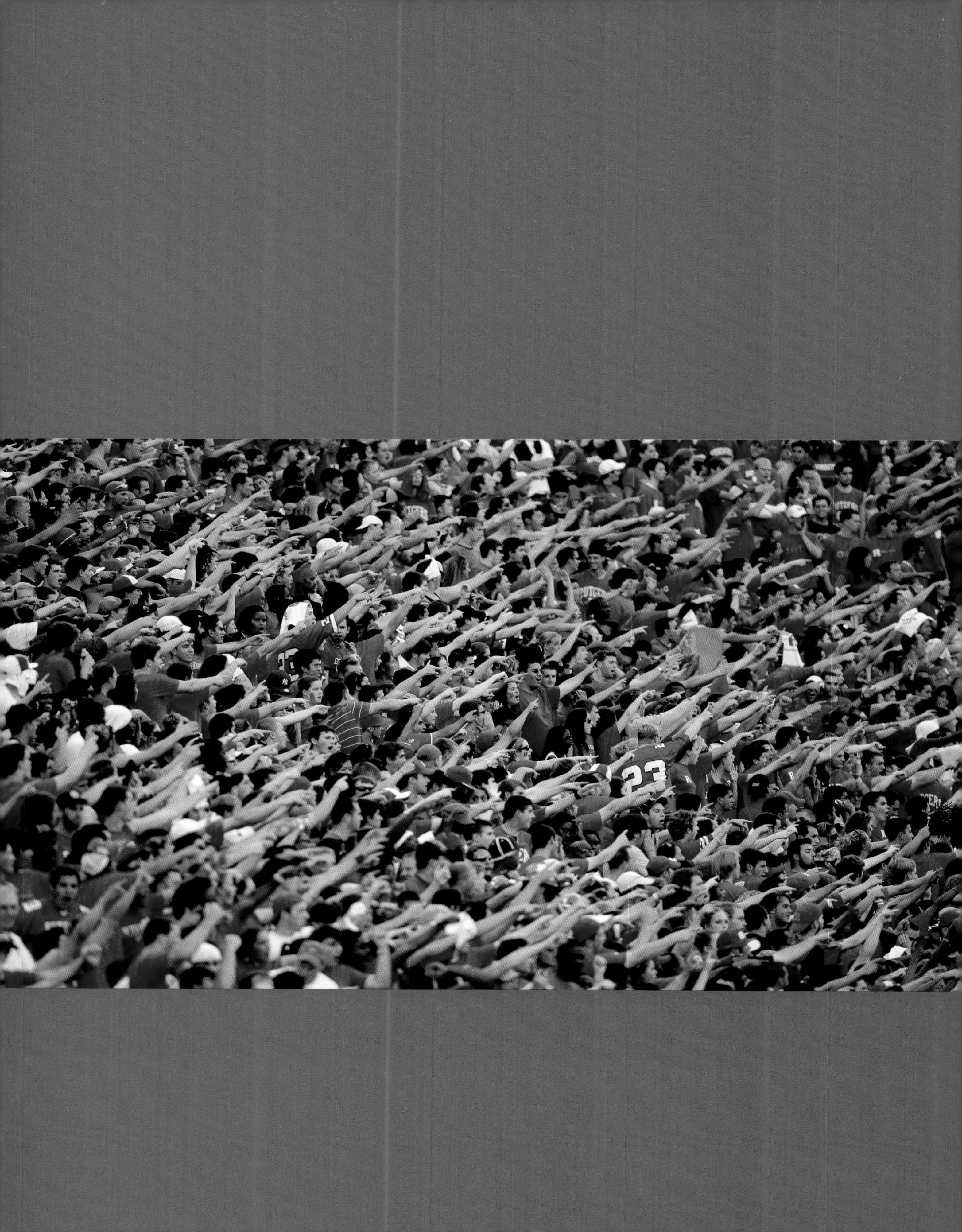
23

ACKNOWLEDGMENTS

My special thanks and appreciation to the following individuals, schools, teams, and organizations that helped make this book possible:

Richard L. McCormick, president, Rutgers University; Robert Mulcahy, director of athletics, Rutgers; Kevin MacConnell, Rutgers deputy director of athletics; Dan Levy, Rutgers Sports Media Archives; Greg Schiano, Rutgers head football coach; Tom Frusciano, Rutgers archivist; Erika Gorder, Rutgers archivist; Terry Beachem, associate director of athletics; Larry Pitt, "Mr. Rutgers"; John Wooding; Doug Kokoski; Tony Oliva; Kathleen Conlin; Pat English; Beth Kressel; Judy Snyder Pellowski; Lee Schneider, dean of students, Cook College; Tim Pernetti, CSTV; Rich Policastro; Bert Kosup; Dwight Lipscomb; Paul Krasnavage; Frank Zukas; Larry Christoff; John Callaghan; Martin Pellowski; Melanie J. Pellowski; Matt Pellowski; Dave Rinehimer; Gary Gibson; Rutgers Football Letterwinners Association; Tim Odell; David Palumbo; Matt Allison; John Miller; Mike Yancheff; Chris Evans; Mike Stephans; Pierce Frauenheim; Matt Bolger; Al Sabo; Andy "Abe" Sivess; Brian "By" O'Hearn; Andy Malekoff; John Cummins; Tosh Hosoda; Clem Udovich; Larry Clymer; Kennan Startzell; Alex and Michelle Falcinelli; Jeremy Ito; Kevin Beattie, Rensselaer Polytechnic Institute; Greg Knowlden, Lafayette College Archives; Mark Langill and Amy Summers and the Los Angeles Dodgers; Scott Ellis and the Miami Dolphins; Lawrence Fan, San Jose State University sports information director; Matt Heidt, Buffalo Bills; Mike Stagnitta, Lehigh University Athletics; Katie Lewis, San Francisco 49ers; Pam Humphrey, Indianapolis Colts; Jancy Briles, Dallas Cowboys; James D. Smith; Kent Brown, University of Illinois Athletics; Scott Strasemeir, U.S. Naval Academy; Syracuse University Athletics; John Looney, Kansas City Chiefs; the Allens, North Miami Beach, Florida; the Tampa Bay Buccaneers; the Washington Redskins; Stephen Abbott, Minnesota Vikings; Charlotte Pellowski Moeller; Carol Goodkind Chernin; Les Unger; Bob Smith; Victor's Photography; West Point Athletics Sports Media; F. J. Higgins; and . . . Morgan Pellowski.

RUTGERS
FOOTBALL

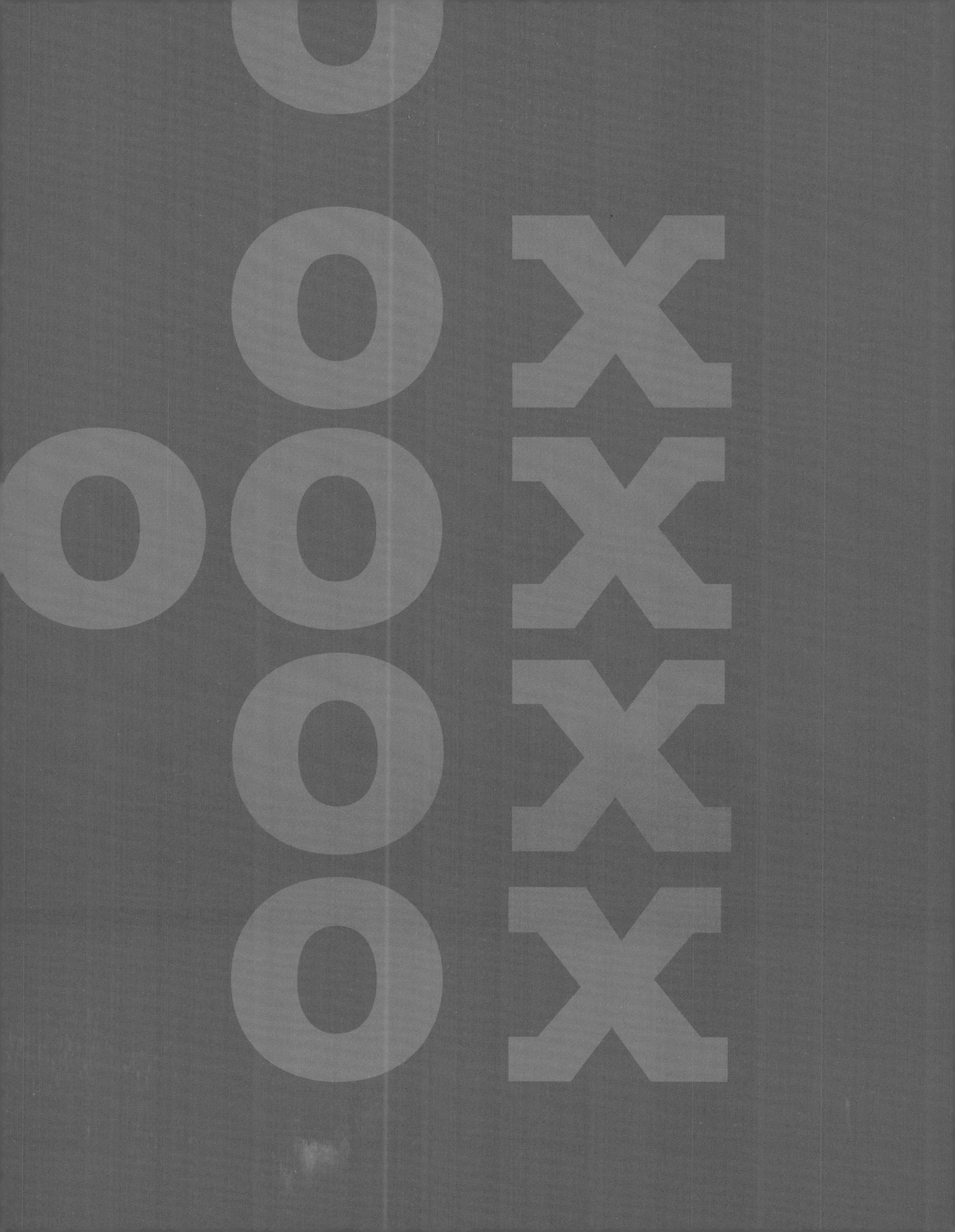

PART ONE 1869–1949

CHAPTER 1

THE BIRTH OF COLLEGE FOOTBALL 1869–1914

The year was 1869. It was ten years after abolitionist John Brown's infamous raid at Harpers Ferry in Virginia. It was four years after Confederate general Robert E. Lee surrendered to Union general Ulysses S. Grant at Appomattox Court House to end the Civil War. It was a year after the first all-professional baseball team, the Cincinnati Red Stockings, was formed. It was seven years before Custer's Last Stand and the publication of Mark Twain's most famous novel, *The Adventures of Tom Sawyer.*

Eighteen-sixty-nine is an important year in the history of sports thanks in part to Rutgers athletes. On November 6, 1869, Rutgers played Princeton in New Brunswick, New Jersey, in the first-ever college football game. So began a sports tradition that has endured for more than 135 years.

Rutgers and Princeton share credit for kick-starting the sport of college football. Kick-starting is an excellent choice of words because American football's origin can be traced to two much older sports: soccer and rugby.

A game similar to modern soccer was played by the ancient Greeks and Romans. It was also played in a variety of forms by the Japanese, the Chinese, and the Aztec Indians. In 1823 English schoolboys at Rugby School converted traditional soccer into a new, exciting sport that adopted the name of the school where it was born. According to football folklore, the sport of rugby spontaneously burst on the scene when a youngster named William Webb Ellis tired of just booting the ball. Ellis scooped up the ball and began to run with it. Angry mates wanted the ball and tried to tackle Ellis to get it back. Thusly, rugby came into being.

In 1871 a football game that combined kicking and carrying the ball sprouted up on school and college campuses in the United States. Athletes at Harvard in Boston were the first college players to experiment with rugby-style football contests. Rugby-style football soon spread to Yale, Columbia, and Princeton. The first Rutgers-Princeton college football game was more like soccer than rugby. However, that didn't make the sports confrontation any less vigorous or violent.

The historic gridiron clash between the two rival New Jersey universities took place at the site of the Old Queen's College campus, which sits on banks rising high above the

A statue of an early Rutgers football player stands along the Scarlet Walk, the path players and coaches take into Rutgers Stadium before a game. (Courtesy Melanie J. Pellowski)

Raritan River. Originally, Rutgers was known as Queen's College. It was renamed Rutgers in 1825 in honor of Colonel Henry Rutgers, a Revolutionary War hero, who served as a Queen's College trustee.

The game was played on a field where the old Rutgers gymnasium (lovingly known as the "Barn" to Rutgers alumni) is located. Even though the field is now mostly covered by an asphalt parking lot, those who pass by should realize that the dirt beneath their feet is hallowed sports ground, because it is the place where college football was born.

What prompted the first college football game to be scheduled is a matter of conjecture. It was not the brainchild of a farsighted college athletic director who envisioned the vast financial rewards generated by modern gridiron competitions. The closest thing the Rutgers Queensmen had to a gridiron mentor in the late 1860s was the Reverend Chester D. Hartranft, the pastor of a Dutch Reformed Church in New Brunswick. Reverend Hartranft was a self-confessed sportsman who enjoyed football. He convinced a group of young Rutgers athletes to pool their funds to buy a communal football to use for practice sessions (even back then, outfitting a football team was expensive). Reverend C. D. Hartranft spent many hours working out with his energetic squad of young footballers. The Queensmen had already adopted scarlet for their team color. Their university mascot was a fierce fighting bird known as "the Chanticleer." Reverend Hartranft's enthusiastic Scarlet squad included Douwe Ditmars Williamson (class of 1870), John Henry Wyckoff (class of 1871) and William James Leggett (class of 1872).

The idea of a football match against Princeton University may have been sparked by a simple, compelling motive: Revenge! Princeton had defeated Rutgers 40 to 2 in a baseball game played between the two schools on May 5, 1866. It was a bitter defeat seared in the

minds of all loyal sons of Rutgers. The newly formed Scarlet football squad decided the time for sports payback had arrived. The members of Rutgers' first football team held a meeting. The group, which counted Ezra D. Delamater (class of 1871), Charles H. Steele (class of 1872), and Abram I. Martine (class of 1873) among its ranks, voted William Leggett their captain and spokesperson. Leggett promptly composed a letter challenging athletes from Princeton to a series of three football games. The challenge was dispatched to Princeton without delay.

Coach Greg Schiano leads players down the Scarlet Walk. (Courtesy Rutgers Athletic Communications)

The base of the statue along the Scarlet Walk commemorates the first college football game, which was played across the Raritan River on the main campus of Rutgers College in New Brunswick, New Jersey. (Courtesy Melanie J. Pellowski)

Princeton's response to the Scarlet challenge was quick and decisive. The athletes from Old Nassau held their own team meeting and elected William S. Gummere (class of 1870) their captain. Gummere was an excellent choice to lead the Princeton squad. Later in life he became a New Jersey chief justice. Gummere sent a formal reply to Leggett's challenge and the date of the two schools' historic meeting on the field of play was set for November 6, 1869.

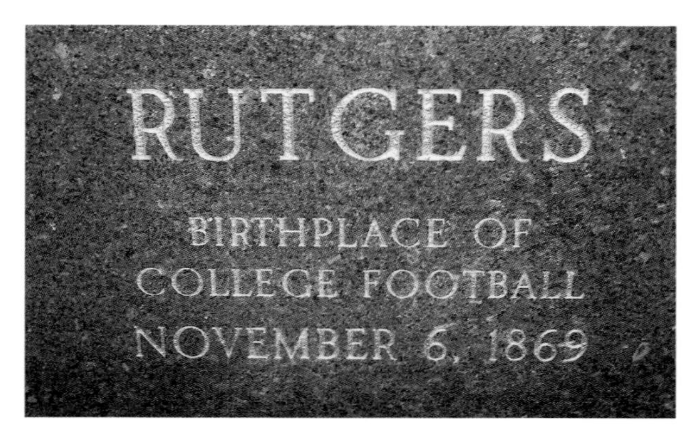

When the Princeton team arrived by train in New Brunswick on November 6, the squad was met and warmly welcomed by the entire Rutgers team. The Princeton footballers were cordially entertained by Rutgers players while the captains sat down to hammer out the rules for their game later that afternoon.

In 1869 rules for football games were not etched in stone. Sports expert Henry Chadwick had laid out a set of football rules in a dime library book published by Beadle and Company of New York in 1866. Chadwick's book outlined two sets of basic rules. One governed the "carry" (Rugby) style of football and the other was for the "kicking" (Association) style of football. Leggett and Gummere chose to play Association style football and added their own personal touches to the game-day rules. College football's first captains quickly agreed on these major points and guidelines:

Rutgers fans celebrate the Scarlet gridiron tradition. (Courtesy Rutgers Athletic Communications)

- The playing field would be 360 feet long and 225 feet wide.
- The goals would be twenty-four feet wide.
- There would be twenty-five players on the field for each team.
- There would be no tripping or holding of opposing players.
- Players would be allowed to bat the ball with their fists or hands.
- The choice of ball possession to start the game would be determined by a coin toss.
- The contest would be refereed by six officials.

Captains Leggett and Gummere also adopted rules dealing with balls kicked out of bounds and free kicks. The groundwork for the game was laid out. The teams were ready for some football. It was time to play.

There was a slight chill in the brisk autumn air as the teams gathered on the athletic field of Queen's College. Small groups of curious spectators clustered on the sidelines eagerly awaiting the kickoff. The athletes stripped off coats and jackets as they prepared for the big game. There were no uniforms, protective gear, or special shoes. However, the Rutgers athletes surprised their opponents when each Queensman donned a fiery red turban cap or a scarlet kerchief. Among those wearing the red that day were John Alfred Van Neste (class of 1872); George Hall Large, who later became a state senator (class of 1872); Claudius Rockafeller (class of 1873); and George Sidney Willits (class of 1873). Douwe Ditmars Williamson dazzled everyone when he removed his overcoat, which had until then hid a shirt as bright as his scarlet headgear. Williamson may well have been football's first showboat player.

Princeton did not yet have any set team colors. Its athletes were dressed in a wild variety of mismatched street wear and athletic gear. Princeton's famous orange and black team colors would first appear in 1876, and L. A. Smock of Princeton would design the university's first football uniforms in 1877. Even though the Princeton footballers were not color-coordinated, they came to New Brunswick ready to play football. As a reporter for the *Targum,* Rutgers' student newspaper, described them, "They were almost without exception, tall and muscular." The Rutgers team did not measure up to their opponents physically. The *Targum* article continued by giving this description of the Rutgers footballers: "The majority of our twenty-five are small and light, but possess the merit of being up to much more than they look."

Before the ball was put in play, the athletes took up set positions on the field. Two players from each team were stationed near their opponent's goal. Those players were known as "captains of the opponent's goal." They served like modern strikers in a soccer game. They hung around the opposing goal area looking for scoring opportunities. Stephen G. Gano (class of 1871) and George A. Dixon (class of 1873) filled those roles for Rutgers. Homer D. Boughner (class of 1871) and George S. Bilmeyer (class of 1871) were captains of the opponent's goal for Princeton.

Other players called "fielders" were assigned to specific areas of the field. It was their assignment to cover that area and not to leave it. The remaining players were called "bulldozers" or "bulldogs." They were free to scramble after the loose ball wherever it was kicked. One of the fiercest "bulldozers" on the field that day was Princeton's Jacob Edwin "Big Mike" Michaels (class of 1871). Michaels was a huge, rough-and-tumble guy who delighted in crashing into opposing players and knocking them to the turf. Along with Big Mike, Princeton's other secret weapon was Hughes Oliphant (class of 1870). Oliphant was a phenomenal all-around athlete.

Princeton kicked off and the historic game began. It was organized mayhem. Princeton chose to play an early form of smash-mouth football while Rutgers tried to finesse its opponent relying on speed, pinpoint passing, and accurate kicks. Reports from the *Rutgers Targum* described play as "headlong running, wild shouting and frantic kicking." Princeton's Big Mike Michaels played the part of the game's enforcer and hardest hitter. At one point during the contest, he hurled his massive bulk into Rutgers' speedy bulldozer, George Large. The two players collided near a wooden fence used as a field boundary. The players smashed through the fence and barreled into a group of shocked spectators huddled behind it. Players and fans were sent flying. George Large had the wind knocked out of him. Large quickly recovered and he and Big Mike frantically scrambled back into the fracas on the field, leaving the startled spectators sprawled in the dirt.

After a long and hotly contested battle to gain possession of the ball, Rutgers scored the first point in college football history. The ball was booted into the Princeton goal. The man who scored the first goal is not known. It has been attributed to both Stephen Gano and George Dixon. Princeton battled back to tie the score with a goal of its own. Who scored the Princeton goal was not recorded either.

As the game continued, Rutgers' smaller and faster players took control of the contest. Rutgers' Madison Ball (class of 1873) gained control of a loose ball and passed it to

In 1869 Rutgers' first football captain was William J. Leggett shown here in an 1872 photo. (Courtesy Special Collections and University Archives, Rutgers University Libraries)

George Dixon, who booted it home for a score. Rutgers jumped out to a 2-to-1 lead. Princeton battled back and their captain, William Gummere, scored to tie the contest at two goals apiece.

The Scarlet squad was unfazed. The red team took a commanding 4-to-2 lead. Again, Princeton rallied to knot the score at 4-all. The Rutgers team didn't fold under the pressure. Led by their captain, William Leggett, the Scarlet played a smart ball-control game. "Keep your kicks short and low," Leggett instructed his teammates. They did and the result was 2 more goals. Rutgers won the first game in the history of college football by the score of 6 goals to 4.

After the game, there were plenty of bruised muscles and bones, but no bruised egos. The Princeton squad was gallant in defeat and the Rutgers team was gracious in its victory. The winners treated the losers to a fine dinner before sending them on their way home.

An article in the *Rutgers Targum* summed up the outcome of the historic football contest. It stated, "Princeton had the most muscle, but didn't kick very well and wanted organization." The article hailed the Scarlet squad for its methodical approach to the game. "Their great point was their organization for which great praise is due to the Captain Leggett (Class of 1872). The right men were always in the right place."

A week later, a second football game between Princeton and Rutgers was held on November 13, 1869, in Princeton. The contest was played in a cow pasture across from the Slidell Mansion, which later became the home of President Grover Cleveland.

According to a college reporter, Princeton took full advantage of playing at home and used special hometown "rooters" stationed on the sidelines to distract and discourage the Rutgers players. The rooters loudly chanted, yelled, and shouted during the contest in support of their squad. On that day, Princeton fans may have invented a crude form of cheerleading. With a little moral support from their rooters Princeton defeated Rutgers 8 to 0 in history's hard-fought second football matchup.

The end result of the second game was a disappointment for the Scarlet twenty-five. However, once again good sportsmanship prevailed. After the game, the teams sat down together to enjoy a delicious meal supplied by the host squad. After dinner Rutgers left for New Brunswick as the Princeton players loudly cheered their opponents. It was such a touching gesture the *Rutgers Targum* reported the defeat in glowing terms. "If we must be beaten," the *Targum* stated, "we are glad to have such conquerors."

The third game between Rutgers and Princeton planned for the 1869 season never took place. Some sports encyclopedias list Princeton as college football's first national champion even though the only games on record in 1869 are two Rutgers-Princeton clashes. Both teams finished the 1869 season with 1–1 records. Princeton scored a total of 12 goals to Rutgers' 6. That is the reason Princeton is considered the first national champion. It is a title that could be debated and disputed.

Rutgers and Princeton once again butted heads on the football field in 1870. The game was played in Princeton and won by the home team 6 goals to 2 goals. Another historical sports first took place in New Brunswick that same year. The Rutgers campus was the site of the first interstate college football game. Columbia University of New York traveled to New Jersey to play the Queensmen. Rutgers defeated Columbia in that gridiron contest by the score of 6 goals to 3.

Rutgers did not play any football in 1871. However, the year was a notable one in college sports history. It was the year Harvard formed its first football squad. A year later,

Yale followed suit. Rutgers played three football games in 1872. They played Columbia twice, winning one game and tying the other. The Scarlet's lone loss was to in-state rival Princeton. In 1873 Rutgers met Yale on the football field for the first time and lost to the Elis by the score of 3 to 1. The Queensmen also beat Columbia 5 to 4 and lost to Columbia 4 to 3.

The 1874 college football season saw a drastic change in the game. Using one's feet to pass and dribble the ball were game methods of the past. Football players started to carry the ball and to run with it. Rutgers, led by its captain, Abram Martine, posted a record of 2 wins and 2 losses.

Another change in football followed in 1875. The round ball was eliminated and the first egg-shaped football came into use. It was also the year Harvard played Yale for the first time. Harvard won 4 to 0. The Rutgers Queensmen posted a 1–1–1 record that season.

The Scarlet squad continued to be part of the evolving college football scene from 1876 to 1879. Some of football's most radical changes occurred for the 1880 football season. It is the year Walter Camp, the man known as the father of football, was a player at Yale University. Camp helped revolutionize the game Rutgers and Princeton had pioneered. In 1880 a football playing field was reduced to 110 yards long by 53 yards wide. A line of scrimmage was adopted and the quarterback position was invented. Before these changes, football games were wild and unruly. The playing area was just too big and there were too many players on the field. It was mass mayhem. Bunches of eager young athletes raced all over a wide expanse in mad pursuit of an elusive ball or ball carrier.

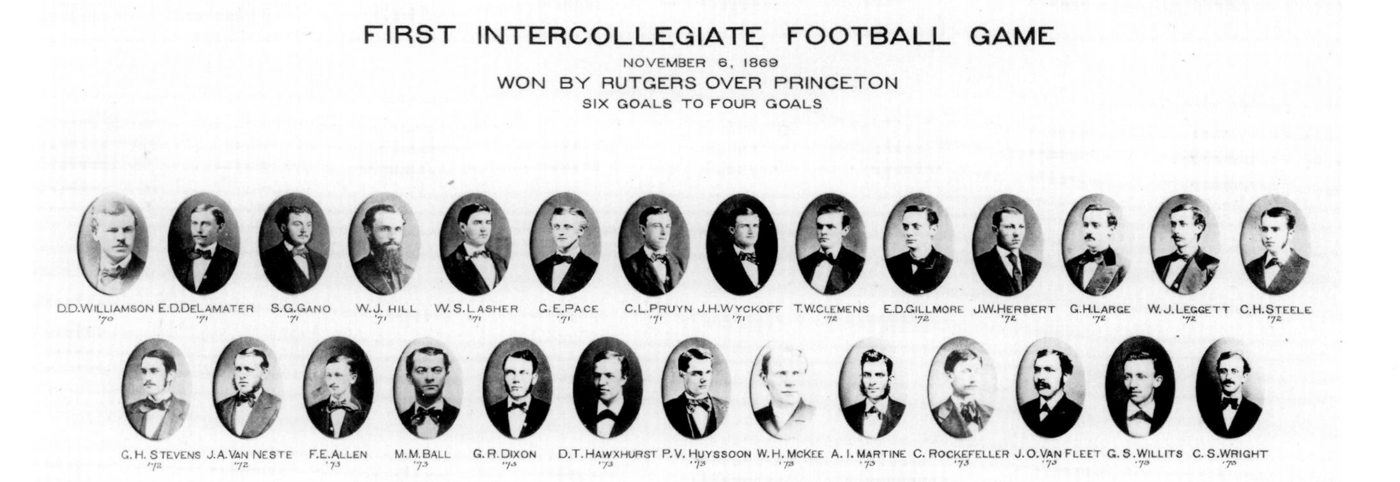

A plaque at Rutgers commemorates the first intercollegiate football game and shows the Rutgers scholar-athletes who played in that historic contest. (Courtesy Special Collections and University Archives, Rutgers University Libraries)

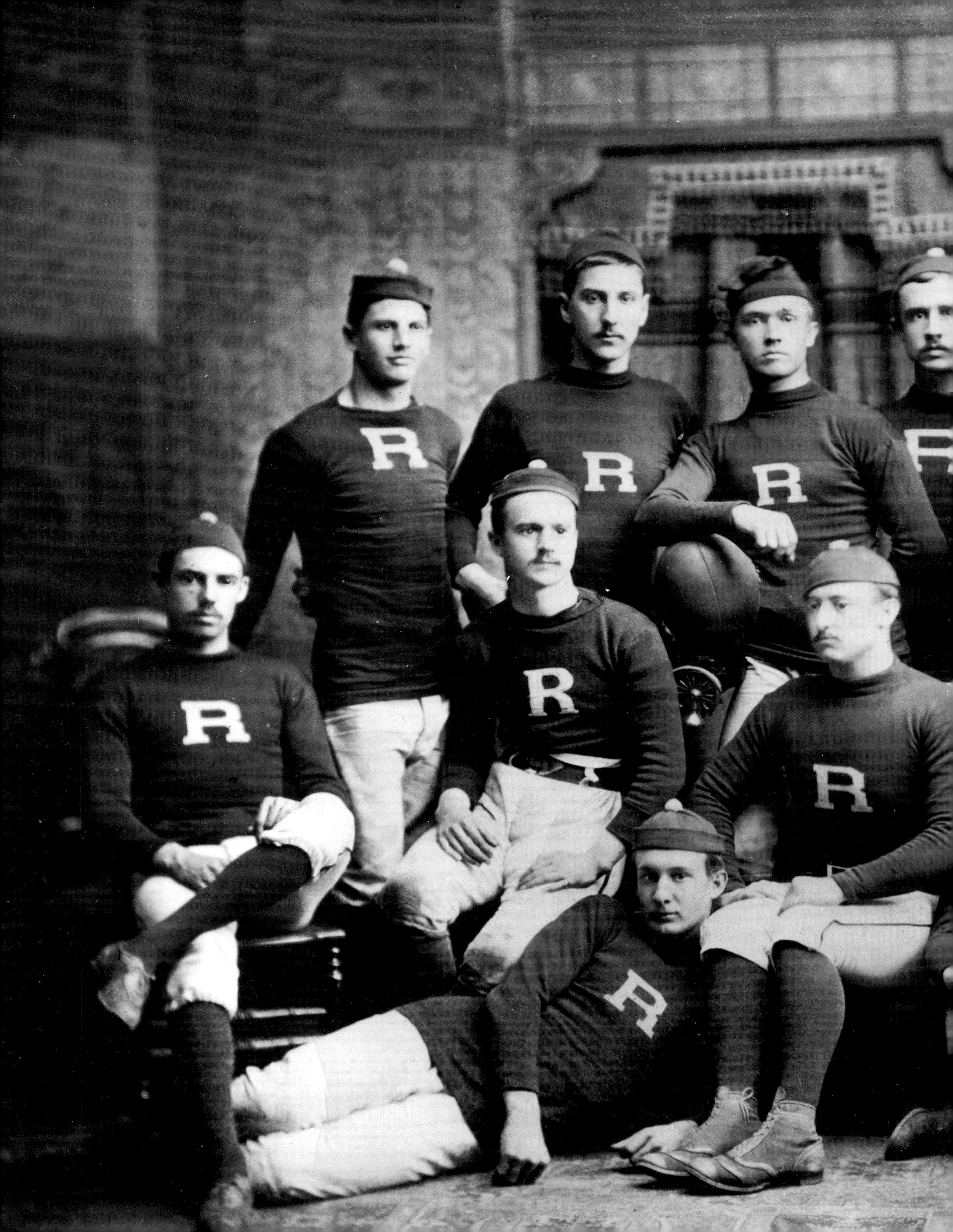

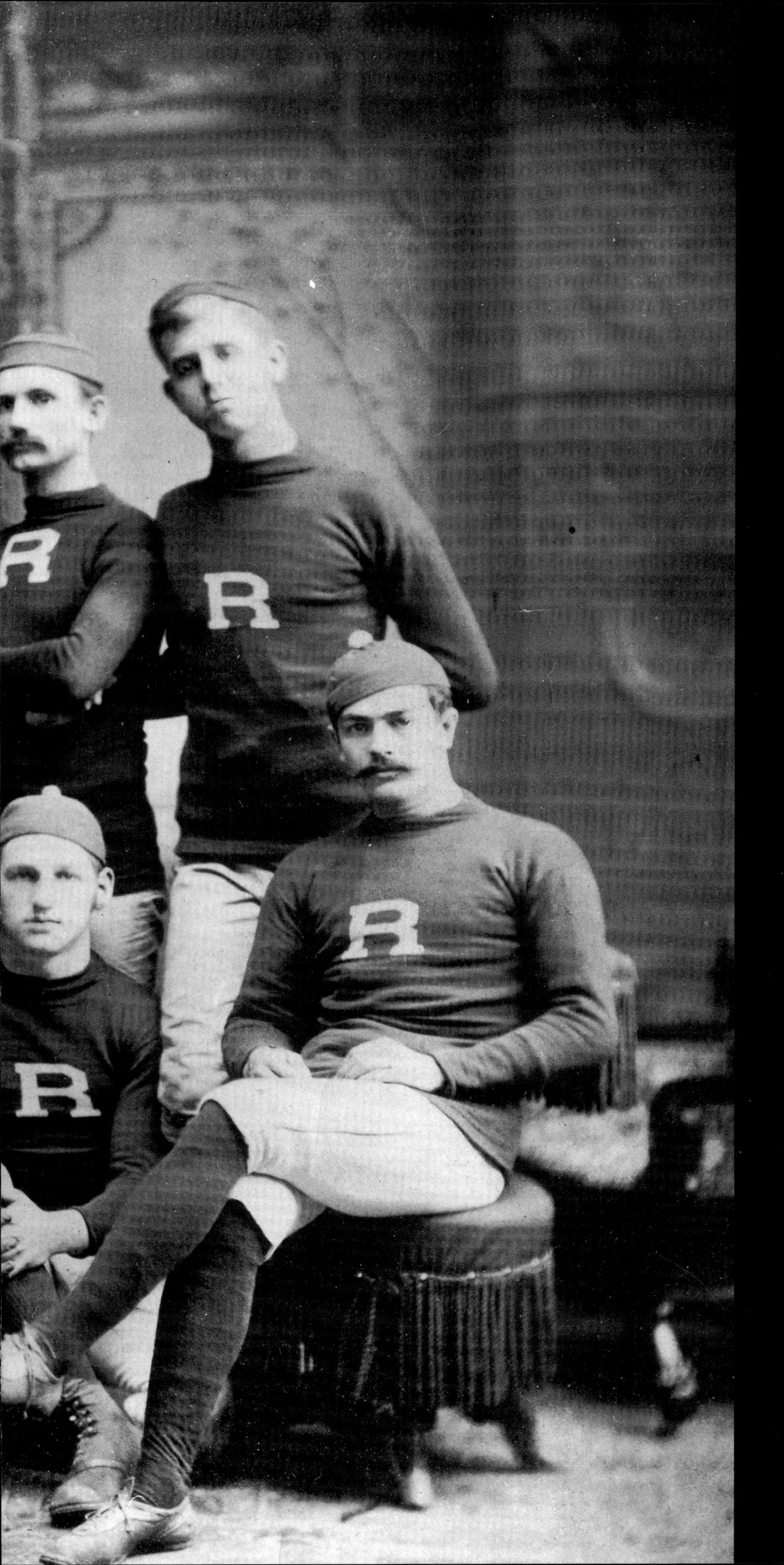

The Rutgers football squad of 1882 poses for a photo. (Courtesy Rutgers Athletic Communications)

Reducing the size of the field required teams to come up with a strategy to advance the ball and to defend their goals. Assigning positions gave each player specific tasks, functions, and responsibilities. A line of scrimmage separated teams on the field to give actual plays a chance to be successful. Football was slowly but progressively becoming a thinking man's game.

Rutgers was there as the game of football improved. In 1880, Captain Jack Morrison led his Scarlet squad to a record of 1 win and 2 losses. One of those losses was to Princeton, which ended up being declared the National Champion.

There were more positive advances in the game of football over the next two seasons. Lines were painted on football fields for the first time in 1882. Set plays and verbal signals were also used for the first time. William Chamberlain captained a Rutgers squad that posted a 6 and 4 record in 1882. Counted among the six victories was a win over Lafayette in the initial meeting between those two schools.

Football's first true scoring system came into use in 1883. For the first time a ball run over the goal line counted as a touchdown and was worth one point.

The following season, Rutgers played Lehigh in football for the first time. The Scarlet footballers lambasted Lehigh 61 to 0 and posted a season record of 3 wins and 4 losses. Eighteen eighty-four was also the year the value of a touchdown was increased to 2 points. An after-touchdown kick was worth 4 points. A field goal counted as 5 points.

The Scarlet gridiron squad suffered through some disappointing seasons from 1885 to 1887. Then, in 1888, Rutgers had the ill fortune to face one of the best teams in the history of college football. The Queensmen were defeated by a powerful Yale squad coached by Walter Camp. Yale went 13 and 0 in 1888. No team scored on Yale that season. Walter Camp's squad was led by football immortals Pa Corbin and William "Pudge" Heffelfinger. Heffelfinger later became football's first paid player. It was no disgrace for Captain Arthur J. Collier and his Rutgers teammates to lose to Yale in 1888.

The first football All-America squad was selected in 1889. It was picked by sportswriter Caspar Whitney and Walter Camp. One of America's first football All-Stars was Amos Alonzo Stagg of Yale. Stagg went on to become one of the game's great coaches and innovators. Stagg came up with the onside kick and offensive motion, which allowed backs and receivers to run parallel before the snap of the ball. He was also the first coach to use tackling dummies and blocking sleds. Another great future coach who was a top player in 1889 was John Heisman, the man for whom the Heisman Trophy is named. Heisman was a player at Brown University. Players at Rutgers were inspired by the leadership of their captain, James Bishop, as Rutgers and the University of Pennsylvania played in the first indoor night football game on January 18, 1889. It was contested in the old Madison Square Garden. Penn won the game 10 to 0.

James Bishop served as the Scarlet captain again in 1890. It was the year football's flying wedge formation became popular. The flying wedge was a dangerous formation in which offensive blockers huddled around the ball carrier in a V shape. The mass of bodies moved like a human steamroller, mashing and mangling tacklers as they tried to fight through the mob to reach the ball carrier. The flying wedge was the cause of many serious and sometimes fatal on-the-field football injuries.

Army and Navy met Rutgers on the gridiron for the first time in 1891. Rutgers, led by its captain, Phillip Brett, lost to Navy 20 to 12, but beat Army 27 to 6. Phillip Brett supposedly came up with the famous sports quote, which has endured the test of time, "I'll die for dear old Rutgers." Brett is credited with muttering this after he was injured in

The Rutgers football team of 1888 poses for a team photo nineteen years after Rutgers and Princeton played the first game in the history of college football. (Courtesy Special Collections and University Archives, Rutgers University Libraries)

Early football action at Rutgers.
(Courtesy Rutgers Athletic Communications)

the Princeton game in 1891. Top players Garrett Voorhees, Chalmers P. Dyke, and brothers George and Howard Ludlum helped their Scarlet squad win 8 games while losing 6. Meanwhile, out on the West Coast, future president Herbert Hoover was helping Stanford organize its first football team. Back on the East Coast, Glenn "Pop" Warner and his brother, Bill, were preparing to play for Cornell the following season (1892). Pop Warner would later become one of the game's greatest coaches and record 319 gridiron victories during his career. Pop Warner Youth Leagues are named after him.

In 1892 Rutgers won 3 games, lost 5 games, and had 1 tie. It was the year Stanford and California met in the first college football game ever played on the West Coast.

Rutgers endured a string of rough football seasons from the early 1890s to the early 1900s. In 1894 the Scarlet Queensmen won 4 games and lost 6. One positive aspect of the 1894 season was that the flying wedge was outlawed in college football.

In 1899 tackling below the waist was made legal. Rutgers tackled a tough schedule that season and posted a record of 2 wins and 8 losses.

Football's T formation came into being in 1902. In the T formation, the quarterback lines up behind the offensive center. The fullback is in line behind the quarterback. Two offensive halfbacks are on either side of the fullback. From above the men in the backfield resemble a letter T.

The year 1902 was also when the first Rose Bowl was played. In the contest Michigan crushed Stanford 49 to 0. Rutgers finished the season with a record of 3 wins and 7 losses, despite the valiant efforts of Rutgers captain Alfred Hitcher. Hitcher would later serve as the Rutgers football coach for one year (1904).

The Rutgers football team of 1913 during practice. (Courtesy Rutgers Athletic Communications)

In 1905 college football came under fire from the public due to the dangers it posed to young athletes. It was the first of several expressions of public concern about the violent aspects of football contests. A published report stated that over the preceding thirty-six years, thirty-five football players had died as a result of serious injuries inflicted on the field of play. The sport of football was deemed brutal and dangerous. President Teddy Roosevelt threatened to ban the playing of college football if the game was not made safer. Representatives of college squads from across the nation met to comply with the president's request. The most violent aspects of rough play in football were eliminated from the game.

Captain Harold Green and teammates Raymond Allen and John MacNeil helped Rutgers win 3 games in 1905. Counted among the squad's 6 losses was a defeat at the hands of first-time opponent Seton Hall.

Scarlet football captain Douglas J. Fisher got Rutgers back on the winning track in 1906. Rutgers had a 5–2–2 record with wins over Fordham, New York University, City College of New York, Stevens, and Ursinus. It was also the year the forward pass was made legal in college football.

Rutgers teams completed identical 3–5–1 records from 1907 to 1909. In 1909 the value of a field goal in college football was reduced to 3 points.

Scarlet coach Howard Gargan snapped the 5-loss trend in 1910 with the aid of his captain, Howard A. Smith. Coach Gargan's team won 3 games, lost 2, and tied 3. Football games were broken down into four quarters for the first time in 1910. Another new rule required teams to have seven offensive linemen on the line of scrimmage.

After a .500 season in 1911 (4–4), Rutgers won 5 games and lost 4 during the 1912 season. Most football players were now wearing leather helmets. Some wore metal nose protectors. Shoulder pads were also starting to come into use. At the Carlisle Vocational School for Native American students in Pennsylvania, football sensation Jim Thorpe was dazzling gridiron fans across the nation. Thorpe scored 198 points to win the national scoring title. Rutgers had its own star running back in young Howard Parker "Tal" Talman. Three seasons later (1915), Talman would score a total of 138 points for the Scarlet. Talman, along with Scarlet captain Theodore Van Winkle and future captains John Elmendorf (captain 1913) and John Toohey (captain 1914), helped Rutgers beat Stevens, Haverford, and Hobart, among others. One of the losses that season was a 19 to 0 defeat by Army. A member of that cadet gridiron squad was future World War II general and U.S. president Dwight D. Eisenhower.

The 1913 Scarlet football squad, coached by George Foster Sanford, won 6 games and lost only 3. Sanford was one of football's early innovators. It was his idea to erect a raised scaffold or tower on the football practice field so he could better see formations and the movement of entire teams. Coach Sanford's elevated viewing position was dubbed "the crow's nest" by his players. All college and pro head coaches now observe team practices from a tower like the one George Foster Sanford originally built at Rutgers.

That same year (1913) teams were allowed four downs to advance the ball ten yards in order to make a first down. Strategy and well-planned offensive plays were becoming more and more important. The thinking aspects of football were being held in higher regard than just brute force.

In the Midwest, two young football players were helping turn Notre Dame into a national football powerhouse. Quarterback Gus Dorias and end Knute Rockne used the forward pass to stun their opponents, including a great Army squad.

The Rutgers team of 1914 counted two outstanding future professional players among its ranks. Those players were fullback Howard Talman and tackle Robert "Nasty" Nash.

Bob "Nasty" Nash also holds the unique distinction of being the player involved in the first football deal in history. In 1920 the Buffalo Bisons paid the Akron Pros three hundred dollars to acquire Nash.

However, before they were great professional players, Talman and Nash were outstanding athletes at Rutgers. They helped the Scarlet post a record of 5 wins, 3 losses and 1 tie in 1914. Rutgers played Syracuse for the first time that season and the result was a 14 to 14 tie. One of the team's losses was a 13 to 0 defeat to an Army squad that ended up winning the National Championship. Rutgers may have lost a few games during the early days of college football, but the Scarlet squad was not an easy team to beat. It was the start of a Scarlet tradition.

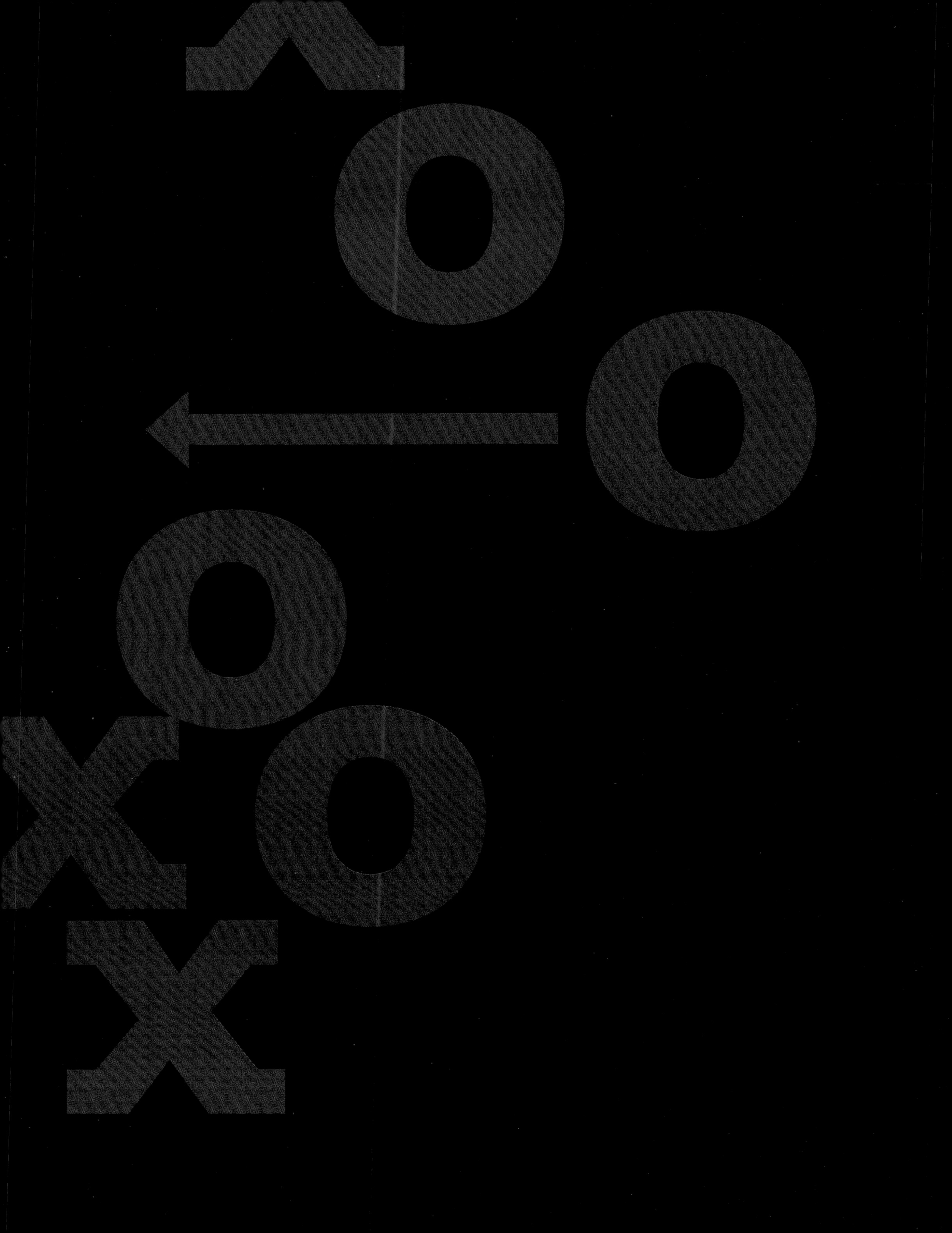

CHAPTER 2

ROBEY RULES THE GRIDIRON

1915–1922

A great group of athletes gathered on the banks of the old Raritan to form Coach George Foster Sanford's Scarlet football squad in 1915. That rough-and-tough bunch of footballers was one of the most talented teams to ever see action on the gridiron for Rutgers University.

The squad was captained by running back Howard Parker "Tal" Talman, a Scarlet scoring machine. Talman led his team to a record of 7 wins and 1 loss in 1915. The lone loss was a 10 to 0 defeat at the hands of intrastate rival Princeton. The fact that the Scarlet team was shut out made the loss an extremely bitter one. The 1915 Rutgers football team scored a total of 351 points, which surpassed the offensive output of any other gridiron squad in the East for that year. Accounting for a great deal of that massive point production was Howard Talman, the Scarlet scoring sensation who tallied 48 points in a single game against Rensselaer Polytechnic Institute on October 9, 1915. Talman racked up 6 touchdowns and 12 extra points in that contest to set several school records.

In his team's victories, Captain Talman tallied 14 touchdowns, 45 PATs, 6 field goals, and a safety for an astounding total of 138 points. He was a one-man wrecking crew when it came to finding ways to score.

On a national level, Talman was considered second best only to Harvard's legendary back Eddie Mahan. Football immortal Jim Thorpe called Eddie Mahan the greatest back in all of football. Mahan was an All-American in 1913, 1914, and 1915. Howard Talman was an All-American selection at the fullback position at the conclusion of the 1915 season. In 1914 Talman had won All-America honors as a halfback. In 1913 he was an All-American guard. Howard "Tal" Talman was as versatile as he was great. After graduation, he continued his football career in the pros, playing with the Detroit Heralds and the Massillon Tigers.

One of Talman's All-American teammates on that 1915 Rutgers squad was hard-nosed tackle Robert "Nasty" Nash. Nash's unique nickname aptly described his no-nonsense style of play. Bob Nash was just plain mean! He was a hard-hitting, relentless competitor from the second he stepped on a football field until the moment he stepped off.

Left: Howard Talman (holding football) was the captain of the 1915 Rutgers team, which had a record of 7 wins and 1 loss. (Courtesy Rutgers Athletic Communications)

Right: George Foster Sanford was Rutgers' head football coach from 1913 to 1923. (Courtesy Rutgers Athletic Communications)

Nash garnered All-American honors in 1914 and 1915. He went on to play for a host of pro teams including the Massillon Tigers in Ohio, which he also coached with Tom Keady. Rutgers' Howard Talman was on that team. Also on that squad were a number of men destined to become football immortals. Listed on the Massillon roster were Gus Dorias at quarterback, Knute Rockne at end, and Lou Little at tackle. Dorias later coached at Detroit University and Gonzaga. Rockne became a famous coach at the University of Notre Dame. Little went on to earn immortality as the head coach at Columbia University. Lou Little coached John Bateman at one point during his career at Columbia, and Bateman later became one of the best football coaches in the history of Rutgers football.

Bob Nash's pro career continued for a number of years. He also played professionally for the Buffalo All-Americans and the New York Giants. In fact, Robert "Nasty" Nash of Rutgers was the Giants' very first team captain. One of Nash's teammates on the Giants was football immortal Jim Thorpe.

Along with Talman and Nash, Coach Sanford's 1915 squad included Alfred "Budge" Garrett. Garrett was a terrific lineman who played guard, tackle, and end. Al Garrett went on to win All-American honors in 1916. After college he had an illustrious professional career as a tackle and end for the Massillon Tigers, the Akron Pros, the Cleveland Panthers, and the Milwaukee Badgers.

Another member of the squad, Elmer "Toady" Bracher, didn't receive as much notoriety as some of his more famous teammates, but he was an outstanding running back. In 1915 Bracher rushed for 1,021 yards in 183 attempts.

Numbered among the other key players on the 1915 team were Francis Scarr, Harry Rockafeller, John Hasbrouck, and John "Mike" Wittpenn. Wittpenn returned an interception 99 yards for a touchdown in Rutgers' 33 to 22 win over Stevens in 1915. Hasbrouck later had a solid pro career with the Rochester Jeffersons and the Rock Island

Independents. Rockafeller earned All-America Honorable Mention for his steady gridiron work during the 1915 season.

Harry Rockafeller eventually became the head football coach at Rutgers and later served as the Scarlet athletic director. His devotion to his beloved alma mater led to him being nicknamed "Mr. Rutgers" later in his life.

Without a doubt, the most famous member of the 1915 Rutgers football squad was an African-American athlete from nearby Somerville, New Jersey. He played college football at a time when very few black athletes were given the opportunity to participate in intercollegiate athletics at major universities. His name was Paul Leroy Robeson. Robeson and Fred "Fritz" Pollard, an outstanding running back at Brown University, were not only talented athletes and outstanding scholars, they were trailblazers in what was, at the time, a world of predominantly white college sports.

In 1915, end Paul Robeson played a significant part in the success of a very talented Rutgers football team. It was the same year a powerful Cornell squad coached by Al Sharpe posted a record of 9 wins and no losses to capture the National Championship. It was Robeson's first year as a varsity football player, and he was just one of many key contributors. But as time passed, Paul Robeson would become the focal point and the cornerstone of Rutgers' gridiron squad. The national sports spotlight was soon to illuminate the many outstanding achievements of Paul "Robey" Robeson.

A group of famous Rutgers football players pose together in this early photo. From left to right: John Wittpenn starred for Rutgers in 1917–18. Elmer "Toady" Bracher rushed for more than 1,000 yards in 1915. Homer Hazel was an All-American in 1923–24. Ken Rendall was captain of the 1917 team. Francis Scarr was captain of the 1916 football squad. (Courtesy Special Collections and University Archives, Rutgers University Libraries)

Above: Rutgers played its home games at Neilson Field from 1892 to 1938. Neilson Field was across the street from Rutgers' original college field. (Courtesy Special Collections and University Archives, Rutgers University Libraries)

Opposite: Paul Robeson was one of the greatest scholar-athletes in Rutgers history. (Courtesy Rutgers Athletic Communications)

Paul Robeson stood 6 feet 2 inches tall and weighed about 220 pounds. He was considered a big athlete of his era. Robeson was quick, powerful, and smart. As a second-year player in 1916, he was a team leader but not yet a star. Elmer Bracher, Al Garrett, and team captain Francis Scarr had returned, but gone were Howard Talman and Bob Nash. William Feitner and Frank Kelley were emerging as top performers, but the Rutgers team had lost the unique chemistry it had the previous season. Even the presence of a promising newcomer named Homer Hazel couldn't help the team jell as a unit. Rutgers' record dipped to 3 wins, 2 losses, and 2 ties in 1916. One of the losses was a 21 to 3 defeat at the hands of a Brown University squad that played Rutgers for the first time that season. Brown was led by its star halfback, Fritz Pollard. Pollard scored touchdowns on runs of 55 and 60 yards against Yale that season. Yale's only loss in 1916 was to Brown. Rutgers' loss to Brown was memorable because that contest matched the nation's top two African-American college football stars against each other. Rutgers' Paul Robeson played end on offense and linebacker on defense. Brown's Fritz Pollard played offensive and defensive back.

Elmer "Toady" Bracher finished his football career at Rutgers with a total of 2,286 rushing yards. Al "Budge" Garrett garnered All-America recognition despite the team's record. Joining Garrett on the 1916 All-America list was back Charles "Chic" Harley. Harley was the first player in the history of Ohio State to earn All-America honors. Charles Harley

has been credited with helping turn the Ohio State football program into the national powerhouse it is today.

The National Championship of college football was won by the University of Pittsburgh in 1916. The Panthers, coached by Glenn "Pop" Warner, were undefeated in eight games.

Homer Hazel, a player destined to be one of Rutgers' greatest gridiron stars, dropped out of school because he couldn't afford to pay his tuition. There were no football scholarships in those days. Hazel would return to the Scarlet football fold several years later. His presence was missed, but the loss was quickly overshadowed by the emergence of two new rising stars. One was back Frank Kelley. The other Scarlet superstar was Paul Robeson. It was time for Robeson to shine on the gridiron.

Paul Leroy Robeson was born the son of a runaway slave. His father came to New Jersey from the South to become a Presbyterian minister. Paul was born in Princeton, New Jersey, in 1898. The Robesons then moved to Somerville, New Jersey. Somerville is only a stone's throw from the Rutgers University campus. Paul "Robey" Robeson attended Somerville High School, where he excelled in athletics and academics. After graduation, he traveled a short distance down the road and enrolled at Rutgers College.

At Rutgers, young Paul Robeson once again proved to be a scholar and an athlete. In addition to football, Robeson lettered in track, baseball, and basketball. In all, he won twelve varsity letters. However it was on the gridiron that Robeson did his best work in athletics. His greatest achievements came during the 1917 and 1918 football seasons. The combined efforts of William Feitner, Captain Ken "Thug" Rendall, and Paul Robeson helped the Scarlet squad open their 1917 season with two impressive wins. Rutgers crushed Ursinus 25 to 0 and blasted a Fort Wadsworth football squad 90 to 0. Syracuse then topped Rutgers 14 to 10 in a hard-fought nail-biter. Easy victories over Lafayette and Fordham followed. The Scarlet team tied the Mountaineers of West Virginia 7-all in its next contest before blanking Springfield and the Long Island Marines. It was in the last game of the 1917 season that Paul Robeson dazzled sportswriters and American football fans coast to coast. Rutgers took on the Newport Naval Reserve football squad at Ebbets Field in Brooklyn, New York. Twelve thousand football fans poured into the stands to watch the contest (that was a lot of fans for the time). The Newport Naval Reserve team was packed with former college All-Americans including Yale's Cupe Black and Cornell's future Hall of Famer Charlie Barret.

Nevertheless, Rutgers' Paul Robeson ruled the gridiron that day. He singlehandedly terrorized the opposing offense, making crushing tackle after tackle. On offense he caught a pass at the 5-yard line and dragged three would-be tacklers into the end zone to score a touchdown. Rutgers won the game 14 to 0. The Scarlet squad finished the 1917 season with a record of 7 wins, 1 loss, and 1 tie.

Georgia Tech, coached by the immortal John Heisman, went 9 and 0 in 1917 and was named the National Champion. However, football icon and sports expert Walter Camp publicly speculated on what the outcome would have been if Rutgers and Georgia Tech had met on the gridiron that season. Camp admitted he could not accurately predict which team would have won. Georgia Tech's best player was star halfback Ev Strupper, but Rutgers had elusive running back Frank Kelley, who scored 12 touchdowns in 1917. And the Scarlet also had defensive bulwark Paul Robeson.

Rutgers footballers Frank Kelley, Ken Rendall, Joe Breckley, and Mike Whitehill all garnered various honors for their outstanding play during the 1917 season. The highest

Paul Robeson (far right) poses with a group of his Rutgers football teammates in the early 1900s. (Courtesy Rutgers Athletic Communications)

honors of all were heaped upon Paul Robeson. Robey became the first Rutgers player to earn First Team All-America honors.

Paul Robeson later recalled the 1917 football season by penning an article for the alumni quarterly. Robeson wrote in part, "The season of 1917 is over, but the memories thereof will fire the hearts of Rutgers men as long as football is football." His words still ring true to this day.

The 1918 season continued the winning tradition established the year before, but fell short in terms of national notoriety. William Feitner, Walter French, and Paul Robeson provided the nucleus of a good team that managed 5 wins and only 2 defeats. One of those losses was a 24 to 14 setback to the Great Lakes Naval Training Station football squad. One player on that team was George Halas. Halas eventually became the first man in pro football history to return a fumble for a touchdown. Halas scooped up a dropped ball in a game against the Marion (Ohio) Oorang Indians and dashed 98 yards for a score. George Halas later won lasting fame as the coach of the Chicago Bears.

A big win for the Scarlet squad of 1918 came in their first gridiron meeting against Penn State. Rutgers beat Penn State 26 to 3. Other victories included a 66 to 0 rout of Ursinus and a 39 to 0 blasting of Lehigh.

Rutgers' record of 5 and 2 in 1918 is impressive when compared to the record of Notre Dame that season. The year 1918 was Knute Rockne's first as the head coach of the Fighting Irish. Notre Dame finished with a record of 3 wins, 1 loss, and 2 ties. However, Notre Dame did rebound to go undefeated for the next two years.

At the conclusion of the 1918 season, Paul Robeson was again named a First Team All-American. He became the first African-American college football player to be a First Team All-American in successive years.

Paul Leroy Robeson graduated Phi Beta Kappa from Rutgers as the valedictorian of his class. He was also named to the senior honor society known as Cap and Skull. Robey played professional football after college with the Akron Pros, the Hammond Pros, and the Milwaukee Badgers. He was a member of the 1920 Akron Pro squad that was unbeaten in 10 games and held 13 straight opponents scoreless.

Cliff Baker, who played quarterback for Rutgers and was a teammate of Robeson, said Robey possessed "football instinct and was able to fathom the attack of every opponent with lightning-like quickness." In short, Paul Robeson was a high-impact player. On the football field he was fast, smart, and a punishing hitter. Off of the field, he was a cultured gentleman and a multitalented performer. After his football career ended, Paul Robeson became an internationally acclaimed singer and actor. He starred on the stage and in movies. In 1995 Paul Robeson was voted into the College Football Hall of Fame. "He was my first football hero," Rutgers historian Larry Pitt said when informed of Robeson's selection. "They told me he was one of the greatest athletes of that era." Indeed he was. It was an era when Robey ruled the gridiron.

Rutgers took on two new gridiron opponents during the 1919 season. The Scarlet played Boston College and Northwestern for the first time. Led by William Gardner, Cliff Baker, Frank Kelley, James Dufft, and John Alexander, Rutgers won both games. Rutgers also enjoyed a victory over North Carolina that year to post a respectable season record of 5 wins and 3 losses. Frank Kelley won mentions on various All-America teams. James Dufft and John Alexander went on to have careers in professional football.

Harvard, coached by Bob Fisher, and Illinois, coached by Bob Zuppke, shared the National Championship with Notre Dame, coached by Knute Rockne. There was no clear-cut National Champion in 1919.

Rutgers suffered through a difficult season in 1920. The Scarlet squad won only two games. The wins came against Maryland and Virginia Tech. Rutgers faced off against Cornell, Virginia, and Nebraska for the first time and lost all three contests plus four others. Notre Dame suffered a more devastating loss that year. Its All-American running back, George "The Gipper" Gipp, suddenly became ill and passed away.

In 1921 the Scarlet gridiron club dared to bump heads with two famous football schools. Rutgers played Notre Dame and Georgia Tech. Unfortunately, the Rutgers squad was not yet up to the challenge and was beaten both times. Another tough loss was to old rival Lafayette. Lafayette produced one of its finest football squads in 1921. The team was guided by legendary coach Jock Sutherland and led by star player Dutch Schwab, who was a two-time All-American. Lafayette went undefeated in 1921 and Rutgers was one of its casualties in gridiron combat.

Paul Robeson played end on offense and linebacker on defense. (Courtesy Rutgers Athletic Communications)

Captain Howard Raub helped his Scarlet squad rebound slightly in the 1922 campaign. Rutgers finished with 5 wins in 9 contests. Three of the Scarlet victories were against Louisiana State University, New York University, and Fordham. Two of the tougher losses were to good Lafayette and West Virginia squads.

Two Ivy League schools shared the national title with California that year. Cornell, coached by Gil Dobie; Princeton, coached by Bill Roper; and California, coached by Andy Smith, were declared National Champions in 1922.

Scarlet football had temporarily faded from the national gridiron picture. In fact, Rutgers football was on shaky financial ground at the end of the 1922 season. Usually the gridiron squad showed a profit of several thousand dollars after the last game. A big money maker for Rutgers was the once-a-year contest the team played at New York's vast Polo Grounds Stadium. Rutgers' home field, Neilson Field, seated only 6,000 fans and never generated enough money to support the operation of the gridiron squad. Rutgers relied on the gate receipts from its Polo Grounds game to make ends meet. In 1922 the Polo Grounds contest against Louisiana State was a fan flop. That year the Rutgers football operation had a net profit of only $69.16. Luckily, Rutgers students and alumni donated and collected enough money to keep the football program around for the 1923 season. It was a good thing they did. Better days were coming for Rutgers on the gridiron.

xo
xo o
xo
xo

CHAPTER 3
HERE COMES HOMER

1923–1933

The man who coined the endearing Rutgers football catchphrase "Upstream, red team," George Foster Sanford, was nearing the end of his coaching career in 1923. Scarlet football had risen to lofty heights under Sanford's expert and innovative guidance. George Foster Sanford came up with revolutionary concepts like two-a-day practices and using movies of players to improve their techniques. Fans referred to Rutgers' performance under Sanford from 1916 to 1923 as the years of the "Scarlet Scourge." It was a fitting compliment to Coach Sanford for a job well done. However, George Foster Sanford still had one outstanding football season diagrammed in his playbook. He also had another Rutgers star on tap. In 1923, Coach Sanford unleashed his old but new Scarlet sensation. It was a big, burly player who returned to the banks of the old Raritan and the Rutgers gridiron after an absence of several years. That player was Homer Hazel. After dropping out of school because he couldn't afford to pay his tuition, Hazel had gone to work in Michigan. He returned to New Jersey and Rutgers as a 28-year-old football player with two years of sports eligibility remaining.

All-American Homer Hazel was a multitalented athlete. Hazel kicked a 49-yard field goal in 1923 and had several 75-yard punts. (Courtesy Special Collections and University Archives, Rutgers University Libraries)

Homer Hazel was quickly nicknamed "Pop" due to the age difference between him and his teammates. Hazel stood 5 feet 11 inches tall and weighed 230 pounds. He was muscular, fast, and agile. He was determined to make the most of his second chance to play college sports. In addition to football, Homer Hazel starred in baseball and track. Hazel was a gifted athlete who could do it all, especially on a football field. Homer could run, block, tackle, kick, and pass. He played fullback, end, and sometimes quarterback. Coach Sanford often used Hazel as a man in motion so Homer could deliver crushing blocks like a pulling guard. A pulling guard is a fast, offensive blocker who leads interference by sprinting out in front of a ball carrier on sweep plays around tackle or end.

John Wallace (far left) was the head football coach at Rutgers from 1924 to 1926. (Courtesy Rutgers Athletic Communications)

Homer Hazel was versatile and multitalented. He could hurt opposing football clubs in many ways. Hazel was an expert punter with a strong leg. He was credited with kicking several 75-yard punts. Homer Hazel also booted extra points and field goals. In 1923, he kicked a 49-yard field goal to establish a Rutgers record. Hazel's mark lasted for forty-five years, until Scarlet kicker Chris Stewart booted a 50-yard field goal in 1968.

Homer Hazel could also pass. In the 1923 game against Villanova, Hazel fired a 69-yard touchdown bullet to end Jack Anderson. It was the longest TD pass recorded in college football that year.

Perhaps most astonishing of all was the speed of Homer Hazel. He was one of the game's first backs to be both big and fast. Hazel was so quick he once kicked off in a game and, when the opposing receiver bobbled the ball deep in his own territory, Hazel recovered the fumble for a Scarlet touchdown.

Homer Hazel was a great player, but his 1923 team was stocked with many good gridiron athletes. Team captain William Kingman, lineman Dave Bender, and backs Carl Waite and Henry Benkert made up the nucleus of a potent defense and offense. The 1923 Scarlet squad opened the season with 4 straight wins, including a 44 to 0 victory over Villanova and a 10 to 0 shutout of Lehigh. Rutgers then encountered an outstanding Lafayette club. The two talented teams met in a rugged, hard-fought contest that ended up deadlocked at 6 points apiece. A strong West Virginia squad was next on the schedule. The Mountaineers surprised the Scarlet Queensmen and handed Rutgers its lone loss of the season—a 27 to 7 defeat.

The red team rebounded with a vengeance and registered a 56 to 0 rout of Richmond, a 61 to 0 blasting of Boston University, and a 42 to 0 flogging of New York neighbor Fordham. Rutgers ended the year with a record of 7 wins, 1 loss, and 1 tie. Homer Hazel tallied 10 touchdowns in 1923 and scored a total of 82 points. That year Hazel was named an All-American at the end position. It was the same year Illinois immortal Red Grange was named All-American at running back for the first time. It was also the year the University of Southern California defeated Penn State 14 to 0 in the Rose Bowl and undefeated Illinois and undefeated Michigan shared the National Championship. Illinois was coached by Bob Zuppke. Michigan was coached by Fielding "Hurry Up" Yost.

Coach George Foster Sanford retired as the head coach of Rutgers at the conclusion of the 1923 season. He went out on a high note. When he was asked to describe his 1923 team, Sanford summed it up in one word: "Great!" George Foster Sanford concluded his Rutgers coaching career with a record of 56 wins, 32 losses, and 5 ties. He was later elected to the College Football Hall of Fame.

Sanford's gridiron successor was John "Jack" Wallace, a former Rutgers running back. Wallace inherited a sound Rutgers squad and would remain as head coach of the Scarlet until 1926.

Illinois's famous coach Bob Zuppke (left) chats with football immortal Harold "Red" Grange, known as the "Galloping Ghost." (Courtesy Illinois Division of Intercollegiate Athletics)

The year 1924 is considered to be one of the glory years of college football. Amos Alonzo Stagg was coaching at the University of Chicago. Pop Warner was coaching at Stanford and had a budding young star at running back named Ernie Nevers. Coach Knute Rockne at Notre Dame had a famous backfield known as the Four Horsemen: Harry Stuhldreher, Don Miller, Jim Crowley, and Elmer Layden. At the University of Illinois, Coach Zuppke had America's most famous backfield star, Harold "Red" Grange. Grange was idolized all across America and known by his nickname "The Galloping Ghost."

Sportswriter Grantland Rice described Red Grange's elusive and unique style of running in flowery prose. Rice wrote, "A streak of fire, a breath of flame, eluding all who reach and clutch. A gray ghost thrown into the game that rival hands may never touch: a rubber bounding blasting soul whose destination is the goal . . . Red Grange of Illinois."

At the outset of the 1924 college football season, no one composed eloquent prose about the running style of Rutgers fullback Homer "Pop" Hazel. He was a big, bruising bulldozer who used brute force to impose his will upon those who dared to impede his progress. Pop Hazel was a punishing runner who plowed into and steamrolled over opposing tacklers. Hazel could use football finesse to outsmart an opponent if the occasion called for it. He had slick moves and could fake out the opposition if necessary. However, it just wasn't his style.

Normally, Pop Hazel left the finesse style of backfield play to his running mate halfback Henry "Harry" Benkert. Benkert was an All-American in 1923. He was favorably compared

Left: Rutgers' Henry "Harry" Benkert was often compared to Red Grange of Illinois and Jim Crowley of Notre Dame. (Courtesy Special Collections and University Archives, Rutgers University Libraries)

Right: Hoyt Terrill (left), Homer Hazel (center), and Henry Benkert made up one of the best backfields in the history of Rutgers football. (Courtesy Special Collections and University Archives, Rutgers University Libraries)

to Red Grange of Illinois and Jim Crowley of Notre Dame. Homer Hazel and Henry Benkert provided the Scarlet offense of 1924 with a powerful one-two punch.

Other key players on the 1924 Rutgers club were William Anderson, Carl Fuchs, Bob Lincoln, and team captain E. Gaynor "Mickey" Brennan. The 1924 Scarlet squad stormed through its first eight gridiron contests without suffering a single loss. The only sour note was a tough 13 to 13 tie with old rival Lehigh. The Queensmen registered impressive victories over Lebanon Valley, St. Bonaventures, Cornell, Franklin and Marshall, Lafayette, and New York University.

The final game of the 1924 season was played under overcast skies at Philadelphia's Franklin Field. The Scarlet took on the Bucknell Bisons in the rain. The game quickly turned into a hard-fought battle as Bucknell provided the Scarlet with its stiffest competition of the season. Eventually, Bucknell emerged from the muddy football fracas victorious and denied Rutgers an unbeaten season. Rutgers finished with a 7–1–1 record.

Once again, Homer Hazel was selected as an All-American. This time it was at the fullback position. In picking Hazel as an All-American, Walter Camp wrote, "Hazel of Rutgers can out-pass and out-kick any of our other stars."

Henry Benkert also received All-Star recognition. Benkert scored a total of 100 points in 1924. He had a career total of 201 points on 32 touchdowns, 6 extra points, and 1 field goal. During his illustrious career, Henry Benkert rushed for a grand total of 2,124 yards. After he graduated, Benkert played pro football as a halfback for the New York Giants.

Homer Hazel completed his Rutgers career with an impressive total of 216 points. He tallied 22 touchdowns, 48 extra points, and 12 field goals. He graduated from Rutgers as the president of his class and went on to become the coach at the University of

Mississippi. The Most Valuable Player trophy awarded annually to Rutgers' top player is named in honor of Homer Hazel. Homer Hazel was voted into the College Football Hall of Fame in 1951.

The mid-1920s saw the emergence of some great college football teams. The University of California, coached by Andy Smith, won 44 games and tied 4 contests in 48 outings. Coach Hugo Bezdek of Penn State lost only one game in three years. That loss was to an amazing Dartmouth squad coached by Jesse Hawley. In 1925 Hawley's Dartmouth club was co-National Champion with Alabama, coached by Wallace Wade. Dartmouth's team was composed of the greatest group of scholar-athletes ever assembled on one squad. Twenty-two members of Dartmouth's 1925 team graduated Phi Beta Kappa.

Rutgers probably had numerous scholars numbered among its footballers in the mid-1920s. Unfortunately, those Rutgers teams did not contain an abundance of outstanding athletes. The Scarlet posted a disappointing record of 5 wins and 13 losses from 1925 to 1926.

Rutgers did have some good players during those bad years. After graduation, guard John Lord played professionally for the Staten Island Stapletons. Back George Fraser collected his Rutgers degree and then played pro football for the New York Yankees (there was a pro football team named the Yankees back then).

A reserve quarterback on those teams named Oswald G. Nelson achieved a different kind of fame. Ozzie Nelson became well known first as a bandleader and then as a television star. Early in the history of TV, Nelson's television show about his family, *The Adventures of Ozzie and Harriet,* became a long-running hit. His son, Ricky

This 1926 team photo shows, from left to right: (top) Head Coach John Wallace, K. D. Gardaniar, J. C. Irwin, H. E. Lorenz, Ozzie Nelson, and Coach John Wittpenn; (bottom) D. Brundage, E. K. Goldschmidt, D. Morse, W. Mason, A. H. Burkhardt, S. Berkowitz, and W. Brundage. (Courtesy Special Collections and University Archives, Rutgers University Libraries)

Ozzie Nelson was a reserve quarterback at Rutgers in 1926–27. He went on to have a long career as a television star. (Courtesy Special Collections and University Archives, Rutgers University Libraries)

Nelson, became a singing and recording star. His grandsons later formed the Nelson musical group.

In 1927 Harry Rockafeller took over the head coaching reins at Rutgers. He was ably assisted by former Rutgers stars Dave Bender, Al Neuschafer, and Mike Wittpenn. Rockafeller immediately steered his red team back upstream, breaking the trend of two straight losing seasons. Rutgers finished the year with a respectable record of 4 wins and 4 losses. Herb Lorenz served as captain of that squad. Other notable members of the 1927 team were Benjamin Greenberg, Walter Morgan, Joe Preletz, and Arthur Burkhardt. Art Burkhardt continued his playing career in the NFL for the New York Giants. Ben Greenberg turned pro as a member of the Brooklyn Dodgers (they were also a football team in those days).

Coach Rockafeller's 1928 team was led by Captain Stan Rosen with help from John Carney, Dave Moscowitz, and James Shedden. Rutgers posted a solid 6 and 3 season with wins over St. John's, Delaware, Albright, Catholic University, Lehigh, and Swarthmore.

One of the losses that season was to New York University, where future All-American Ken Strong was blossoming into a gridiron great. In fact, Ken Strong of NYU led the nation in scoring in 1928 with 160 points.

Rutgers' Stan Rosen also proved to be a player of star quality. He later played in the National Football League for the Buffalo (N.Y.) Bisons.

In 1929 All-American Bronko Nagurski of Minnesota burst upon the college football scene. He was a player cut from the same mold as Rutgers' Homer Hazel. Nagurski would eventually be named an All-American tackle and fullback. Rutgers, led by its captain Richard Crowl and Scarlet comrades George Cronin, Bert Harris, and Richard Knauss, posted a record of 5 wins and 4 losses. One of the better victories was a 17 to 0 shutout of Providence. Crowl later enjoyed a pro football career with the Brooklyn Dodgers.

The 1930 football season concluded Harry Rockafeller's first stint as Rutgers' head coach. The red team was a gridiron club in transition. It was stocked with a few solid lettermen and an abundance of new young talent. Captain Richard Knauss spearheaded the experienced lettermen. Newcomer Jack Grossman was the cream of the fresh crop of athletes. Grossman excelled in football, baseball, soccer, and several other sports at Rutgers.

Jack Grossman quickly distinguished himself as a future star of the Scarlet football squad. He made key contributions in Rutgers victories over George Washington, Johns Hopkins, Delaware, and Lehigh. However, it was in a hotly contested 31 to 26 loss to Lafayette that Grossman made a lasting impression on sportswriters nationwide. In that contest, Jack Grossman tossed a 58-yard touchdown pass to Scarlet receiver Don Coursen. It was the longest TD toss in college football that season.

The year 1930 also marked a historic moment in Rutgers football history. The Scarlet game against Holy Cross was the first Rutgers homecoming contest.

The Scarlet Queensmen posted a record of 4–5 in 1930. Coach Harry Rockafeller finished with a career record of 19 wins and 16 losses. J. Wilder Tasker became the new Scarlet gridiron mentor in 1931.

College football suffered one of its greatest losses in 1931. Knute Rockne, the beloved head coach of Notre Dame, perished when the aircraft he was in plummeted out of the sky and smashed into a cattle pasture in Kansas. Football fans everywhere mourned his passing.

The new Rutgers coach, J. Wilder Tasker, was an admirer of Knute Rockne and utilized some of Rockne's gridiron tactics. It took the Rutgers club a while to adjust to a new coach and a new style of play. Even with Jack Grossman and teammates Jerry Cronin, Joe Julien, and Harry Karakas leading the way, the Scarlet could manage only 4 wins, 3 losses, and 1 tie in 1931. In his final game as a Scarlet footballer, Jack Grossman turned in a memorable individual performance. In the game, a home contest against Lehigh, Jack Grossman had a 45-yard pass completion to receiver Les Horton, an 85-yard kickoff return, and a 60-yard punt return for a touchdown. Coach Tasker called Jack Grossman "the greatest back I ever saw!"

At the conclusion of the 1931 season, Rutgers back Jack Grossman was named an Honorable Mention All-American. He graduated and began a pro football career with a Brooklyn Dodgers team coached by gridiron immortal Benny Friedman. Grossman later played pro baseball and pro soccer in addition to professional football.

Gerry Cronin went on to play pro for the Brooklyn Dodgers.

Another often-overlooked star of the 1931 team was back Les Horton. Horton was a three-year letterman in football who played professionally for the Newark Tornadoes along with another former Scarlet star, Carl Waite.

Rutgers appointed its first permanent athletic director in 1931. It was George E. Little. Little quickly established a junior varsity football program and a lightweight football program (no player could weigh over 150 pounds) at Rutgers.

Meanwhile in New York State, Coach Andy Karr at Colgate was putting together a phenomenal gridiron squad which would cruise through the 1931 football season undefeated, untied, and un–scored upon.

The Rutgers varsity squad couldn't match Colgate's marvelous wonder season that year despite the Herculean efforts of Captain Andy Wiley, center Al "Red" Twitchell, and backs Lou Hermerda and Nick Prisco. The team did rack up 6 wins in 10 outings. Rutgers' victories included wins over Johns Hopkins, Delaware, and Lafayette. Its one tie was 6 to 6 against Providence. The season was actually more successful than it might first appear. The losses included a 6 to 0 defeat to Holy Cross and a 7 to 6 loss to Manhattan. The Manhattan contest was an extra game played in New York's Polo Grounds before fifteen thousand fans.

Harry Rockafeller (right) played football at Rutgers and was head coach of the team for the first time from 1927 to 1930. (Courtesy Rutgers Athletic Communications)

The ability of Rutgers senior Nick Prisco did not go unnoticed by pro football scouts. Prisco played for the Philadelphia Eagles after his college football career ended.

The year 1933 unveiled a new, improved, and redesigned football. It was easier to throw and teams began to fling the ol' pigskin with reckless abandon. At Texas Christian University, quarterback Sammy Baugh earned the nickname "Slingin' Sammy" by connecting for 11 touchdown passes that season.

The University of Alabama also stepped up its passing attack. Quarterback Dixie Howell and end Don Hutson made up a lethal southern pass-and-catch combo.

Rutgers had its own scaled-down but somewhat successful version of a pass-catch combination. Passer Arnold Truex and receiver Walt Winika proved to be a formidable offensive weapon when needed. The Scarlet squad also boasted a bevy of gridiron bulwarks in Wilho Winika (Walt's brother), Bill Demarest, Harold Updike, and George Kramer

Above: Jack Grossman, a star running back and kicker at Rutgers, punts against Drexel in 1931. (Courtesy Special Collections and University Archives, Rutgers University Libraries)

Below: George E. Little was Rutgers' first permanent athletic director. Little was appointed in 1932. (Courtesy Rutgers Athletic Communications)

(who later became the director of admissions at Rutgers). The Scarlet posted an impressive record of 6 wins, 3 losses, and 1 tie in 1933.

Oddly enough, some of the Scarlet losses that year were almost as impressive as the team's wins. Rutgers lost to Colgate 25 to 2. However, Rutgers was the first team to score against a Colgate squad that had gone unbeaten, untied, and un–scored upon the year before.

Rutgers broke Colgate's scoreless streak when Scarlet tackle Mo Bullard blocked a Colgate kick and tallied a safety for Rutgers.

Rutgers also lost to a powerful Princeton team 26 to 6 that season. Coach Herbert "Fritz" Crisler's Princeton club went undefeated in 1933. Crisler was the first Princeton head coach in school history not to have attended Princeton. Fritz Crisler was a graduate of the University of Chicago, where he had been an All-American player for gridiron immortal Amos Alonzo Stagg.

Only one opponent scored against Coach Crisler's 1933 Princeton squad. It was Rutgers. Scarlet QB Arnold Truex fired a 45-yard touchdown pass to end Walt Winika for the score. The contest was played in front of more than forty thousand fans in Princeton. At the conclusion of the 1933 season, end Walt Winika received All-America Honorable Mention for his gridiron work that year. Center Al Twitchell's accomplishments were also rewarded with All-America Honorable Mention. Twitchell would eventually become one of the most admired figures in Rutgers athletics. Tackle Harold Updike went on to play with the New York Yankees.

The 1933 college football season concluded with an amazing upset that is recognized as an all-time great football achievement to this day. In January of 1934, Ivy League Columbia, coached by Lou Little, defeated vastly favored Stanford in the Rose Bowl by the score of 7 to 0. The winning touchdown was scored on a trick play. On that one day Columbia and Lou Little—both of whom had football ties to Rutgers—became college football immortals.

Left: Star halfback Nick Prisco blocks Harry Karakas during practice in the 1930s. (Courtesy Special Collections and University Archives, Rutgers University Libraries)

Right: Early photos of a field goal attempt. (Courtesy Rutgers Athletic Communications)

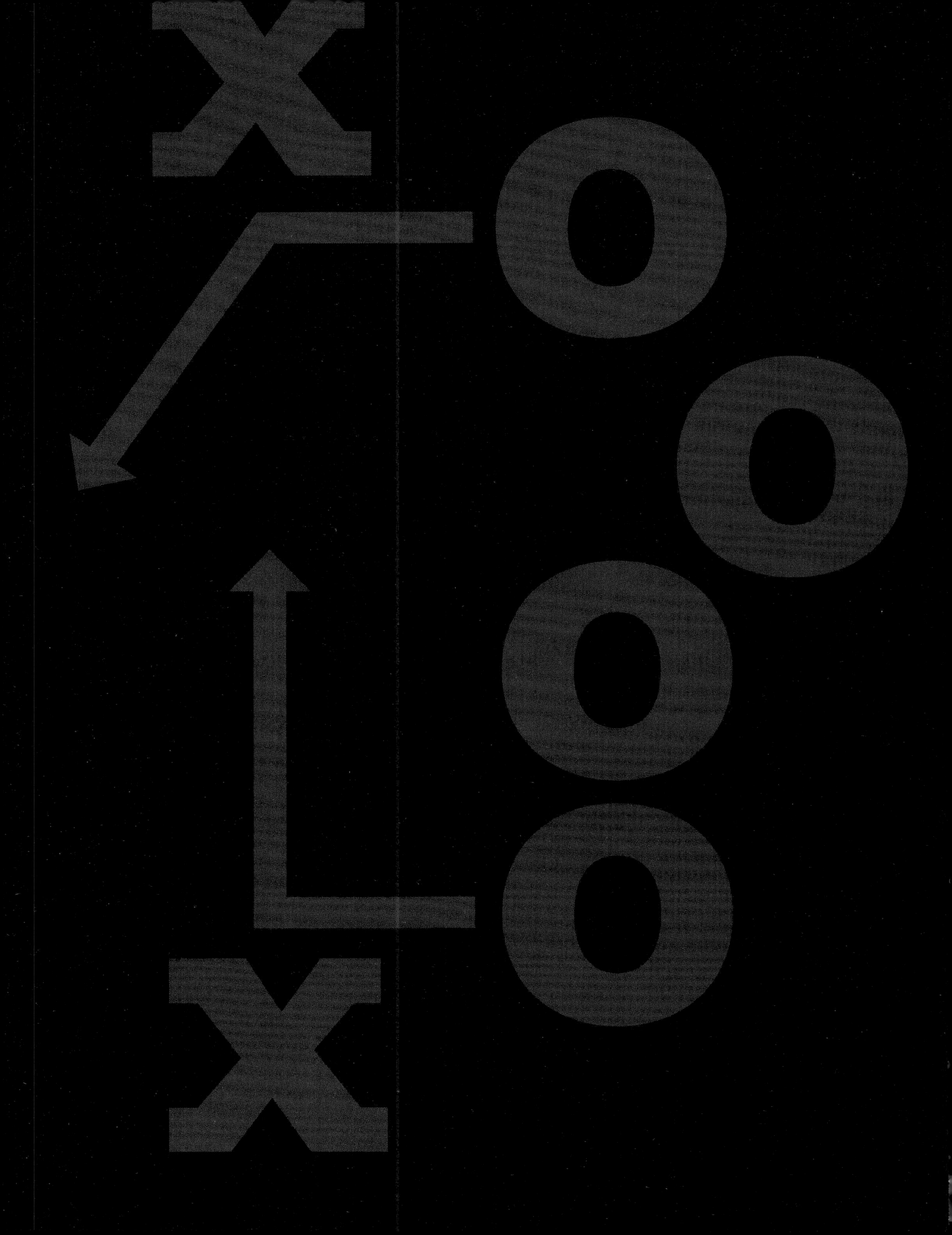

CHAPTER 4

FLINGING FRANKIE BURNS

1934–1949

The mid-1930s was a thrilling time for fans of college football. The offensive T formation was being reinvented. It was the time of a new wave of innovative coaches including Jim Crowley (the former Notre Dame star) at Fordham, Earl "Red" Blaik at Dartmouth (and later Army), Frank Leahy at Boston College (and later Notre Dame), and Harvey Harman at Penn (and later Rutgers).

It was an exciting time of college football firsts. The first official national college-football statistics were compiled during this period. The Associated Press began to rank college football teams for the first time in the mid-1930s. The first Heisman Trophy was awarded to honor college football's top player. And, last but not least, college football was broadcast on television for the first time.

The late 1930s and the 1940s also saw the emergence of a new type of college football quarterback. The college QB of this period was a smart athlete who could not only run well, but who could also throw accurately and for distance. The new breed of quarterback included players like Sid Luckman of Columbia, Slingin' Sammy Baugh of Texas Christian University, Davey O'Brien also of TCU, Otto Graham of Northwestern, and Johnny Lujack of Notre Dame. The names of other quarterbacks who could well be included in a second tier of those famous team leaders are Columbia's Paul Governali (who finished second in the Heisman Trophy race in 1942), Mississippi's Charlie Conerly, and Rutgers' Frank Burns. Rutgers' killer gridiron coach-and-quarterback combination of Harvey Harman and Frank Burns would mesh in the postwar year of 1946.

In 1934, the Scarlet coach was still J. Wilder Tasker, an excellent gridiron tactician and mentor in his own right. Tasker's team captain in 1934 was star center Al "Red" Twitchell. Other key performers on the Scarlet squad, which posted a season record of 5 wins, 3 losses, and 1 tie, were Arnold Truex, Lou Hermeda, Al Chizmadia, Tony Naparano, and the Winika brothers, Walter and Wilho. The Scarlet eleven notched solid wins over Boston University, Lafayette, and Lehigh, among others.

Tough losses came at the hands of Franklin and Marshall, powerful Penn coached by Harvey Harman, and a strong Colgate club which played at Rutgers for the first time that season.

At the end of the year, Scarlet lineman Al Twitchell was once again honored with various All-Star mentions for his gridiron work. After graduating, Twitchell took a coaching job at North Plainfield High School in New Jersey, where he mentored future Rutgers star lineman and linebacker Ernie Gardner. Eventually, Al Twitchell became the Rutgers athletic director.

The 1935 football season was historic for a number of reasons. Halfback Jay Berwanger of the University of Chicago made national sports headlines by earning the first Heisman Trophy ever awarded. Berwanger rushed for 4,108 yards over his three-year career at Chicago.

Quarterback William Shakespeare of Notre Dame was the composer of a fitting end to the 1935 gridiron matchup between the Fighting Irish and the Buckeyes of Ohio State. Shakespeare tossed a touchdown pass to Wayne Miller with thirty-two seconds remaining in the game to give Notre Dame a stunning 18 to 13 upset victory.

Rutgers dropped five out of nine contests in 1935. Captain Mo Bullard and teammates Art Perry, Dan Van Mater, Bob Zimmerman, Cuno Bender, Jack Keating, and Joe Nilan registered wins over Marietta, Lehigh, Lafayette, and Boston University. Scarlet fans were cheered by a decision to build a new and larger stadium across the Raritan River in Piscataway, New Jersey. The stadium would be erected on a 256-acre tract and be constructed as part of President Roosevelt's WPA Depression program, which created jobs for the unemployed. The new Rutgers stadium would be horseshoe shaped and would seat twenty thousand fans. It would have a construction cost of $1,310,000, of which the WPA would supply $1,104,696. Rutgers made up the difference. News of the new stadium prompted cries for Rutgers to play a big-time football schedule. Rutgers president Robert C. Clothier issued a statement of athletic policy reaffirming the university's belief that sports should continue to reflect only part of the total education experience. "We like to win our games and have tremendous satisfaction when we do so," wrote Clothier, "but we refuse to make a fetish of victory; we believe in sports for sports' sake." The new stadium would be a welcome upgrade from the aging athletic facilities of Neilson Field on the New Brunswick campus.

Fordham University in New York, coached by Jim Crowley, had its famous Seven Blocks of Granite in 1936. One of the blocks was Vince Lombardi, who later became an NFL coaching legend. The Seven Blocks of Granite gave up only one touchdown that season. It was a 1-yard plunge in Fordham's final game of the season against New York University. Fordham lost the game 7 to 6 and missed out on going to the Rose Bowl that year.

Rutgers ran into a brick wall on the gridiron in 1936 and won but a single game. However, playing college football on the East Coast in 1936 was no easy task. Yale thumped Rutgers 28 to 0 in 1936, but Yale had two Heisman Trophy winners on its squad. End Larry Kelley, who was known as "Laughing" Larry Kelley because of his demeanor, was voted America's top player in 1936 and won the Heisman Trophy. Kelley's teammate, halfback Clint Frank, was named the recipient of the Heisman Trophy in 1937. Yale's biggest rival, Harvard, did not have a Heisman hopeful in 1936 or 1937. It did have a budding football player who would eventually become president of the United States. John F. Kennedy was an end on the Harvard freshman squad in 1936 and played on the junior varsity football squad in 1937.

Lou Little was coaching the Columbia Lions in 1937 and his team captain was a stout guard named John Bateman. Bateman later became the head coach at Rutgers.

The first official college-football statistics were compiled in 1937. Center Alex Wojciechowitz of Fordham finished fourth to Clint Frank in the Heisman Trophy race.

Halfback Marshall Goldberg of Penn finished third. The runner-up in the Heisman balloting was Colorado halfback Byron "Whizzer" White, who led the nation in rushing yards (1,596) and scoring (122 points) in 1937.

The Scarlet football squad posted a winning record in 1937. Rutgers opened the year with victories over Susquehanna, Hampden-Sydney, Delaware, and Springfield. After a brutal 6 to 0 loss to Princeton, Rutgers rebounded with a 34 to 0 rout of Lehigh. Lafayette, guided by Hooks Mylin (the eventual American Football Coaches Association Coach of the Year in 1937), managed a slim 13 to 6 win over Rutgers. After being shut out by Ohio University, the Scarlet ended its season with a nail-biting 7 to 6 loss to Brown. Captain Art Perry and team leaders Bill Tranavitch, Arthur Gottlieb, and Doug Hotchkiss had to be satisfied with a respectable record of 5 wins and 4 losses.

Coach J. Wilder Tasker concluded his Rutgers coaching career in 1937 with a positive record of 31 wins, 27 losses, and 5 ties. Tasker turned over the helm of the Rutgers team to Harvey J. Harman, the outstanding Penn coach schooled in gridiron tactics by football immortal Glenn "Pop" Warner. Harman, an ex-tackle in the Warner system, was a firm believer in emphasizing offensive football. He was a smart playmaker who was also a strong advocate of holding spring football practice.

Rutgers' new football stadium in Piscataway, New Jersey, would be open for gridiron business in 1938. One of the first major moves orchestrated by Coach Harman was to reschedule the Rutgers-Princeton clash of 1938 from Princeton's Palmer Stadium to the new Rutgers stadium. Princeton and its head coach, Tad Wieman, agreed to make the switch.

Coach Harvey Harman's revamped Scarlet squad opened the 1938 season with an easy victory over Marietta. Captain Paul Harvey, Al Hasbrouck, and Ben Herr were all part of

Rutgers constructed a new stadium across the Raritan River from its New Brunswick campus in the late 1930s. The stadium, which is in Piscataway, New Jersey, opened in 1938. (From the personal collection of Frank Zukas/Courtesy Rutgers Athletic Communications)

Coach Harman's first win at Rutgers. In the second game of the season, Vermont proved to be a much tougher opponent. A 15 to 14 Scarlet victory was recorded with a little help from Herman Greif, John Casey, and Nelson Hopkins. A disappointing defeat to NYU came next. The loss was followed up with a shutout victory over Springfield.

On October 22, 1938, Rutgers dedicated its new stadium. Rutgers' first opponent in its new home was Hampden-Sydney. It was the second and last time the two schools played. A crowd of ten thousand turned out to christen the new Rutgers stadium. The visiting team was clearly no match for Rutgers. The Scarlet's Burt Hasbrouck tallied the first touchdown in the new stadium on a 2-yard plunge. Joe Varju, Art Gottlieb, and John Mullen all scored touchdowns for Rutgers in the Scarlet's 32 to 0 shutout victory. The following week Rutgers shut out Lehigh for its fifth win of the year.

Finally it was time for the much anticipated Rutgers-Princeton game at the new Rutgers stadium. A crowd of more than forty thousand turned out to watch the clash between the New Jersey rivals. Princeton had dominated Rutgers on the gridiron for many years. The loyal sons of Rutgers, playing for a new coach and in a new stadium, were not concerned with past results. It was the future and the start of a new trend that sparked the enthusiasm of a determined Scarlet squad. Besides that, it was payback time, gridiron style!

Princeton drew first football blood. Jack Daniel staggered into the end zone after a fine run to make the score Princeton 6 and Rutgers 0. The try for the extra point was no good.

The Princeton advantage was short-lived as Rutgers' Art Gottlieb fired a long pass completion to Parker Staples. Bill "Big Train" Tranavitch then tallied a touchdown to knot the score at 6-all. Len Cooke trotted on for the PAT and calmly booted the ball through the uprights to give Rutgers a 7 to 6 advantage over Princeton.

Princeton roared back. Dick Purnells added another touchdown for the visiting team. Stan Pearson then scampered 7 yards for another Princeton score. No extra points were made so Princeton led 18 to 7 late in the second period. With only a minute left in the first half, Scarlet lightning struck! Herm Greif scored for Rutgers. The extra point failed and Princeton led 18 to 13 at halftime.

The third period of the game was scoreless. It was in the fourth and final quarter that Rutgers mustered its offense for one last surge of power. Art Gottlieb was on target to receiver John "Moon" Mullen and the result was a touchdown pass that put Rutgers out in front of Princeton 19 to 18. Walter Bruyere came on and added the extra point for the Scarlet. The score was Rutgers 20 and Princeton 18, but time still remained in the game.

Late in the fourth quarter Princeton was driving when a punishing tackle by a Scarlet defender separated a Princeton runner from the pigskin. The bouncing ball was recovered by an alert Doug Hotchkiss of Rutgers and the Scarlet victory was in the bag. Rutgers beat Princeton by the score of 20 to 18.

The final game of the 1938 season was against Lafayette. Rutgers topped the Leopards 6 to 0 to notch their fifth win in a row. Coach Harvey Harman won 7 games and lost only 1 in his first season as the Scarlet's head coach. In a 1938 poll of some two hundred coaches, Harvey Harman was voted one of the five outstanding college football coaches of 1938. The honor was well deserved. However, it was just the start of a streak of gridiron successes for Coach Harman and his Scarlet footballers.

TV came to a college football game for the first time in 1939. A television camera mounted on a dolly at the 40-yard line used the industry's first telephoto lens to broadcast the gridiron contest between Fordham and Waynesburg. Fordham won the game 34 to 7.

Texas A&M, led by All-America fullback John Kimbrough, captured the National Championship. Iowa's star athlete, Nile Kinnick, won the Heisman Trophy.

Curiously, Rutgers was ignored by national pollsters in 1939 despite the fact that the Scarlet put together a string of thirteen straight games without a loss from 1938 to 1939.

The Scarlet beat Wesleyan University and Wooster in its first two games of 1939. A tie against Richmond followed. Rutgers then scored with easy wins over Maryland, Lehigh, and New Hampshire. Tougher victories came in games against Lafayette and Springfield. The only loss of the year was a 13 to 0 defeat by Brown in the final game. Rutgers compiled a record of 7 wins, 1 loss, and 1 tie. The Scarlet were not ranked nationally even though the team had a better record than nine of the twenty teams ranked and a win record equal to two additional ranked teams.

However, team captain William Tranavitch was rewarded for his outstanding play in 1939. Bill "Big Train" Tranavitch played in the North-South All-Star Game in Montgomery, Alabama. He also later played for the Detroit Lions in the National Football League.

Back Art Gottlieb continued his football career as a pro for the Buffalo Indians.

Harvey Harman (second from left) was appointed the Rutgers head coach in 1938. Harman's coaching staff in the 1940s included (left to right) Art Matsu, Ed Masavage, and Al Sabo. (From the personal collection of Andy Malekoff/Courtesy Rutgers Athletic Communications)

In 1940, halfback Tom Harmon of Michigan won his second straight scoring title. Harmon topped all college players by totaling 102 points in 1939 and 117 points in 1940. Harmon also won the Heisman Trophy in 1940. (Many years later, Tom Harmon's daughter, Kristen, would wed singer Rick Nelson, the son of former Rutgers quarterback Ozzie Nelson.)

The Rutgers football team of 1940 was a solid, well-balanced squad. They won 5 games and lost 3. Big wins came over Springfield, Lehigh, Marietta, Connecticut, and St. Lawrence. The three defeats, all of which were close contests, were at the hands of Princeton, Lafayette, and Maryland.

Key players on the 1940 squad included Ray Foster, Vince Kramer, Alex Szot, Jim Wallace, and center Milt Nelson, who served as team captain.

The world was on the verge of total war when the Scarlet squad led by co-captains Vinnie Utz and Ralph Schmidt took the field for the 1941 football season. Top college teams in the country included Duke, Notre Dame, Penn, Fordham, Navy, and Duquesne.

The Rutgers record that season may have been good enough for some national recognition, but the squad was once again overlooked by pollsters. The Scarlet club began the year with impressive victories over Alfred (34 to 0), Springfield (26 to 0), Lehigh (16 to 6), and Fort Monmouth (26 to 0). A midseason loss to Syracuse (7 to 49) spoiled the string of victories. Additional wins over Maryland (20 to 0), Connecticut (32 to 7), and Brown (13 to 7) were broken up by a loss to traditional rival Lafayette (0 to 16).

Key players on that 7–2 Rutgers team of 1941 were Steve Capestro, Gilbert Greenberg, Ford Ratti, and center Otto Hill, a three-year letterman. After graduation, Hill would serve Rutgers as an assistant coach and then as the business manager of the athletic department. Otto Hill's sons, Jim and John, later went to Lehigh to play football.

The end of the 1941 season saw the United States enter World War II after the Japanese bombing of Pearl Harbor. The war changed the world of college football and Rutgers was no exception. Coach Harvey Harman temporarily gave up his head coaching position to serve in the Navy. The war years halted the academic and athletic careers of many young men at Rutgers. Rutgers University historian Dr. Richard McCormick noted the Scarlet response for a national call to arms. Dr. McCormick wrote, "Altogether 5,888 Rutgers men, 1,700 of them undergraduates . . . served in the Armed Forces. . . . Inscribed in the service book in Kirkpatrick Chapel [on Rutgers' main campus] are the names of 234 men . . . who gave their lives in the line of duty." Those loyal sons of Rutgers made the ultimate sacrifice for their country. It proves that loyal sons (and now daughters) of Rutgers are loyal to more than just their school.

College football was dominated by two schools during the war years. Those schools were Army (West Point), coached by Earl "Red" Blaik, and Notre Dame, coached by Frank Leahy. From 1943 to 1949 Notre Dame won four national championships (1943, 1946, 1947, and 1949) and Army won two (1944 and 1945). Notre Dame had three Heisman Trophy winners (Angelo Bertelli in 1943, Johnny Lujack in 1947, and Leon Hart in 1949). Army had back-to-back Heisman winners in 1945 and 1946 with fullback Doc Blanchard and halfback Glenn Davis, who were dubbed Mr. Inside and Mr. Outside by the press.

At Rutgers, Harry Rockafeller took a second turn at coaching football and filled in for Harvey Harman, who had posted a record of 26 wins, 7 losses, and 1 tie before his departure. Harman's excellent assistant coaches also left to contribute to the war effort. Gone were assistants Frank Long, Ed Masavage, and Al Sabo. Sabo was particularly hard to replace. Al Sabo had been a star football and baseball player at Fordham. He'd also played pro baseball and served as a baseball coach at Rutgers. To fill the coaching spots vacated by Sabo, Long, and Masavage, Harry Rockafeller recruited Tom Kenneally, Dave Bender, Art Matsu, and former Rutgers star Bob Nash.

The Scarlet, with a substitute coaching staff in place, could muster only 3 wins in 8 contests during the 1942 season. There were wins over Bucknell, Vermont, and Springfield, and a tie with Fort Monmouth. A high point in the Scarlet loss to Maryland was a 99-yard kickoff return for a touchdown by Rutgers' Harold Connors. Another top performer on that 1942 club was center Ken MacDonald, who played professionally with the Chicago Cardinals after graduation.

Due to wartime travel restrictions, Rutgers played Lehigh and Lafayette four times each from 1944 to 1945. Rutgers topped Lehigh all four times, but dropped three out of four contests to Lafayette. The Scarlet also played Brooklyn College for the first and only time during that period. Brooklyn College forever won bragging rights over Rutgers by beating the Scarlet 12 to 6 in that gridiron contest.

Bob Goldberger captained the 1943 Scarlet squad and Joe D'Imperio was the captain of the 1944 red team. Art Price, who starred for the 1944 Scarlet, went on to play for the Pittsburgh Steelers.

The 1945 Rutgers football squad had the nucleus of a great team in the making. The team included Bert Manhoff, Art Mann, Andrew "Abe" Sivess, and young quarterback Frank Burns. Sivess and Burns would become cornerstones in Rutgers athletics for many decades to come.

Andy Sivess would win letters in three sports and later become an assistant coach and the head trainer of the university. His son, Greg, would later play football at Rutgers in the mid-1960s.

Frank Burns played baseball and football at Rutgers. He became one of Rutgers' best football players ever. Later, he enjoyed a pro career and became an assistant coach and then the head football coach at Rutgers. Both Sivess and Burns won the respect and admiration of generations of Rutgers athletes. They were unique individuals.

"You never saw any dirt on the back of Frank Burns's uniform," Andy Sivess once said. What he meant was Burns never got knocked on his can by an opponent. Frank Burns

Frank Burns, pictured circa 1947, was one of Rutgers' all-time great athletes. (From the personal collection of Andy Malekoff/Courtesy Rutgers Athletic Communications)

The 1947 Rutgers team included Andy Sivess, Jim Taigia, Bob Ochs, Al "Boomy" Malekoff, Harvey Grimsley, Ernie Gardner, Henry Pryor, Frank Burns, Herm Hering, and many other all-time Rutgers greats. (Courtesy Special Collections and University Archives, Rutgers University Libraries)

was tough! In addition to excelling at quarterback, Flinging Frankie Burns also played linebacker on defense. His nickname stemmed from the fact that passer Frank Burns could really fling the football.

Burns passed the Scarlet to a record of 5 wins and 2 losses in 1945. In 1946 Rutgers football celebrated a gridiron marriage made in heaven. Harvey Harman returned to coach the Scarlet, relieving Harry Rockafeller of duty. Coach Rockafeller willingly stepped aside, but not before he introduced Coach Harman to quarterback Frankie Burns. The Harman-Burns combination would prove lethal to most of Rutgers' gridiron opponents over the next few years. Counted among the Scarlet teammates of Burns and Sivess were a throng of excellent athletes. Center Ernie Gardner was also a vicious tackler from his linebacker position. Gardner, who had entered World War II as a private, emerged from the conflict as a major with the 352nd Fighter Group. He joined the Scarlet squad after being mustered out and was nicknamed "Pappy" by his college comrades. Speedster Richard Cramer could really move. He'd been timed at 9.9 seconds in the 100-yard dash. Other offensive scoring threats were Herm Hering and Al "Boomy" Malekoff. The team received added punch from Captain Joe D'Imperio and linemen Bob Ochs, Fred Sowick, Oakley Pandick, Frank Thropp, Mike Kushinka, Bill Vigh, and Jim "Chief" Taigia.

After losing two of the first three games to open the 1946 season, Rutgers began to roll. The Scarlet thumped George Washington, NYU, Harvard, Lafayette, Lehigh, and Bucknell. Added to an earlier victory over Johns Hopkins, Rutgers won a total of 7 games in 1946 while dropping only 2 games (to Princeton and Columbia). Frank Burns tossed 9 touchdown passes in 1946 and led his team to a 252-to-48-point advantage over Scarlet opponents. The 7 and 2 record of 1946 was the start of something big.

John Garrabrant, Pete Butkus, Irwin Winkelreid, Harvey Grimsley, John Sabo, and William "Bucky" Hatchet joined forces with veterans of the previous season and the net result was an even better record in 1947.

Rutgers opened the year with a loss to a tough Columbia club that had been ranked in the AP Top 20 two out of three seasons since 1945. The game was hotly contested, but the Scarlet went down to defeat. Rutgers did not lose again for the remainder of the gridiron year. The Scarlet won eight games, beating Western Reserve, Princeton, Fordham, Harvard, NYU, Brown, Lafayette, and Lehigh.

In the Lafayette contest, back Harvey Grimsley was inserted into the game in the fourth quarter. Grimsley scored 3 touchdowns in less than 14 minutes to help Rutgers post a 20 to 0 victory.

In Rutgers' homecoming game against Lehigh, the Scarlet squad really flexed its offensive muscle. Harvey Grimsley rushed for 2 touchdowns. Bucky Hatchett snared 2 touchdown tosses. (Hatchett grabbed a total of 7 touchdown passes that season.) John Sabo and Dick Cramer also tallied a touchdown each. Even big tackle Bob Ochs got in on the Scarlet scoring frenzy. Ochs snatched a Lehigh fumble out of midair and rumbled 23 yards for a Rutgers touchdown. The final score of that lopsided contest was Rutgers 46 and Lehigh 13.

Left: William "Bucky" Hatchett caught 7 touchdown passes in 1947. He was one of Rutgers' first great receivers. (From the personal collection of Andy Malekoff/Courtesy Rutgers Athletic Communications)

Right: Mike Kushinka was one of Rutgers' top linemen in the late 1940s. (From the personal collection of Andy Malekoff/Courtesy Rutgers Athletic Communications)

Rutgers outscored its opponents 234 points to 59 points in its 8 wins in 1947. Herm Hering was the leading Scarlet scorer with a total of 51 points. Hering had a rushing average of 5.9 yards. Ernie Gardner, Fred Sowick, Frank Thropp, Mike Kushinka, and Frank Burns received various All-East honors.

Frank Burns's 1947 stats were equal to or better than the stats of the top quarterbacks in the land that season. Burns completed 45 of 104 passes for 911 yards and 11 touchdowns. He also scored 2 touchdowns himself. Thanks to his work behind center, Rutgers ended up ranked 14th in total offense in the country. Burns ranked 18th in the nation in total yards and was second to Heisman Trophy winner Johnny Lujack of Notre Dame in average gain per pass.

In 1948 Rutgers once again stumbled in its opening game against Columbia. The team quickly regained its balance and, with additional manpower provided by Leon Root, Joe Furnari, Henry Pryor, and Mike Pannucci, went on to thump Colgate, Temple, Princeton, and Lehigh before losing a second game to Brown. The 1948 Scarlet finished the season with wins over Lafayette, NYU, and Fordham. It was the end of an impressive four-year run for Frank Burns and his Scarlet cohorts. In 1948 Burns completed 40 of 97 passes for 623 yards and 5 touchdowns. Over a four-year period Frank Burns had guided Rutgers to 27 wins against only 7 defeats. Of course, Burns was not the only reason for the outstanding success of the Rutgers squad over that span. Herm Hering, Harvey Grimsley, Henry Pryor, John Sabo, Dick Cramer, Bucky Hatchett, and Bill Vigh were all potent offensive weapons. Vigh played in the 1947 Blue-Gray college football All-Star game.

Henry Pryor starred as a return specialist and running back for Rutgers in 1948. (Courtesy Special Collections and University Archives, Rutgers University Libraries)

Ernie Gardner, Al Malekoff, Bob Ochs, Jim Taigia, Mike Kushinka, and Oakley Pandick provided punch on both sides of the ball. Gardner became a beloved high-school coach and community leader. The Rutgers Alumni Association now presents an annual award in Ernie Gardner's name to former Rutgers athletes in recognition of outstanding community service.

Jim "Chief" Taigia went on to become a successful high-school football coach. In the 1960s he returned to Rutgers as an offensive line coach. He remained in service to the Scarlet football program for many years.

However, the key element to Rutgers' overwhelming gridiron success in the late 1940s was Flinging Frankie Burns. He was an All-East selection in 1947. Burns was captain of the 1949 squad and won All-America Honorable Mention that season. Frank Burns played in the 1949 East-West College All-Star game in San Francisco. In the contest Burns was credited with making 17 tackles and was voted the game's Most Valuable Player. He was a second-round pick of the Philadelphia Eagles in the NFL draft and later played for the Cleveland Browns.

Flinging Frankie Burns threw for a total of 2,751 yards and 30 touchdowns during his years at Rutgers.

Rutgers reloaded in 1949. Another fine group of young athletes appeared on the scene for the 1949 season. Those budding stars included Robert D'Amato, Vic Archambault, Jim Monahan, and Bill Pellington. Returning lettermen Herm Hering, Henry Pryor, Harvey Grimsley, Fred Sowick, John Sabo, Leon Root, Bucky Hatchett, Al Malekoff, and Oakley Pandick welcomed them into the Scarlet gridiron fold. The meshing of new and old clicked to produce a fine season record of 6 wins and 3 losses. The Scarlet football squad of 1949 closed out the decade on a high note with its fifth consecutive winning record.

At the conclusion of the 1949 season, end Bucky Hatchett was named First Team All-East. Herm Hering became an NFL draft pick and later played for the Green Bay Packers. Harvey Grimsley closed out his stellar Rutgers career with a total of 28 touchdowns scored. Return specialist Henry Pryor ended his Rutgers career with 643 yards on punt and kickoff returns for a 21.3-yard average per runback. Al "Boomy" Malekoff turned his attention to high school football after graduation. Eventually he became the head football coach at Somerville High School in New Jersey. Somerville was the high school former Rutgers football star Paul Robeson had attended.

Left: Herm Hering, shown here in 1948, was an NFL draft pick and played for the Green Bay Packers. (From the personal collection Andy Malekoff/Courtesy Rutgers Athletic Communications)

Right: Jim "Chief" Taigia, who was a lineman at Rutgers in the late 1940s, is shown here as an offensive line coach at Rutgers in the late 1960s. (Courtesy Paul Krasnavage)

PART TWO 1950–1972

CHAPTER 5

THE FIRST HEISMAN CANDIDATE 1950–1958

Rock-and-roll revved up the American music scene in the 1950s. College football also began to move to the beat of a different drummer. Fast and flashy backs like Vic Janowicz of Ohio State, Johnny Lattner of Notre Dame, and Tommy McDonald of Oklahoma astonished gridiron fans with dazzling displays of open-field running. College football was changing. Linemen became bigger and stronger. Backs became quicker and more agile. Plays were now considerably more complex.

The fan base of college football exploded. People flocked to high profile football contests. The sport began to generate vast revenues for some colleges and universities. The increased revenue made more money available for student-athletes, who in some cases became athlete-students. That was not the case at Rutgers, even though some fans and alumni campaigned for a bigger-time schedule. Rutgers' high entrance requirements turned away many potential gridiron stars who could make the cut on the field but not in the classroom. Some outstanding athletes got into Rutgers, but could not stay in and flunked out. Rutgers had to compete with schools like Harvard, Yale, and Princeton for scholar-athletes. Rutgers couldn't go big-time and it had a hard time luring good players it needed away from Ivy League schools. In football Rutgers was caught between a rock and a hard place when it came to recruiting players. Rutgers needed a little help.

Support for Rutgers' unique brand of football came from varied sources. Over the years, Rutgers football survived thanks to the devotion of many unsung heroes who never made a tackle or block, caught a pass, or scored a touchdown. Those pillars of Scarlet include people like Leonor F. Loree (president of Delaware and Hudson Railroad), Fred "Pop" Hart (unofficial statistician for more than fifty years), David "Sonny" Werblin (play producer and former president of MCA-TV), Richard Hale, Herb Goodkind, Thomas T. Barr, Jack Anderson, Peter Hendricks, Mark Hershhorn, and Peter Jennings, to name just a few. On-the-field individuals who put in long hours of support time included team physician Dr. Hyman Copleman, team dentist Joel Fertig, equipment manager John Powers, trainers Jake Besas and Mike Stang, and many tireless team managers like Charles Sweetman, Tony Oliva, Terry Beachem, and Carol Goodkind.

Left: Rutgers center Leon Root (left) stands with Scarlet head coach Harvey Harman. Root was one of Rutgers' greatest linemen and later played with the Chicago Cardinals. (Courtesy Special Collections and University Archives, Rutgers University Libraries)

Right: Jim Monahan was an all-around athlete who starred in football and baseball for Rutgers. (Courtesy Special Collections and University Archives, Rutgers University Libraries)

Eventually Rutgers would make the adjustments necessary to play a big-time schedule without compromising its academic standards. However, in 1950 Rutgers was still an all-boys school where athletes had demanding class requirements that made playing sports a difficult task. So when a player with big-time potential appeared on the banks of the old Raritan, football fans sat up and took notice.

In 1950 Rutgers captain Leon Root and teammates Bill Pellington, Bob D'Amato, Joe Scaliotta, and Jim Monahan plowed through a tough schedule with games against Penn State, Syracuse, and a Princeton team led by All-American Dick Kazmaier. Rutgers posted a record of 4 wins and 4 losses in 1950. Three-year letterman Earl Read went on to play in the North-South All-Star Game. Leon Root won All-East honors and continued his playing career in the pros with the Chicago Cardinals. Linebacker Bill Pellington won gridiron fame in the NFL as a star for the Baltimore Colts. Pellington played in the classic 1958 NFL Championship between the New York Giants and the Baltimore Colts, won by the Colts in sudden death overtime (in which the first team to score wins). Many football historians consider that contest to be the greatest pro football game ever played, and a Rutgers player was part of it.

The frequency of televised college football games increased during the 1950s.

Rutgers' schedule in 1951 did not include any televised contests, nor did it include Princeton. Once again Rutgers was 4 and 4. However, down the road in New Jersey Princeton went undefeated thanks to the efforts of Heisman Trophy–winning halfback Dick Kazmaier.

At season's end Rutgers captain Jim Monahan was named All-East. He was later named an All-American in baseball. Monahan played in the North-South All-Star football game and continued his gridiron career as a pro for the Dallas Texans. Jim Monahan's 89-yard touchdown run against Temple in 1951 is still one of the longest scampers in Rutgers history.

Monahan wasn't the only member of the 1951 Scarlet squad to turn pro. Halfback Bob D'Amato later played for the Baltimore Colts in the NFL.

The two-platoon system in college football was voted out in 1952. Players could no longer specialize by playing just offense or defense. A team had to play both ways. There were no individual substitutes. Coaches had to substitute for the entire team. Generally teams alternated squads. One team played a full quarter, a second squad played the next quarter, and so on. Ivy League schools decided to ban spring football in 1951. They felt it put too much emphasis on sports. In those days spring drills were usually held at the end of the semester, not around or during spring break. Football players had to spend extra days at school, which posed a problem for some athletes. Rutgers decided to follow the Ivy League policy.

Rutgers had a .500 record (4–4–1) for the third straight year in 1952. The team was captained by Russ Sandblom and Howard Anderson.

In 1953, a back named Jim Brown was embarking upon a historic career at Syracuse University. Brown blasted into the end zone numerous times during the next few years. Unfortunately for Rutgers, touchdowns were tough to come by in 1953. Captain Don Duncan's squad managed only two wins that season. Scarlet center Joe Daddario had an outstanding season and was awarded Honorable Mention All-America honors for his fine gridiron work.

Rutgers got off to a disastrous start in 1954, but salvaged some respect thanks to the leadership of team captains J. Brian "By" O'Hearn and Angelo Iannucci. The team suffered a number of tough losses, including a defeat at the hands of a Penn State squad that featured future NFL stars Milt Plum at quarterback and Lenny Moore at halfback.

Left: Rutgers center Brian "By" O'Hearn was an Associated Press Honorable Mention All-American in 1954. (From the personal collection of By O'Hearn/Courtesy Rutgers Athletic Communications)

Right: Running back Angelo Iannucci (far left) and center Brian O'Hearn talk football with head coach Harvey Harman in 1954. (From the personal collection of By O'Hearn/Courtesy Rutgers Athletic Communications)

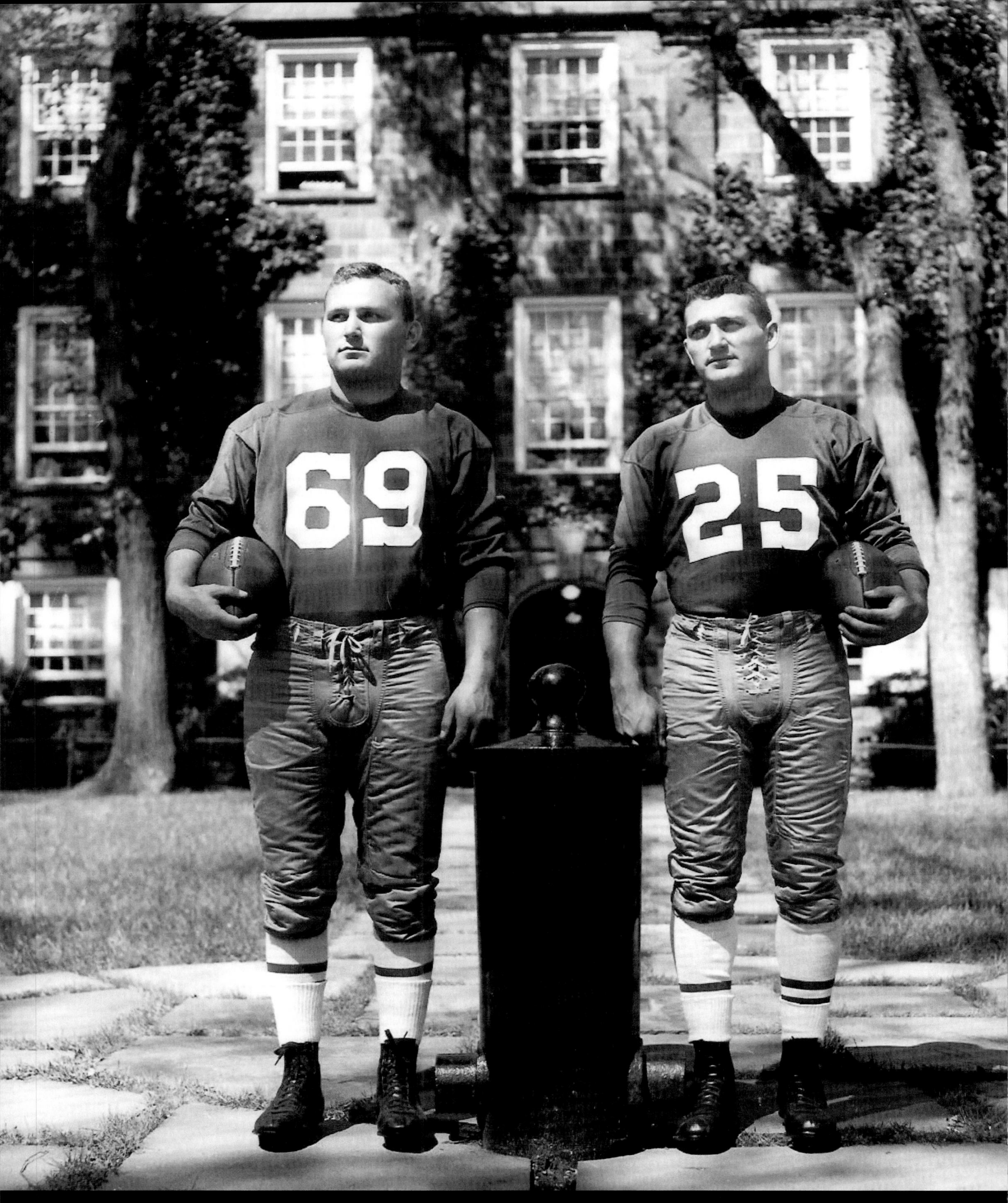
69
25

Rutgers, bolstered by the inspired play of quarterback John Fennell, rebounded to win 3 of their last 4 games.

At the conclusion of the season, center J. Brian O'Hearn earned First Team All-East and Honorable Mention All-America honors.

Eastern football was a tough place to ply the gridiron trade in 1955. Five of Rutgers' opponents were ranked nationally. Captains Ed Evans and Bob Kelley guided their Scarlet teammates to 3 wins in 8 games.

Another interesting note to the season was the role of an undersized but gutsy player named Tosh Hosada. Hosada may have been the first player of full Japanese descent to letter in football at Rutgers. Hosada booted two extra points in Rutgers' 14 to 12 victory over Brown in 1955.

Kojiro Matsugata, another footballer of Japanese ancestry, had played at Rutgers before Hosada, but was a member of the 1889 freshman team and did not earn a varsity letter.

Scarlet guard Bob Howard also made his gridiron presence known in 1955. Howard was All-East and Honorable Mention All-America.

The 1955 season concluded Harvey Harman's brilliant coaching career. The man who had guided Rutgers to numerous outstanding seasons finished with a career record of 48 wins, 37 losses, and 1 tie. Harvey Harman was later voted into the College Football Hall of Fame.

Scarlet football fans said good-bye to Coach Harman in 1955 and also bid farewell to Rutgers' fighting Chanticleer mascot. A contest was held at the university to replace the Chanticleer. Two popular suggestions were the Pioneers and the Cannoneers. The winning idea was submitted by student Oscar Huh. Huh's original suggestion was to dub Rutgers' new mascot the Red Knights. The name was altered slightly and became the Scarlet Knights of Rutgers. Oscar Huh later became a professor emeritus at Louisiana State University.

Rutgers' new head football coach was selected from more than seventy-five applicants by an alumni committee representing classes and coaching eras from 1918 up to 1955. The person determined to be the right man after an extensive search was John R. Steigman.

Steigman had competed in football, hockey, swimming, and lacrosse as an undergraduate at Williams College. He'd worked as an assistant for Coach Charlie Caldwell at Princeton. John Steigman knew football and he knew how to win.

Pigskin pollsters in the East focused their attention on Syracuse during the 1956 season. Syracuse, coached by Ben Schwartzwalder, ended up ranked 8th in the nation thanks to the efforts of their star running back Jim Brown. Brown capped off his college career by personally scoring 43 points (6 TDs and 7 PATs) in Syracuse's season-ending rout of Colgate.

Rutgers, with a new head coach and a new team mascot, was faced with tough gridiron sledding in 1956. Coach John Steigman decided to switch to a single-wing offense, and the new formation had not yet jelled with his players.

Scarlet co-captains John Laverty and Art Robinson, along with lettermen Ed Burkowski, Don Simone, and LeRoy Lusardi, could muster only enough punch to kayo three opponents in ten games.

The 1956 Rutgers team included a group of fine prospects, including Rich Oberlander, Ron Sabo, Bob Naso, Fred Simms, Charles Wermuth, Dave Pooley, and halfback William "Bill" Austin. In limited action, Austin led the squad with 661 all-purpose yards (rushing,

Opposite: Brian O'Hearn (left) and Angelo Iannucci were co-captains of the 1954 Scarlet Knights. (From the personal collection of By O'Hearn/Courtesy Rutgers Athletic Communications)

All-American Bill Austin was Rutgers' first Heisman Trophy candidate. (Courtesy Rutgers Athle Communications/Archives)

passing yards, punt returns, and kickoff returns combined). He'd also scored 7 touchdowns and gained 380 yards rushing. It was obvious to everyone who saw the Rutgers squad play in 1956 that Bill Austin was something special.

In his second season as coach of the Scarlet Knights, John Steigman named Bill Austin his starting halfback. Austin stood only about 5 feet 11 inches tall and weighed about 170 pounds. He was quick, but not exceptionally fast. People who studied his running style claimed he sort of slithered through the line in serpentine fashion, managing to wiggle past opposing defenders. Former assistant football coach Al Sabo once said, "Austin was light on his feet, but he ran heavy. He could smash into a would-be tackler with the brute force of an athlete twenty or twenty-five pounds heavier. He surprised guys by running them over."

The 1957 college football season was surprising in a number of ways. Notre Dame shocked the nation by ending Oklahoma's 27-game winning streak (7 to 0).

The 1957 Rutgers squad did not play Notre Dame or Oklahoma, but the Knights shocked many early-season skeptics by winning two of their first three games. Led by Bill Austin and team captain Richard Pfeiffer, Rutgers also racked up victories over Richmond, Lafayette, and Columbia. In the Columbia win, Austin ran and passed for 305 yards.

The Scarlet Knights, under Coach John Steigman, won five games in 1957. A highlight of the season was Bob Max's 67-yard punt return against Delaware.

Bill Austin fired 10 touchdown passes in 1957. He rushed for a total of 946 yards and scored 74 points to lead the team in both categories. Bill Austin's 1,425 total yards ranked second nationally (Bob Newman of Washington State totaled 1,444 yards). At the conclusion of the season, Bill Austin was named All-East.

The next season, Rutgers hailed Bill Austin as its first Heisman Trophy candidate. Sports experts regarded Austin as one of college football's elite players in 1958. His name was mentioned in the same breath as stars like Billy Cannon of LSU, Dick Bass of Pacific, and quarterback Don Meredith of SMU.

Other Rutgers stars in 1958 included Bruce Webster, Charles "Dutch" Wermuth, Larry Muschiatti, and Bob Simms.

Thirty thousand gridiron fans filled the stands of Princeton's Palmer Stadium to watch the Tigers take on the Scarlet Knights on opening day in 1958. An early stalemate was broken when Rutgers' Sam Crosby intercepted a Princeton pass. The pick set up a quick touchdown toss from Bill Austin to Bob Simms and Rutgers jumped out in front. Pinpoint passing by the Knights' Bruce Webster set up another touchdown, which Bill Austin scored. In the second half, Austin found the end zone again and fired another touchdown toss to receiver Bob Simms. The net result was a decisive 28 to 0 victory over Princeton.

Rutgers began to roll up victories. The Scarlet bested Colgate, then met and dismantled Richmond. Next on the schedule were the Bucknell Bisons. Heisman hopeful Bill Austin had a field day against Bucknell. He rushed for 189 yards and tallied 2 TDs. Bob Simms, Arny Byrd, Bill Tully, Paul Mullert, and Larry Brown all scored touchdowns in the 57 to 12 blasting of Bucknell on Parents' Day at Rutgers.

The Scarlet Knights beat Lehigh in the fifth game of the season. Next, Delaware went down to defeat. Then, Rutgers blasted Lafayette. In the Lafayette game, however, the undefeated Scarlet Knights squad suffered a bad break. The misfortune took the form of a broken bone in the hand of Scarlet star Bill Austin. Austin was labeled doubtful for a game against the Quantico Marines.

Opposite: A poster for the college football all-star game in 1959. (Courtesy Rutgers Athletic Communications)

The 7 and 0 Scarlet Knights were two games away from an undefeated season. Austin wanted to play. The trainers tried to get the Rutgers Heisman Trophy candidate ready for action, but Coach John Steigman wouldn't consider using Austin against Quantico. Bill Austin sat out the contest. Rutgers went into gridiron battle against the powerful and talented Marines without their star field general. Quantico played head to head and nose to nose with the Knights. In the fourth quarter, Quantico had a 13 to 6 lead over Rutgers. With the clock running down, halfback Bill Wolff (who played in place of Bill Austin) threw a terrific touchdown pass to Bob Simms to make the score 13 to 12 in favor of Quantico. Rather than take a tie and preserve the undefeated season, Rutgers coach John Steigman made a gutsy decision. He chose to go for two points and the win. When the two-point play failed, Rutgers tasted defeat for the first time that season. The Knights lost to Quantico by a single point.

The last game of the year was against Columbia at home. Bill Austin was cleared to play in the contest. After a scoreless first quarter, the Rutgers offensive floodgates gushed open. The Scarlet Knights put up 32 points in the second quarter. Bill Austin, playing with a padded hand, had a 64-yard TD scamper, a pass interception he returned for 52 yards, and another touchdown run from scrimmage. In all, Bill Austin tallied 5 touchdowns in his last college game. He scored a total of 34 points that day. The last score of the afternoon was a 31-yard touchdown pass from Bill Wolff to Jay Hunton, which made the final score 61 to 0 in favor of Rutgers. The Scarlet Knights finished the year with a record of 8 wins and 1 loss. The lone loss was by a single point.

The Scarlet Knights ended up ranked number 20 in the country in the final poll of the Associated Press. There were many individual honors for Rutgers players. Dutch Wermuth and Bob Simms received All-East recognition. Simms snared 9 touchdown passes in 1958. Guard Larry Muschiatti also garnered All-East honors. Bill Austin was named All-East and First Team All-American in 1958. He did not win the Heisman Trophy. The trophy was awarded to halfback Pete Dawkins of Army that year. All-American Bill Austin played in the Blue-Gray college All-Star game and later continued his football career as a pro with the Washington Redskins. In addition to being an All-American in football, Bill Austin won Honorable Mention All-America honors in lacrosse.

Austin's teammate Bob Naso also earned All-America mention in lacrosse. After graduation Naso went on to coach both lacrosse and football at Rutgers.

Bill Austin is one of the top players in the long history of Rutgers football. Austin rushed for 2,073 yards during his college career. He had 9 games in which he rushed for 100 or more yards. He had 3,066 yards of total offense (2,073 rushing and 993 passing). Bill Austin had a career average of 4.5 yards per carry. He scored 32 touchdowns and amassed 2,851 all-purpose yards in his Rutgers football career. His longest scoring scamper was an 87-yard touchdown run against Connecticut in 1957. He scored a total of 204 points in his career. In addition to his many offensive gems, Bill Austin excelled on defense. He had 13 interceptions during his three-year varsity career and returned those picks for a total of 371 yards. He had an 85-yard interception return against Richmond in 1957. The Scarlet Knights' Bill Austin was an all-around student-athlete. In a public interview after his football days at Rutgers ended, Austin described his experiences on the college gridiron in the simplest terms. "It has been a lot of fun," said Bill Austin.

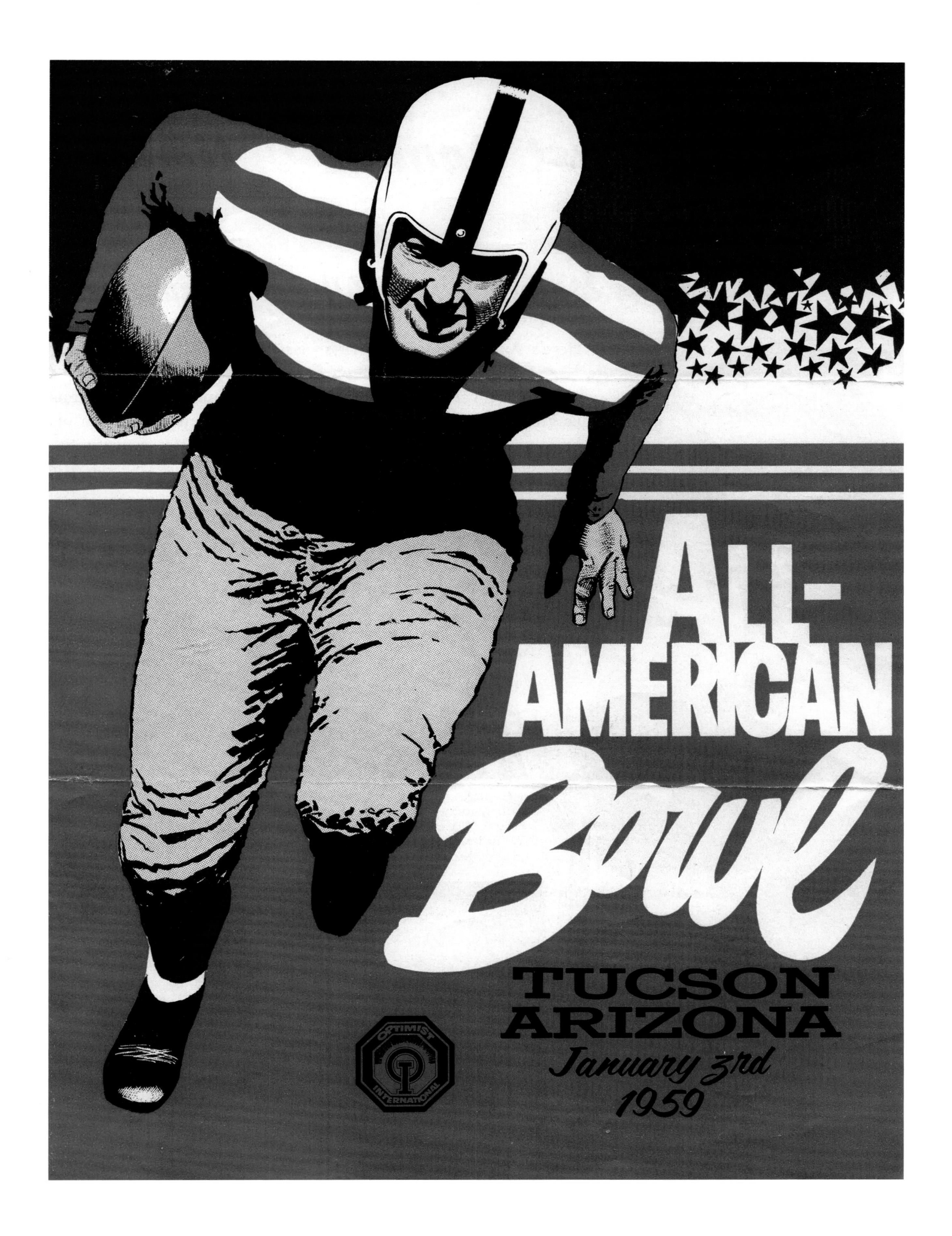
ALL-
AMERICAN
Bowl
TUCSON
ARIZONA
January 3rd
1959
OPTIMIST
INTERNATIONAL

CHAPTER 6
UNDEFEATED

1959–1961

In 1959 college football teams got their kicks by attempting and making more field goals. College kickers were delighted when the rules committee widened the gap between goalposts from 18 feet 23 inches to 23 feet 4 inches wide. The end result was that successful field goals increased on the college gridiron by more than ninety percent over the previous year.

That same year, Syracuse had phenomenal success under Coach Ben Schwartzwalder. Syracuse finished the year undefeated and won the National Championship. Halfback Billy Cannon of LSU took home the Heisman Trophy as college football's top player.

Coach John Steigman's 1959 Scarlet squad was led by its captain, Bob Simms. Bob was the second of four Simms brothers to play football at Rutgers. Gene Simms was Bob's older brother and a guard. Steve and Dick Simms were younger than Bob and played fullback and end respectively. All the Simms brothers were fine athletes, but it was tight end Bob Simms and fullback Steve Simms who starred for the Scarlet Knights on the gridiron. Bob and Steve were starters for the 1959 Knights.

Other top players on that Scarlet squad included Arnold "Arny" Byrd, Lester Senft, Dick Pencek, and newcomers Bill Speranza, Richard Lawrence, and Sam Mudie.

Rutgers opened the 1959 gridiron season against its traditional rival, the Princeton Tigers. Scarlet QB Bill Wolff fired a first-period touchdown pass to Arny Byrd. Rutgers then added a 2-point conversion. Princeton soon battled back to score, but failed on the conversion try. Strong defense was then the name of the game until the final gun. The 8 to 6 score held up and Rutgers chalked up win number one. Wins two and three came against Connecticut and Colgate.

The following week, undefeated Rutgers was shocked by Bucknell and lost to the Bisons. Rutgers then rode an erratic win-lose roller coaster for the rest of the season. A record of 6 wins and 3 losses was the end result of the up-and-down ride.

Captain Bob Simms was named First Team All-East. Simms had 4 touchdown catches in 1959 and led the team with 345 receiving yards. He also led in scoring with a total of 20 points.

John Bateman, a former star player at Columbia, became the head coach of the Rutgers Scarlet Knights in 1960. (Courtesy Rutgers Athletic Communications/ Archives)

Over his career Bob Simms led Rutgers in receiving from 1957 to 1959. In all, Simms had 13 touchdown catches. Bob Simms continued his football career in the pros playing tight end for the New York Giants and the Houston Oilers.

At the end of the decade, another page turned in the long history of Scarlet Knights football, concluding John Steigman's stint as the Rutgers head football coach. Steigman wanted to return to the Ivy League coaching ranks. He left Rutgers to take the top gridiron post at the University of Pennsylvania. Coach Steigman's career record at Rutgers ended with 22 wins, 15 losses, and 0 ties.

In a sort of fair-exchange coaching swap, Penn assistant coach John Bateman was announced as the new head coach of the Rutgers Scarlet Knights. Bateman was a perfect fit for Rutgers. He was not only a gridiron innovator and play master, but also a well-respected scholar. John Bateman was a graduate of Columbia. He'd played guard for gridiron icon Lou Little and was captain of the Columbia Lions squad his senior season. Bateman had a master's degree in political science and a doctoral degree in education. The doctorate entitled Bateman to use the title Dr. John Bateman. He quickly became known as Dr. John to Rutgers football fans.

Dr. John Bateman's original gridiron staff included Warren Schmakel, Chuck Klausing, Dewey King (who later became the head coach at San Jose State), and Matt Bolger (who later became a Hall of Fame baseball coach at Rutgers).

In 1960, the door opened on a new era of college football. Standing in the breach waiting to take their first steps toward football coaching immortality were a group of budding gridiron greats. Those football masterminds included Joe Paterno of Penn State, Dan Devine of Missouri, John McKay of USC, Frank Broyle of Arkansas, Vince Dooley of Georgia, Bud Wilkinson of Oklahoma, Woody Hayes of Ohio State, Ara Parseghian of Notre Dame, Wayne Hardin of Navy, and Jordan Oliver of Yale.

Coach John Bateman of Rutgers quietly aspired to elevate the Rutgers football program to loftier heights. The Scarlet players were up to the challenge. In 1960 the Knights began a gridiron rise to power which raised the eyebrows of football pollsters nationwide.

The single-platoon system of college football was still in effect in 1960. There were no specialists or single substitutions. Rutgers was blessed with two outstanding quarterbacks in Sam Mudie and Bill Speranza. Mudie was the big-play guy. Speranza was the steady and reliable field general. The squad also had a double dose of super centers in Captain Lester Senft and newcomer Alex Kroll.

Rutgers sports stationery in 1960 had drawings of team captain Lester Senft and the Rutgers coaching staff. (From the personal collection of Charlotte Moeller Pellowski)

Kroll had been an All–Ivy League lineman as a sophomore at Yale. Unhappy with Ivy League life, Alex Kroll left Yale for Rutgers. He found Rutgers appealing both academically and athletically.

The Scarlet squad of 1960 featured a long list of star players on its roster, which included veterans Bill Tully, Paul Benke, Justin Pahls, and Larry Brown. Young stars on the rise were Lee Curley, Tony Simonelli, Rich Webb, and backs Steve Simms and Pierce Frauenheim. Frauenheim also excelled as a defensive back and punt returner. He had great respect for the unique individual abilities of his teammates.

"Alex Kroll had charisma," said Frauenheim in describing the Scarlet's rugged center. "He was a mature person who was a smart offensive player." Pierce Frauenheim had equally high praise for quarterback Sam Mudie, who shared duties as a pass defender with Frauenheim, Bob Yaksick, and Joe Kowalski. "Sam Mudie was a quiet leader," said Frauenheim. "He was a very versatile athlete. Mudie was a fine quarterback, an outstanding safety, and a good punter."

Dr. John Bateman planned to utilize the athletic abilities of his versatile players, especially on offense. Bateman scrapped John Steigman's old single-wing formation, which featured Bill Austin. Bateman's multiple-wing T formation would give various players a chance to carry the ball and catch passes.

Defensive coach Dewey King also added some new concepts on the other side of the ball. He believed that good pass defense was actually an offensive weapon. He emphasized picking off opponents' passes rather than just breaking up completions. He wanted his defensive backs to be aggressive. King decided to reward his defenders with helmet decals for big plays. Rutgers was one of the first college football programs to use helmet decals as a motivating force for players.

Dewey King was Rutgers' defensive coordinator in the early 1960s. He later became head football coach at San Jose State. (Courtesy San Jose State Athletics)

With the offense and defense ready to go, Rutgers took on Princeton in the first game of the 1960 season. In the opening quarters defense ruled and the teams went into the lockers at halftime with goose eggs on the scoreboard. In the third period Rutgers' Bill Tully turned in the big play of the day. He tucked the pigskin under his arm and jetted 83 yards for a Scarlet score. Paul Benke added the point after. Rutgers' lead seemed comfortable until Princeton's Jack "Silky" Sullivan fielded a Scarlet punt in the fourth quarter and sprinted 60 yards for a touchdown. The Tigers' Hank Large snared a pass for a 2-point conversion and Princeton was out in front 8 to 7 over Rutgers.

Time began to run out for Rutgers. With precious seconds ticking by, the Tigers' offense misfired. A fumble was recovered by a Rutgers defender in Princeton territory. There was a little more than a minute remaining in the game. It was enough time for Rutgers QB Sam Mudie to make a big play. Mudie, utilizing the blocking power of his center, Alex Kroll, ran a quarterback sneak and rumbled into the end zone for the go-ahead points. Time expired and Rutgers won!

The Scarlet traveled to Connecticut to register win number two. In the first home game of the season, Rutgers pasted Colgate. Bucknell came visiting and found Rutgers Stadium an inhospitable place. The Bisons were beaten by the Knights. Rutgers then crossed the state line to take on Lehigh in Pennsylvania. The result of the trip was a win for the Scarlet. The Knights were riding high with a 5 and 0 record when Villanova came into New Brunswick to play the State University of New Jersey.

Rutgers' bid for an undefeated season was spoiled in stunning fashion. Villanova shocked Rutgers by beating the Knights 14 to 12 with a little help from a failed 2-point conversion try.

Rutgers roared back from its narrow defeat to wreak havoc upon its remaining opponents. The Knights battered Lafayette, shut out Delaware, and crushed Columbia in the final game of the season. Rutgers' Arny Byrd had a 70-yard punt return in the Columbia contest.

For the second time in three years, Rutgers finished the season with 8 wins and only 1 loss.

Rutgers center Alex Kroll was named All-East and garnered Honorable Mention All-America honors. Fullback Steve Simms also earned All-East honors and was Honorable Mention All-America. In 1960, Steve Simms led the Scarlet in scoring with 36 points. Since Bob Simms had led Rutgers in scoring in 1959, the Simms siblings were the first brothers in Rutgers football history to accomplish that back-to-back feat.

Arny Byrd led Rutgers in reception yards and was named the winner of the Homer Hazel Trophy as the team's Most Valuable Player. Paul Benke was honored for his diligent work on the football field and in the classroom. Benke earned a National Football Foundation Scholar-Athlete Award.

John Bateman made his Rutgers head coaching debut in remarkable fashion. His trademark shout of "Everybody up!" at the start of games and at halftime helped inspire the on-field performance of his team. When a coach loses only one game at the start of his career there is very little room for improvement. It's only logical that the next step is . . . an undefeated season!

The 1961 college football season was a year of firsts. Coach Paul "Bear" Bryant guided Alabama to a perfect 11 and 0 season and its first National Championship. Syracuse halfback Ernie Davis became the first African-American football player to win the Heisman Trophy (tragically, Davis would die a short time later of leukemia). Tackle Merlin Olsen became the first player from Utah State to win the Outland Trophy as America's top lineman. Another historic first was about to occur at the State University of New Jersey, where college football was born back in 1869. The elusive unbeaten record, which had slipped through the fingers of various Rutgers squads in the past, would once again be within the grasp of a Scarlet squad. All Dr. John Bateman's team had to do was grab it.

Prior to the start of the 1961 season, Rutgers athletic director Harry Rockafeller stepped down from his post. "Mr. Rutgers" Rockafeller was replaced by his able assistant Al Twitchell, the former Scarlet football and lacrosse star.

Coach Bateman's 1961 coaching staff included two new faces. One was ex-Scarlet quarterback Frank Burns. The other was Bob Naso, who had played with Bill Austin. Both Burns and Naso were veterans of past Rutgers squads that had narrowly missed posting perfect season records.

As usual, Rutgers' season began at Palmer Stadium in Princeton. A crowd of more than forty thousand fans crammed into the Tigers' home stadium to watch the contest. After a scoreless first period, Princeton's Bill Merlini blasted into the end zone to give Princeton the lead.

Inspired by team captain Alex Kroll, Rutgers embarked upon a long offensive drive that ended with Steve Simms smashing into the end zone for a touchdown. With the score 7 to 6 in favor of Princeton, Sam Mudie once again made the big play. The 6-foot-5-inch QB ran the pigskin across the goal line on a 2-point play. The first half ended with the Knights enjoying a slim 8 to 7 advantage.

Neither team could mount much offense in the second half. Rutgers clung to a 1-point lead with time running down. Suddenly, offensive lightning struck for Rutgers. Second

Head Coach Dr. John Bateman prowls the Rutgers sidelines. (Courtesy Rutgers Athletic Communications)

unit quarterback Bill Speranza spotted Scarlet receiver Lee Curley in the open. Speranza threw a dart. Curley caught it and streaked for the Tiger end zone. Lee Curley bolted 87 yards for an insurance touchdown with less than three and one-half minutes to go in the game. Dave Brody then found his way across the goal line on the 2-point play. The Rutgers lead was a comfortable 16 to 7 bulge.

Princeton refused to roll over and concede defeat. The Tigers stormed back in valiant fashion. A long touchdown toss trimmed Rutgers' lead to 16 to 13. The Scarlet Knights held on and recorded their first win of the season. The game set the tone for the rest of the year.

The second game of the season was a home contest against Connecticut. Rutgers easily outclassed the Huskies. The Scarlet Knights then traveled to Pennsylvania for a game

Rutgers beat Penn to win its fifth game in a row in 1961. (Courtesy Pierce Frauenheim)

against dangerous old rival Bucknell. The Knights beat the Bisons and left Pennsylvania with a record of 3 wins and 0 defeats.

Next came Lehigh at Rutgers Stadium. With the help of Pierce Frauenheim's 70-yard punt return, Rutgers spanked Lehigh. Up next was the University of Pennsylvania. Former Penn assistant John Bateman butted heads with Penn's current head coach and former Scarlet gridiron mentor John Steigman. Bateman's squad won the battle. Next, the Scarlet Knights traveled to Easton, Pennsylvania, for a contest against Lafayette. The Knights easily tamed the Leopards. The Rutgers Scarlet Knights were steamrolling over their foes.

National pollsters took notice of Rutgers. The Scarlet Knights were undefeated in six outings and John Bateman was being heralded as football's coaching flavor of the month. Everyone wondered, What was the secret to the new Scarlet success?

"John Bateman let his coaches coach," stated Tony Oliva, who served as team manager of the 1961 squad along with William Huber. Oliva and Bateman maintained a long friendship and working relationship throughout their lives. They were both later involved in the early development of Rutgers' Scarlet R sports support program.

What Oliva meant is that Dr. John Bateman utilized all the individual skills and attributes of his staff. Bateman saw to the overall supervision of his team. However, he gave his offensive and defensive coordinators the freedom to govern their respective units. Bateman maintained control of his staff without suffocating the enthusiasm and creativity of his assistant coaches.

Bateman's approach to coaching in 1961 proved successful beyond question. Rutgers demolished Delaware for win number seven.

Win number eight came in an away game against Colgate. In the Scarlet victory, Rutgers' Sam Mudie showed off his skills on the defensive side of the ball. Mudie established a Rutgers record by intercepting 3 passes and returning them for a total of 115 yards. In all, Rutgers defenders pilfered a total of 5 Colgate passes in that contest.

Rutgers stood at 8 wins and 0 losses after the Colgate contest. There were whispers of possible bowl invitations. Some said Rutgers was headed to the Sun Bowl. Others speculated the Knights would travel to the Liberty Bowl. A number of bowl possibilities were discussed whenever fans of Rutgers football met that year.

The bowl rumors were abruptly terminated when Rutgers officials publicly announced that the university would not consider any bowl invitations whatsoever because of academic concerns for the players. A bowl appearance might cut into the exam schedule. Athletic Director Al Twitchell announced to the press, "If the team is fortunate enough to conclude its schedule undefeated, then it would be regarded as the greatest in Rutgers history—and that's glory enough for any squad."

The goal of the Rutgers coaches and players quickly became focused on a single target. There was but one game remaining on the 1961 schedule. Rutgers set its sights on the attainment of an unbeaten and untied season.

The Columbia Lions were the final opponents of the Rutgers Knights that year. Columbia and Rutgers had a long football tradition. The teams first played against each other in 1870. Columbia spoiled Rutgers' perfect record in 1947. Rutgers football fans wondered if the 6 and 2 Lions of Columbia would play the role of spoilers once again.

An anxious crowd of 25,000 packed into Rutgers Stadium for the Scarlet home contest against Columbia. There was a resounding collective gasp of shock as Columbia jumped out to a 3 to 0 lead on a successful field goal. A sigh of relief followed as Scarlet halfback Pierce Frauenheim took a handoff and dashed for the go-ahead touchdown. The extra

Rutgers quarterback Bill Speranza looks back after handing off to Pierce Frauenheim (#23) for an off-tackle run in 1961. (Courtesy Pierce Frauenheim/Photo by Will Gainfort)

point conversion gave Rutgers a 7 to 3 advantage, which the Knights maintained at the half break.

In the third period, the Columbia Lions clawed their way back into the game. Walt Congram of Columbia caught a TD toss. Almost immediately afterwards the Lions' Mike Hassam intercepted a Rutgers pass and returned it for a score. Suddenly, Columbia was out in front of Rutgers 19 to 7. The home crowd was stunned into silence. Columbia was 12 points ahead of undefeated Rutgers with only minutes to go in the third quarter.

Suddenly, Scarlet return specialist Dave Brody ignited a spark of offensive life. Brody returned the ensuing kickoff 58 yards. Moments later field general Bill Speranza hooked up with his favorite receiver, Lee Curley, for a touchdown to start the fourth quarter. Rutgers had quickly whittled down the Columbia lead to 6 points.

Columbia went back on offense. Rutgers' defensive line came up big and pressured the Lions' quarterback. The Scarlet's Pierce Frauenheim made a key interception and returned the ball to the Lions' 28-yard line. Rutgers' offense took charge and Bill Speranza tallied the tying touchdown behind a crushing block by All-Star center Alex Kroll. The game was now knotted at 19-all after a failed conversion try.

Rutgers sensed that Columbia was beginning to buckle under the Scarlet onslaught and poured on the pressure offensively and defensively. After Columbia gave the ball back to Rutgers, the Scarlet scoring machine shifted into overdrive. A 60-yard drive ended with fullback Steve Simms plunging into the end zone. Rutgers added the point after touchdown and the Scarlet climbed on top by a 26 to 19 score.

Columbia began a drive of its own. Ball hawk Pierce Frauenheim picked off his second pass of the afternoon. This time the speedy halfback returned the interception 30 yards for another Rutgers score. Frauenheim's heroics closed the door on any possible Columbia comeback and Rutgers went on to clinch a 32 to 19 win. Rutgers iced its first undefeated season in history. Pierce Frauenheim was the star of the day, but many Rutgers stars had glowing gridiron moments during the course of the 9 and 0 season. It was truly a team effort. At the conclusion of the game, Rutgers University president Mason Gross

Left: Rutgers center Alex Kroll was named an All-American in 1961. (Courtesy Rutgers Athletic Communications/Archives)

Pages 70–71: The Rutgers football team was undefeated (9–0) in 1961 and ended up ranked number 15 in the country. (Courtesy Pierce Frauenheim/Photo by Will Gainfort)

23

33
50

Opposite: Center Alex Kroll and fullback Steve Simms of Rutgers played in the 1962 Senior Bowl.
(Courtesy Rutgers Athletic Communications)

anointed the 1961 squad as Rutgers' "Greatest Team." As time passed, the 1961 Scarlet Knights would always be remembered as one of Rutgers' greatest gridiron clubs.

The 1961 Knights were recognized by national pollsters for their accomplishments. The team ended up ranked number 15 in the country, ahead of teams like UCLA, Penn State, Rice, and Arizona.

The Rutgers secondary, which had 26 interceptions in 9 games in 1961, led the nation in that category.

Coach John Bateman was named the College Coach of the Year by the Washington, D.C., Touchdown Club.

Quarterback and safety Sam Mudie led the nation in pass return yards in 1961 (167 yards). He also led the Scarlet in total offense with 703 yards and in scoring with 70 points. Mudie was voted All-East and was selected to play in the North-South All-Star Game. In addition, Sam Mudie was named Rutgers' Most Valuable Player.

Fullback Steve Simms had a banner year and career for Rutgers. He led the team in rushing with 614 yards and topped the squad with 627 all-purpose yards. In 1961 Steve Simms concluded his Rutgers career with 1,240 yards on 205 carries for a stunning average of 6 yards per carry. In 1961 Steve Simms garnered All-East and Honorable Mention All-America honors. He played in the North-South and Senior Bowl All-Star games.

Other Rutgers players received a variety of awards. Rutgers' Tom Kocaj was named New York's Athlete of the Year. The Scarlet's Joe Kowalski was presented with a National Sportsmanship Award from the Gridiron Club of Boston.

Scarlet center Alex Kroll received the most recognition. He was named All-East by the Associated Press and the Eastern College Athletic Association. In addition, he was voted First Team All-America by the AP, the Newspaper Enterprise Association, and *Sports Review*. Kroll played in the Senior Bowl All-Star Game.

Alex Kroll was a Henry Rutgers Scholar and graduated with a perfect grade-point average. He was the winner of a National Football Foundation Scholar-Athlete Award. Kroll later served as the president and CEO of Young and Rubicam, one of the world's largest advertising companies.

Sam Mudie and Alex Kroll continued their football careers after graduation. Mudie spent time with the Pittsburgh Steelers in the National Football League. Kroll spent a year snapping the ball for the old New York Titans of the American Football League. The Titans later became the New York Jets. Alex Kroll is a member of the National Football Foundation Hall of Fame.

Several members of the undefeated team went on to have illustrious coaching careers. Pierce Frauenheim, the hero of the 1961 Columbia game, became legendary in New Jersey as the head football coach at Immaculata High School. Frauenheim's squads won numerous New Jersey private-school state championships. Bill Speranza, one of the heroes of the 1961 Princeton game, became a successful high school coach in New Jersey and returned to Rutgers as a longtime assistant coach to John Bateman and then to Frank Burns.

Eddie Wilson
QB.
Alex
Kroll
C.
All America
ARIZONA
RUTGERS
NORTH
RUTGERS
Steve Simms, FB.
Jimmy Carpenter, B.
Dan Grego, T.
Pete Kakela, T.
OKLAHOMA
WYOMING
MICH. STATE

CHAPTER 7

SPEED BUMPS

1962–1968

The college football scene of the mid-1960s featured a long line of famous running backs. Topping the list was O. J. Simpson of USC, who captured the Heisman Trophy in 1968 (and many years later had a horrifying fall from grace). Included among those notable gridiron thoroughbreds were Brian Piccolo of Wake Forest (who turned pro with the Chicago Bears and tragically died of cancer), Calvin Hill of Yale (the father of NBA star Grant Hill), Larry Csonka of Syracuse, Franco Harris of Penn State, and Cosmo Iacavazzi of Princeton.

Rutgers had its own comet in cleats in the form of halfback Bryant Mitchell, who kept pace with most of the elite ball carriers of the period. In the later part of the sixties, Mitchell established a multitude of rushing records at Rutgers.

However, before Bryant Mitchell ever donned a Scarlet uniform, Rutgers quarterback Bob Yaksick was faced with the difficult task of guiding a Rutgers squad ravaged by graduation. Gone were most of the stars of the 1961 unbeaten team. Bob Yaksick and captains Tony Simonelli and Tom Tappen didn't have to rebuild, but the team did have to reload at key positions.

The 1962 squad suffered through tough losses to Princeton and Connecticut to start the season. The Knights then regrouped to record wins over Colgate, Lehigh, Lafayette, and Penn. In the Penn victory, Rutgers' Bill Thompson had a dazzling 94-yard kickoff return. Unfortunately, disappointing losses to Delaware, Villanova, and Virginia erased any hopes of a better than .500 season. A solid victory over Columbia resulted in a 5 and 5 record, which proved to be an unsatisfying postscript to an undefeated squad.

Bob Yaksick led the 1962 team in scoring with 36 points and was named the Knights' Most Valuable Player. Yaksick was selected in the NFL draft by the Chicago Bears.

Tight end and team captain Tom Tappen was named All-East.

In 1963 quarterback Roger "The Dodger" Staubach of Navy won the Heisman Trophy as America's top player in his junior year. Staubach was nicknamed "The Dodger" because of his ability to scramble when under pressure from defensive linemen.

Princeton's Cosmo Iacavazzi shared the national scoring title with Dave Casinelli of Memphis State. Each man tallied a total of 84 points. Rutgers had a tough time scoring

Opposite: Rutgers quarterback Jack Callaghan carries the ball for a first down against Lehigh in 1965. (Courtesy Jack Callaghan)

points in 1963 and opened the year with successive shutout losses to Princeton and Harvard. Team captain Tony Hoeflinger received help from Dave Stout, Jack Hohnstine, and Don Viggiano in scratching out wins over Lehigh, Lafayette, and Boston University. Rutgers finished the year with a record of 3 wins in 9 games.

Dave Stout led the team with 634 passing yards and was the winner of the Homer Hazel Award as the Most Valuable Player of 1963. Tony Hoeflinger was voted First Team All-East as a guard. After graduation Hoeflinger became an assistant football coach at New Jersey's Franklin High School and later helped steer several Franklin athletes into the Rutgers football program.

Ara Parseghian became the head coach of Notre Dame in 1964. Brian Piccolo of Wake Forest led the nation in scoring with 111 points and in rushing with 1,044 yards. Linebacker Dick Butkus of Illinois finished third in the Heisman race behind quarterback Jerry Rhome of Tulsa and QB John Huarte of Notre Dame, who took home the award as America's top college player.

After hitting a gridiron speed bump in 1963, Rutgers bounced back in 1964. The season began with some changes in John Bateman's coaching staff. Assistant coach Warren Schmakel left to take the head coaching position at Boston University. Former Scarlet quarterback Bill Speranza returned to his alma mater as an assistant.

In September of 1964 Rutgers was ready to rumble on the gridiron. Veteran players Roger Kalinger, Peter Savidge, Gene Renna, and Captain Bob Norton provided spirit and leadership. Newcomers Charlie Mudie, Ron Kenny, Bob Schroeder, and John "Jack" Emmer added youthful punch on both sides of the ball.

The opening game against Princeton in 1964 could have gone either way. The powerful Princeton offense, led by Tiger star Cosmo Iacavazzi, managed a single touchdown, which was scored by Don McKay. Princeton's premier kicker, Charley Gogolak (who would go on to star in the pro ranks for many years), booted a 41-yard field goal to give the Tigers a 10 to 0 lead over the Scarlet Knights. Rutgers roared back in the fourth quarter as Roger Kalinger tossed a touchdown pass to Bill Green. Time ran out on Rutgers and the Knights dropped a 10–7 opening day decision at Palmer Stadium. Coach Dick Colman's Princeton Tigers went on to win eight more games and finished the year unbeaten and ranked number 13 in the country.

The Scarlet Knights put together a nice win streak of their own. Rutgers beat Connecticut, topped Lehigh, and dumped the University of Pennsylvania. Ralf Stegmann's 51-yard touchdown scamper helped Rutgers notch the win over Penn.

Coach John Bateman's club then edged Columbia for its fourth victory. Next Rutgers bested Boston University and blasted Lafayette. Season-ending losses to Delaware and Colgate spoiled what could have been another great Rutgers season.

The 6 and 3 record of 1964 suggested that Rutgers was once again ready to accelerate back onto the winning track. Unfortunately, another speed bump lay ahead.

Rutgers' Roger Kalinger had an outstanding season in 1964. He led the Scarlet in passing and total offense. Kalinger was named the team's MVP.

College football flip-flopped on its playing rules in 1964. Free substitution and two-platoon football were legalized. Players could once again specialize on offense or defense. Few if any athletes would play both ways from then on. It was good-bye to single-platoon football forever.

College football fans also bid farewell to one of the game's true icons in 1965. Gridiron pioneer Amos Alonzo Stagg, the inventor of the onside kick and men in motion as well

14
80
74

as the first coach to use tackling dummies and blocking sleds, passed away at 102 years of age.

Rutgers suffered a loss of momentum in 1965 and found wins very hard to come by. Captain Pete Savidge and a crew of lettermen headed up by Tom Connelly, Jack Callaghan, George Lamb, Don Riesett, and Bob Stohrer gave the game their best efforts week after week. Kicker Jack Hohnstine remained a reliable source of points. Top linemen Ron Kenny and Sampson Brown made key contributions. Speedy return specialist Jim Baker was a bright spot, along with pass-catching phenom Jack Emmer. However, the team just did not mesh quickly enough to produce many victories. Army returned to the Rutgers schedule for the first time since 1914 and outflanked the Knights on the field. Princeton and Boston University proved to be formidable foes. The Scarlet Knights mustered enough gridiron determination to notch hard-fought and well-deserved wins over Connecticut, Lehigh, and Holy Cross. Newcomer Jim Baker had a spectacular 95-yard kickoff return for the Scarlet Knights against the Crusaders of Holy Cross.

At season's end, Tom Connelly was anointed as the Knights' Most Valuable Player. Jack Callaghan was tops in passing yards and total offense. Rutgers guard Gene Renna went on to score fame as a business executive. Renna eventually became the chief operating officer of Mobil Oil.

Army, which had bested Rutgers the year before, named Tom Cahill as their new head coach in 1966. Army went 8–2 in 1966 and Tom Cahill was named the College Coach of the Year. Two quarterbacks made national sports headlines as they went nose to nose in their competition for the Heisman Trophy. Quarterback Steve Spurrier of Florida won the coveted trophy as America's top college performer. QB Bob Griese of Purdue finished second in the balloting.

Rutgers found itself in quarterback controversy in 1966 as Fred Eckert shared signal-calling duties with sophomore Pete Savino. The Scarlet Knights mustered one of their strongest groups of defensive and offensive linemen that season. On defense there were Scott Lewendon, Sampson Brown, Doug Kenny, and Co-captain Bob Schroeder. The offense boasted the likes of Alan Greenberg, Jim Julian, and big tackle Rick Koprowsi. Sorting out who played where and when was new line coach Don "Bud" Heilman. In 1966 Heilman began a long stay at Rutgers, which would see him eventually being named a deputy athletic director.

Head Coach John Bateman speaks to a football recruit at the Franklin High School (New Jersey) Sports Banquet in 1966. (Courtesy M. J. Pellowski)

Team co-captain Jack Emmer was one of the Scarlet squad's brightest stars in 1966. His amazing pass-catching ability dazzled fans.

Another shining Scarlet nova that season was a young running back with breakaway speed and agile moves that confounded would-be tacklers. His name was Bryant Mitchell. "Pound for pound Bryant Mitchell is the equal of any running back in the country," Coach John Bateman once said. Bateman had high hopes for the 1966 Scarlet Knights. On paper Rutgers looked strong and balanced. Paper predictions, however, are not always accurate. The 1966 team turned out to be good, but not as good as it might have been.

Princeton just managed to squeak past Rutgers in the season opener for both squads. Quarterback Fred Eckert fired an 83-yard pass completion to Bryant Mitchell at Princeton's Palmer Stadium, but the Tigers still managed to edge the Knights.

The Scarlet team was pitted against another top Ivy League opponent the following week. A Yale squad that featured two future pros took on Rutgers at the Yale Bowl. One of Yale's quarterbacks was Brian Dowling, who later played professionally with the Minnesota Vikings and New England Patriots. A running back on that same Yale squad was Calvin Hill. Hill later starred in the NFL for the Dallas Cowboys. His son Grant Hill later would star in the NBA.

Rutgers refused to be dazzled by Yale's young stars and emerged from the Yale Bowl with a victory. A good win over Lehigh and a gritty loss to Army followed.

The Lions of Columbia were next. Columbia was led by quarterback Marty Domres, one of the greatest passers in that school's long football history. Years later, Domres would be a first-round pick in the NFL draft and play for the San Diego Chargers and the Baltimore Colts.

Marty Domres lived up to his advance billing and passed Columbia to a 34 to 30 lead over Rutgers late in the fourth quarter. The chances for a Rutgers victory seemed slim at best as time ticked under a minute. Suddenly, Rutgers exploded offensively with quarterback Fred Eckert and receiver Jack Emmer clicking like a professional pass-and-catch combo. There were only seconds left in the contest when Eckert hit Emmer with the winning touchdown pass. Jack Emmer's amazing reception in the end zone gave Rutgers a 37 to 34 victory.

Boston University fell victim to Rutgers that season. Scarlet kicker Jim Dulin booted three field goals against BU and Rutgers notched another win. The following week, the Scarlet Knights bested the Lafayette Leopards 32 to 28 for win number five of the season. Rutgers' momentum stalled and the team agonized over tough year-ending losses to Holy Cross and Colgate.

In the Holy Cross contest, Rutgers' Jack Emmer set a Scarlet record for receiving yardage. Emmer caught 13 passes for 237 yards against the Crusaders. Rutgers finished the season with 5 wins and 4 losses.

Bryant Mitchell led the squad with 540 rushing yards and 42 points scored.

Co-captain Jack Emmer had a total of 701 yards in receptions in 1966. He was named All-East at the split end position. Emmer had a total of 76 catches in his career at Rutgers and 1,158 total receiving yards. In addition, Jack Emmer was an All-American lacrosse player. He later became the head lacrosse coach for Army at West Point.

In 1966, All-East wide receiver Jack Emmer was also a Second Team All-American in lacrosse. Emmer later became the head lacrosse coach at West Point. (Courtesy West Point Army Athletics/Athletic Communications)

Rutgers linemen Ron Kenny and Sampson Brown also made their marks in football after graduation. Kenny was picked by the Dallas Cowboys in the NFL draft. Brown eventually became a varsity line coach at Rutgers. Most impressive of all was the life path selected by Scarlet quarterback Fred Eckert. At a time when the Vietnam War was a cold, harsh, life-threatening reality, Eckert got his wings as a military helicopter pilot after graduation.

There was important news for the Rutgers football program prior to the 1967 season. Rutgers received a three million dollar donation from Scarlet alumnus Thomas T.

Barr. The money was to be used for football scholarships. Barr had been the manager of the 1912 Rutgers football squad and was an avid supporter of the Scarlet gridiron program.

Other important news affected the team on the field. Rutgers agreed to hold spring practice on the banks for the first time since 1954. Spring practice was not popular with some athletes who played other sports like baseball, track, and lacrosse. At that time many athletes played multiple sports and were not restricted from doing so. Many football players viewed spring practice as both a curse and a blessing.

In 1967, Rutgers coach John Bateman and his staff were looking for a way to best utilize their well-stocked stable of outstanding athletes headed by co-captains Tom Vitolo and Bob Higgins. The offense featured Bryant Mitchell, Don Riesett, Jim Baker, Paul Hohne, and sophomore sensation Bruce Van Ness.

Rutgers summer camp drills in 1968.
(Courtesy M. J. Pellowski)

The defense, spearheaded by Rich Bing, John Pollock, Denny Dutch, and Scotty Lewendon, welcomed sophomore starters Rich Bonsall, Lee Schneider, and Jim Renshaw. Rutgers looked loaded at the beginning of the season.

Once again the starting gun misfired. The Tigers handed the Knights a heartbreaking 22–21 defeat in the opening game even though Bryant Mitchell tallied three touchdowns for Rutgers.

The Scarlet Knights shook off the depression of a stinging opening-day loss and won successive home games against Lehigh and Delaware.

Two tough losses followed. Bruce Van Ness was now operating as the team's quarterback in place of Pete Savino, who'd shifted to split end.

Coach Bateman's club bobbed through the remaining games on the schedule, winning 2 games and losing 2. The net result was a lackluster 4 and 5 record. It was another speed bump.

Nevertheless, newcomer Bruce Van Ness turned in a spectacular performance in his first varsity season. Van Ness was named All-East and voted the Rookie of the Year. Halfback Bryant Mitchell led Rutgers in rushing and scoring for the second straight year. Mitchell ran for 542 yards and tallied 36 points.

Bryant Mitchell led Rutgers in rushing in 1966, 1967, and 1968. (Courtesy Rutgers Athletic Communications)

Jim Baker concluded his career at Rutgers by returning 54 kickoffs for a total of 1,234 yards. He was named the Most Valuable Player of the 1967 squad. Kicker Jim Dulin finished his playing days at Rutgers with a total of 12 field goals.

The year was 1968. Coach Joe Paterno of Penn State was named the Associated Football Coaches of America Coach of the Year. In the Ivy League, unbeaten Yale played unbeaten Harvard for the League Crown in the final game of the season. The contest resulted in a 29 to 29 tie as Harvard scored on the last play of the game in dramatic fashion.

At Rutgers there was increased drama. The Barr Scholarship brought new football blood into the system. Members of an undefeated freshman team were primed to play varsity (freshman could not play varsity football in Division I at that time). Two key transfers from Virginia Military Institute were also now eligible to play as juniors. One was split end Jim Benedict from nearby Berkeley Heights, New Jersey. The other was a strong-armed quarterback from Highland Park, New Jersey. Highland Park High School was a top feeder school for potential Rutgers football players. Past star Bob Ochs had played at Highland Park. In the future, Highland Park stars Bruce Presley and L. J. Smith would attend Rutgers. In 1968, the Highland Park native about to embark upon a stellar Rutgers career was field general Richard Policastro.

Policastro's turn behind Scarlet center Jack Orrizzi did not come at the outset of the season. At the start of the year, super all-around athlete Bruce Van Ness was the man taking snaps. He was part of a solid Scarlet backfield that featured halfback Bryant Mitchell and fullback Mel Brown. The potent Rutgers running attack functioned behind bone-crushing blocks from linemen Bruce Rockwell, Mike Kizis, and Co-captain Dave Zimmerman. New offensive line coach

Jim Taigia (who was a former Rutgers offensive lineman) called the shots for those bruising blockers. Another new coach was Tom Faulkner, who would depart from Rutgers a few years down the road to assume coaching duties at Holy Cross.

Rutgers' defense was solid in 1968. A terrific trio of linebackers headed a fast, hard-hitting unit. They included Co-captain Rich Bing, Lee Schneider, and Drew Forgash. The secondary was led by John Pollock, Jim Renshaw, and Pete Savino, who was playing his third varsity position in as many years.

Joining the varsity starters for the start of the 1968 season were sophomores Al Fenstemacher at flanker, Mike Pellowski at defensive end, and Larry Clymer at defensive rover back. Other players who would quickly distinguish themselves during the season were sophomore defensive end Andy Naporano and defensive tackle Mo Hill. Hill was the grandson of former Rutgers basketball coach Frank Hill, who guided the Scarlet hoop squad from 1935 to 1942.

There were no speed bumps in sight when the 1968 edition of the Scarlet Knights took the field for their opening game. The Knights were ready to put the pedal to the metal.

For the first time in many years, Rutgers began its season against an opponent other than its in-state rival Princeton. Rutgers' first game of 1968 was against a Lafayette team coached by Harry Gamble. Gamble later went to work for the Philadelphia Eagles. On Harry Gamble's staff at Lafayette in 1968 was young assistant coach Dick Anderson. Anderson would serve as the Rutgers head coach in the mid-1980s.

The Rutgers-Lafayette game was played in blazing heat of nearly one hundred degrees. After a scoreless first period of action, Bryant Mitchell and Mel Brown scored touchdowns for Rutgers. In the second half Al Fenstemacher caught his first varsity touchdown pass. Rich Policastro came in for Bruce Van Ness at quarterback and fired his first two touchdown passes at Rutgers. The Scarlet Knights won big over Lafayette.

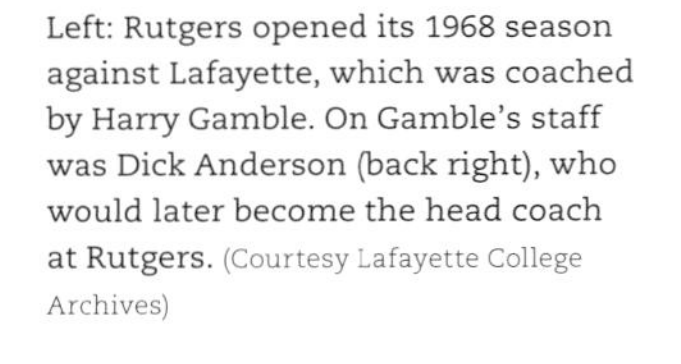

Left: Rutgers opened its 1968 season against Lafayette, which was coached by Harry Gamble. On Gamble's staff was Dick Anderson (back right), who would later become the head coach at Rutgers. (Courtesy Lafayette College Archives)

Right: Rich Policastro took over the starting quarterback job midway through the 1968 season. (Courtesy Rutgers Athletic Communications)

Rutgers rolled into Princeton's Palmer Stadium to take on the Tigers in game two of the 1968 season. The Scarlet Knights opened the scoring when Jim Julian got his foot into a successful field goal. After an interception by defensive captain Dave Bing, Rutgers quarterback Bruce Van Ness bolted into the end zone for a touchdown. The Scarlet Knights jumped out to a quick lead.

Princeton battled back as the Tigers' Ellis Moore powered into the end zone. The Rutgers defense tightened and held fast. After a punt the Scarlet offense methodically advanced forward play by play. Finally field general Bruce Van Ness threw a screen pass to fullback Mel Brown, who rumbled into the end zone. The Scarlet lead over Princeton increased to 17 to 7. Late in the game Scarlet safety John Pollock intercepted a Tigers pass, which led to a 50-yard field goal booted by Rutgers kicker Chris Stewart. Princeton's Scott McBean scored with time running out to make the final score Rutgers 20, Princeton 14.

Coach John Bateman's squad recorded its second win of the year by using balanced offense and defense. Bryant Mitchell ran for 109 yards in the contest. It was his second 100-plus-yard rushing game in a row. Linebackers Lee Schneider and Drew Forgash each made 11 tackles in the winning effort. It was truly a team victory.

The Scarlet Knights next traveled to New York State to take on the Big Red of Cornell. Rutgers and Cornell butted heads in a defensive tussle that produced a scoreless first period. In the second period, the teams exchanged short field goals, which knotted the score at 3-all. Suddenly, Rutgers gridiron flash Bryant Mitchell broke free behind an Alan Greenberg block and raced 77 yards for a touchdown. Rutgers led at the half.

Cornell came back in the third to score two touchdowns, one on an interception return. The Big Red led the Scarlet Knights 17 to 10 when Cornell was forced to punt. Rutgers safety John Pollock gathered in the ball and raced 80 yards for an apparent touchdown. However, a disputed clipping call against Rutgers wiped out the score.

Late in the fourth period, Rutgers put up more points thanks to the efforts of Rich Policastro, who'd replaced Van Ness at quarterback. Policastro tossed a pass to Paul Hohne, who was in for an injured Bryant Mitchell. Hohne caught the ball and raced for a TD. The score was Cornell 17 and Rutgers 16 when Coach John Bateman made a gutsy decision. He could have tied the game with a PAT kick, but opted to try a 2-point play instead. Bateman coached to win. Bruce Van Ness came back in at quarterback to run an option play. Van Ness rolled out and was tackled short of the goal line. Cornell held on to win 17 to 16.

Lehigh was the next Scarlet opponent. Starting halfback Bryant Mitchell was injured in the Cornell loss and could not play. His replacement, Paul Hohne, was more than capable of handling the task. Hohne would have been a starting halfback on most other teams. It was his misfortune to be slotted behind one of Rutgers' greatest runners.

Tight end Bob Stonebraker, who was a pro prospect, opened the scoring for Rutgers by grabbing a scoring strike from Bruce Van Ness. An interception by ball hawk Pete Savino set up another Rutgers score. Halfback Paul Hohne ran the pigskin over the goal line to give the Knights a 14 to 0 lead. Just as the half was about to end, Lehigh's Jack Paget scored to make it a 14 to 7 game.

In the third period, fleet Paul Hohne of Rutgers broke free for a 31-yard scoring scamper. Lehigh's Jack Paget then tallied the second of his four touchdowns on the day to knot the score.

John Pollock, one of the all-time great Rutgers pass defenders and punt returners, then made the big play of the day. Pollock intercepted a pass and returned it 54 yards for a

Rutgers defense (light jerseys) in action against Lehigh in 1968. The Scarlet Knights' Kevin O'Connor and Pete Savino rush in to make the tackle. (Courtesy M. J. Pellowski)

touchdown. Pollock had a remarkable outing against Lehigh. In addition to the interception return for a TD, he made 15 tackles, recovered a fumble, intercepted a second pass, and also intercepted a pass on a 2-point conversion try by Lehigh.

"He [Pollock] has to be one of the finest athletes we have had at Rutgers," Coach Bateman told reporters after the game. Rutgers handed Lehigh a stinging 29 to 26 defeat as the Knights notched their third win of the season.

Rutgers then took on Army at home in the rain. The Cadets handed the Knights their second loss of the year.

Rutgers unveiled a new offensive weapon the following week against Columbia. Rich Policastro took over the quarterbacking duties and Bruce Van Ness was switched to running back. The decision proved to be a brilliant one. Policastro quickly began to rewrite every passing record in the Rutgers stat book.

Tight end Bob Stonebraker was the first Scarlet receiver to take advantage of the change. Policastro hit Stonebraker with two scoring strikes.

Columbia quarterback Marty Domres staged an aerial circus of his own. At halftime the game was tied.

It was Rutgers running back Bryant Mitchell's turn to shine in the second half. He churned up a total of 153 yards rushing on the afternoon and scored 2 touchdowns. The only points the Columbia Lions could muster in the second half came on a field goal. Rutgers won its fourth game of the year.

The backfield combo of Bryant Mitchell and Mel Brown shredded the Delaware defense in game seven. Together they rushed for 277 yards. Mitchell gained 160 yards and scored 2 touchdowns. One came on an amazing 84-yard weave through a wave of Delaware defenders. Brown ran for 116 yards on the day.

Rutgers' other scores were the result of a Jim Julian field goal and a touchdown pass from Rich Policastro to split end Jim Benedict. Rutgers defeated Delaware for win number five.

Next came Connecticut. The Huskies were led by big running back Vinny Clements (who would later enjoy a career in the pros) and by quarterback Rick Robustelli (who was the son of former NFL star Andy Robustelli). Rutgers got off to a fast start in the contest thanks to a Jim Julian field goal and a Jim Benedict touchdown catch.

Vince Clements tallied 2 touchdowns for Connecticut, but Rutgers won the game 27 to 15. Bryant Mitchell gained 157 yards in the contest. It was his sixth 100-plus-yard rushing game. QB Rich Policastro fired 3 touchdown passes.

Up next was a home contest against Holy Cross. The Scarlet Knights quickly located the weak points in the Crusaders' armor. Rutgers' John Pollock fielded a Holy Cross punt early in the contest and bolted 73 yards for a touchdown. Holy Cross surprised Rutgers by scoring 2 quick touchdowns and held a shaky 14 to 7 edge over the Knights at halftime.

After the break, Bryant Mitchell showcased his talent. He scored 2 touchdowns. Rich Policastro also grabbed a share of the offensive spotlight. He hit tight end Bob Stonebraker and flanker Al Fenstemacher with scoring strikes. Rutgers won again. The Knights were 7–2 going into the final game of the season against Colgate.

Coach John Bateman's Scarlet squad closed out its season at home. The last game of the year turned out to be a wild offensive shootout between quarterbacks Ron Burton of Colgate and Rich Policastro of Rutgers. The Red Raiders put up 34 points led by Burton, who amassed more than 4,000 running and passing yards during his career at Colgate.

The Scarlet Knights, led by Rich Policastro and Bruce Van Ness, topped that total by registering 55 total points. Rich Policastro had touchdown tosses of 50 yards, 34 yards, 36 yards, and 60 yards. Bruce Van Ness had a 51-yard pass completion for a touchdown. He also had a 38-yard TD run. Flanker Al Fenstemacher hauled in 2 touchdown passes. Bob Stonebraker, Mel Brown, and Paul Hohne also snared TD passes. In addition, Hohne had a 36-yard touchdown run. Rutgers halfback Bryant Mitchell gained 175 yards rushing. Scarlet safety John Pollock tied a Rutgers record by intercepting 3 Colgate passes. It was a grand finish to an outstanding season. The 1968 Scarlet Knights finished the year with 8 wins and 2 losses. One of those losses was a 1-point defeat helped by a disputed call that was later found to be a judgment error. Despite Rutgers' fine record, the team was ignored by bowl scouts and national pollsters.

Individual achievements of members of the 1968 squad were impressive. During the year quarterback Rich Policastro threw for 994 yards and 15 touchdowns. Tight end Bob Stonebraker had 31 receptions and 6 touchdown catches. Safety John Pollock had 9 interceptions to set a Rutgers single-season record. He also had 35 punt returns that year to establish another record. Over his Rutgers career, John Pollock returned 58 punts for a total of 652 yards. In addition, Pollock had a career total of 14 interceptions, which he returned for a total of 236 yards.

Halfback Bryant Mitchell established numerous rushing and scoring records. Mitchell rushed for 1,204 yards in 1968 and scored 9 touchdowns. Bryant Mitchell had 5 consecutive 100-plus-yard rushing games in 1968. He rushed for 100 yards or more 8 times in 10 games. Mitchell concluded his Rutgers career with 2,286 rushing yards. He averaged 4.62 yards per carry and scored a total of 22 touchdowns. Bryant Mitchell had 12 100-plus-yard rushing games in three years at Rutgers. In 1968 he was named All-East and team MVP. Co-captain Dave Zimmerman continued his football career by working as an assistant coach at Boston University. Peter Savino later became a member of the Rutgers coaching staff.

Left: Scarlet trainer Abe Sivess (left) and manager Terry Beachem watch action from the Knights' sidelines in 1970. Beachem later became an associate director of athletics at Rutgers. (Courtesy M. J. Pellowski)

Below: Bryant Mitchell runs behind the blocks of Alan Greenberg, Dave Zimmerman, and Rich Koprowski. (Courtesy Rutgers Athletic Communications)

xo
xo
xooo
xo
xo

CHAPTER 8

ONE HUNDRED YEARS OF FOOTBALL | 1969–1972

The year was 1969. It was the year Neil Armstrong set foot on the moon. It was a year after the Tet offensive in Vietnam resulted in one of the most brutal battles of the war. It was six years after President John F. Kennedy was assassinated.

Fall of 1969 was also five years before news of the Watergate scandal broke and toppled the administration of U.S. president Richard M. Nixon. It was ten years prior to the overthrow of the Shah of Iran and twenty years before the Berlin Wall was torn down for good.

A time of social and political upheaval in the United States and in the world, 1969 was the dawn of awakening for many young Americans. It was a time of peaceful protests and hippies. It was a year of conflicts, contrasts—and contact sports. For, along with all the other things that marked the year, 1969 was the one-hundredth anniversary of college football. Rutgers and Princeton had begun America's obsession with college football in 1869. It was time to commemorate that historic event.

The game that officially celebrated college football's centennial would be played at Rutgers Stadium in Piscataway, New Jersey. The stadium was across the Raritan River from the New Brunswick site where that first gridiron brawl had taken place one hundred years before. In honor of the occasion, Rutgers, Princeton, and the National Collegiate Athletic Association staged a variety of events, from parades to the selection of a National College Football Centennial Queen. Miss Barbara "Bobbie" Specht, a junior at Texas Tech, was picked by the NCAA to reign as its Centennial Queen. Miss Specht was a twirler for the Texas Tech Red Raider band, a government major, and an A student. In the city of New Brunswick, a commemorative football stamp was issued by the Post Office in honor of college football's one-hundredth birthday. The Rutgers-Princeton football clash was slated to be broadcast on ABC television, which was a big deal at the time. Cable TV was not around and ESPN was just a grouping of letters without any meaning. In the 1960s the American Broadcasting Company was the TV home of college football, and only a few select games were aired.

Prior to the one-hundredth-anniversary meeting of Rutgers and Princeton on the field, there were indications that President Nixon would attend the big game in person. Nixon

Right: The New Brunswick Post Office issued a special collectors' stamp and cover envelope to honor college football's centennial on September 26, 1969. (From the personal collection of Martin Pellowski)

Below: The 1969 Rutgers media guide commemorated the centennial. (From the personal collection of M. J. Pellowski/ Courtesy Rutgers Athletic Communications)

had been a reserve quarterback on the Whittier College football team in the 1930s and was a big football fan.

However, before Rutgers took on Princeton in the historic gridiron contest, the Knights were scheduled to meet another of their oldest rivals in the season opener. Rutgers would first travel to Easton, Pennsylvania, to take on the Leopards of Lafayette.

The centennial edition of the Rutgers Scarlet Knights appeared solid on both offense and defense. The offense was led by record-setting quarterback Rich Policastro and bolstered by the potent running attack of veteran Bruce Van Ness and newcomers Steve Ferrughelli, Bill Donaldson, and Larry Robertson. Robertson was a swift, agile scatback. A strong offensive line included Jim DiGiacinto, John Bauer, John "J. L." Langenus, Bob Coppola, and Jack Orrizzi.

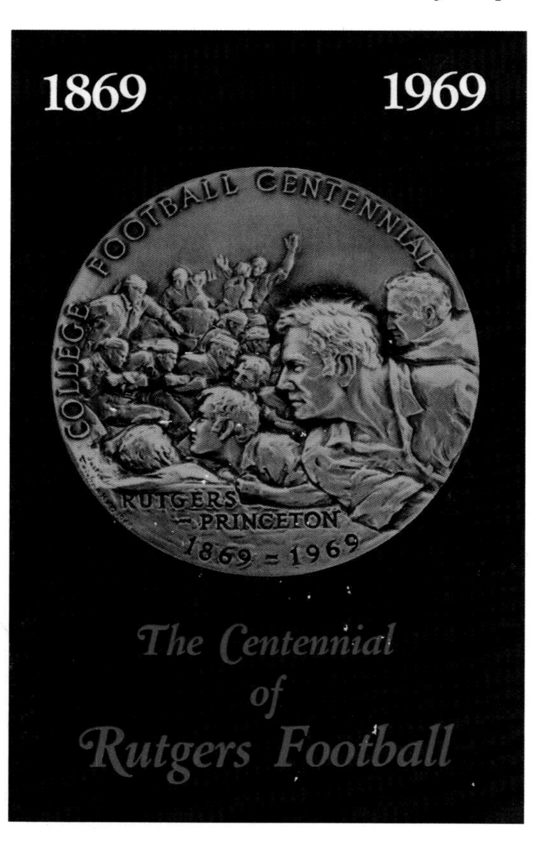

Rutgers field general Rich Policastro had excellent receivers to throw to. The list of potential targets included co-captain and tight end Bob Stonebraker, flanker Al Fenstemacher, and split end Jim Benedict.

An experienced defense was led by senior co-captain and linebacker Lee Schneider. Rutgers' linebacking corps was composed of fierce hitters Drew Forgash, Larry Clymer, Larry Walsh, and sophomore Sam Picketts.

A fast defensive secondary included ball hawks John Miller and Sam Chapman and Jim Renshaw.

The defensive line was spearheaded by tackles Paul Milea and Len Novelli and defensive ends Mike Pellowski and Andy Naporano. Mike Yancheff was the team's backup quarterback and team punter.

The Rutgers-Lafayette series dated back to 1882. On the field, the Leopards were led by their outstanding quarterback, Ed Baker. Baker would later play with the New York Giants, the Houston Oilers, and the Oakland Raiders in the pro ranks. Although Baker was a great passer, he never got the opportunity to showcase his talent in the opening game of the centennial season. On that day, Rutgers' gridiron general Rich Policastro ruled the football roost. Policastro

Left: The 1969 Rutgers team had many players from New Jersey high schools on its roster. Top row, left to right: Paul Milea (New Brunswick), Rich Bonsall (Franklin/Somerset), John Angelillo (Old Bridge), Rich Policastro (Highland Park), and Greg Sivess (South River). Bottom, left to right: Mike Pellowski (Franklin/Somerset), Coach John Bateman, Drew Forgash (South Plainfield). (Courtesy Rich Policastro)

Right: Rutgers captains Bob Stonebraker (#84) and Lee Schneider (#70) pose with University president Mason Gross in 1969. (Courtesy Lee Schneider)

completed the first four passes he threw and quickly tossed touchdown passes to Jim Benedict, Bruce Van Ness, and Al Fenstemacher.

Rutgers' new fullback, Steve Ferrughelli, contributed to the offensive cause with a 51-yard run and a 4-yard touchdown plunge.

The Scarlet defense also had a field day in that opening game of 1969. Lafayette QB Ed Baker was pressured, pursued, and harassed all afternoon. Larry Clymer, Sam Chapman, and Rich Spizuoco all had interceptions. Defensive end Mike Pellowski had four quarterback sacks to set a single-game record that lasted for more than thirty years. The Knights beat the Leopards 44 to 22.

The Rutgers-Princeton football clash of 1969 started with a no-show from Washington, D.C., as President Richard Nixon abruptly declined his invitation to attend the game. Perhaps now, in light of events to follow, it was a decision in the best interest of all concerned. However, the president did compose a letter directed to all college football squads in America in 1969. The letter was reproduced in college football programs across the country. It provided its readers with a keen insight to President Nixon's views on football. The letter is worth reprinting.

THE WHITE HOUSE
WASHINGTON
COLLEGE FOOTBALL'S CENTENNIAL

One hundred years ago, the first intercollegiate football game was played in the United States. Since that November day when students from Princeton and Rutgers began it all, the game has thrilled generations of Americans as players and spectators.

During its first hundred years, football has become more than a game. It has become a familiar and beloved part of American life and has provided an opportunity for young boys to first learn the discipline and rewards of teamwork. The boundaries of the one-hundred-yard field mark a special place for most Americans: a place in which are born legends of great skill, endurance and courage.

I have always loved football. I consider the time I spent as a member of a college football squad as one of the most rewarding periods of my life. I discovered there—mostly from that unique, if often frustrating, vantage point offered by the bench—that football is a game which engages the skills and talents of the whole man, his spiritual as well as his physical endurance, his mental attitude as well as his emotional conditioning.

My congratulations go to intercollegiate football—and to all those who play the game, whether it be on a makeshift field or in the great stadiums—on its one hundredth birthday. It is a game which not only has thrilled generations of Americans but has also helped to develop qualities of sportsmanship and competitiveness in those generations.

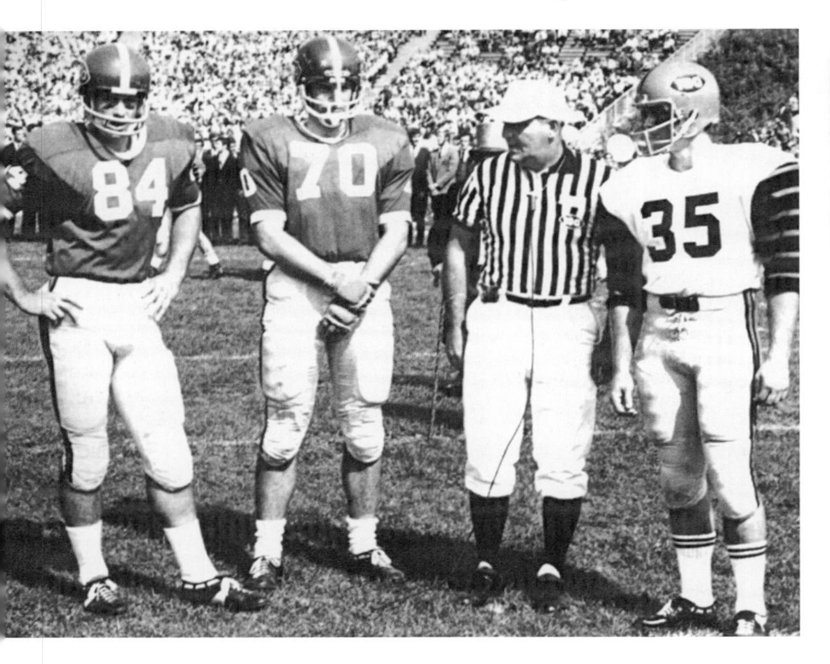

Left: Co-captains Bob Stonebraker (#84) and Lee Schneider (#70) of Rutgers meet before the centennial game with Captain Ellis Moore of Princeton for the coin toss. (Courtesy Rutgers Athletic Communications)

Right: In the 1969 centennial game, Rich Policastro (#12), Rutgers' record-setting quarterback, passes against Princeton while Rutgers' Hall of Fame running back Bruce Van Ness (#10) blocks. The contest was shown on ABC-TV. (Courtesy Rich Policastro)

The letter was signed by President Richard Nixon.

There was a gala parade in the city of New Brunswick the day before the 1969 Rutgers-Princeton game. It was complete with marching bands, decorative floats, and a personal appearance by college football's centennial queen, Bobbie Specht. On the afternoon of game day, more than thirty thousand excited fans packed Rutgers Stadium to view the contest. Famous past players from both schools as well as celebrities and benefactors gathered on the sidelines before the kickoff. Rutgers president Mason Gross greeted television stars Ozzie and Harriet Nelson (family sitcom stars of the 1950s and '60s) and well-known Broadway producer David "Sonny" Werblin. (Werblin was one of the driving forces behind the reshaping of the old New York Titans pro football team into the New York Jets. He helped lure quarterback Joe Namath to the team.) Former Scarlet gridiron greats Bill Austin and Alex Kroll were on hand to support their alma mater, as was William Van Dyke, the captain of the 1894 Rutgers football team.

Finally, after all the hoopla died down, it was time to play football.

A collage shows all members of the Rutgers Scarlet Knights who played football during the Centennial Celebration season of 1969. The Rutgers-Princeton contest marked the one-hundredth anniversary of college football. (From the personal collection of M. J. Pellowski/Created by Victor's Photography)

Scarlet quarterback Rich Policastro piloted the Rutgers aerial circus with pinpoint accuracy. Policastro was on target with 12 of his first 14 passes. Finally, Policastro rolled out and scored a 1-yard touchdown on a well-executed option play. Rutgers defense held, thanks to key stops by Drew Forgash and Lee Schneider. The Scarlet offense returned and mounted another drive. It culminated with Bruce Van Ness scoring a touchdown on a 1-yard dive into the end zone. Again the Rutgers defense stopped the Princeton offense cold thanks to the stellar plays by Jim Renshaw and Andy Naparano.

Rutgers offense, directed by Rich Policastro, scored almost at will. When the Knights got the ball back, Policastro passed to Bob Stonebraker for another touchdown. Later quarterback Mike Yancheff came on to connect with end Joe Barone for the final touchdown of the day.

Split end Jim Benedict of Rutgers had a big day. He caught 8 passes. The defense was led by linebacker Drew Forgash, who made 10 unassisted tackles.

Rutgers walloped Princeton 29 to 0 on TV in college football's one-hundredth anniversary game. The contest signaled there was trouble ahead for football's oldest rivalry. Princeton football fans began to wonder if playing Rutgers was still such a good idea after all.

Above: Rutgers co-captains Bob Stonebraker (left) and Lee Schneider appeared on *The Ed Sullivan Show* with Head Coach John Bateman after the Scarlet Knights' 29 to 0 victory over Princeton in the centennial game. (Courtesy Lee Schneider)

Below: Rutgers linebacker Larry Clymer (#41) prepares to make a tackle in 1969. (From the personal collection of Larry Clymer/Courtesy Rutgers Athletic Communications)

After the contest ended, the coaches and captains of both teams were invited to appear on Ed Sullivan's television show in New York City. They would be introduced by the show's host to his national TV audience on Sunday night. *The Ed Sullivan Show* was the most widely watched variety show on television at that time. It was like being on *The Late Show with David Letterman* or *The Tonight Show* today.

Princeton's invitees declined for personal reasons. Rutgers coach John Bateman and co-captains Bob Stonebraker and Lee Schneider accepted. Rutgers football was in the spotlight on that Saturday afternoon and Sunday night in September of 1969.

The Big Red team of Cornell University came to New Brunswick for the first time ever in 1969. It was only the fifth meeting between the two schools on the gridiron. Rutgers welcomed Cornell to the Scarlet's home field with a cannonade of pass completions and stingy red-zone defense.

Cornell was led by its super sophomore running back Ed Marinaro, a New Jersey native. In three short years, Marinaro would become one of college football's greatest ground gainers. In 1971 he would win the Maxwell Trophy as America's best college football player and finish second in the Heisman balloting. Ed Marinaro would gain a total of 4,715 yards rushing from 1969 to 1971 and average a record 174.6 rushing yards per game. He would turn pro with the Minnesota Vikings and, after a successful NFL career, would become an actor. Marinaro later costarred on the TV shows *Laverne & Shirley* and *Hill Street Blues*.

In 1969, tailback Ed Marinaro of Cornell came to Rutgers looking for a gridiron win. The Rutgers defense would deny it to him. Linebacker Larry Clymer made 15 tackles in the Scarlet's 27 to 7 victory.

The Knights were 3 and 0 when Lehigh rolled into Rutgers Stadium with plans to pop the undefeated Scarlet's big red balloon. Lehigh was led by two tough offensive linemen who would move on to the pros after graduation. One was tackle Thad Jamula. The other was center John Hill. Hill was the son of former Rutgers player and Associate Director of Athletics for Finance Otto Hill. John Hill would eventually play in the NFL for many years with the New York Giants and the New Orleans Saints. Lehigh topped Rutgers and dealt the Knights their first defeat of the centennial season.

Navy sailed into New Jersey to wage gridiron war with Rutgers. The Midshipmen were a well-coached squad. Head coach Rich Forzano had an able crew of assistants that included future NFL coaches Leeman Bennett and Joe Bugel. On the field the Midshipmen were led by quarterback Mike McNallen and running back Dan Pike.

Several Rutgers players had injuries. The most serious was a knee injury to end and offensive captain Bob Stonebraker. The injury ended his season and terminated a possible pro career.

The Scarlet Knights did most of their offensive damage in the second period of the game. On a fourth down in Navy territory, the Scarlet's Mike Yancheff came on to punt. Instead of kicking, he took the snap and passed to reserve running back Bill Donaldson. Donaldson made the catch and rumbled for a pickup of 22 yards and an important first down.

Sophomore halfback Larry Robertson of the Knights made the most of his first starting role. He tallied 2 touchdowns in the second period.

In the third period, Mike Yancheff had a key 70-yard punt that pinned the Navy offense at their own 2-yard line. When the Scarlet defense held, Rutgers' Larry Robertson added a third touchdown to his day's work. Rutgers sank Navy to improve their record to 4 and 1 on the season.

The Knights' Mike Yancheff proved to be a super backup hero in the game against Columbia the following week.

As usual, Rich Policastro started at quarterback for Rutgers. He fired a touchdown toss to end Randy Bokesch in the second period. Bokesch and Jim Fallon now filled the tight end spot vacated by the injured Bob Stonebraker. Columbia, guided by its quarterback

Above: Rutgers assistant coach Hank Small later became the head football coach at Lehigh University. (Courtesy Lehigh University Athletics)

Below, left: Defensive end Mike Pellowski (#81) led Rutgers with 9 sacks in 1969. Safety Sam Chapman (#26) had 5 interceptions that same year. (Courtesy M. J. Pellowski)

Below, right: Mike Yancheff (#15) took over the starting quarterback job in 1970. Seen blocking are Murray Bakst (#63), John Bauer (#75), and Mike Kizis (#74). (Courtesy Mike Yancheff)

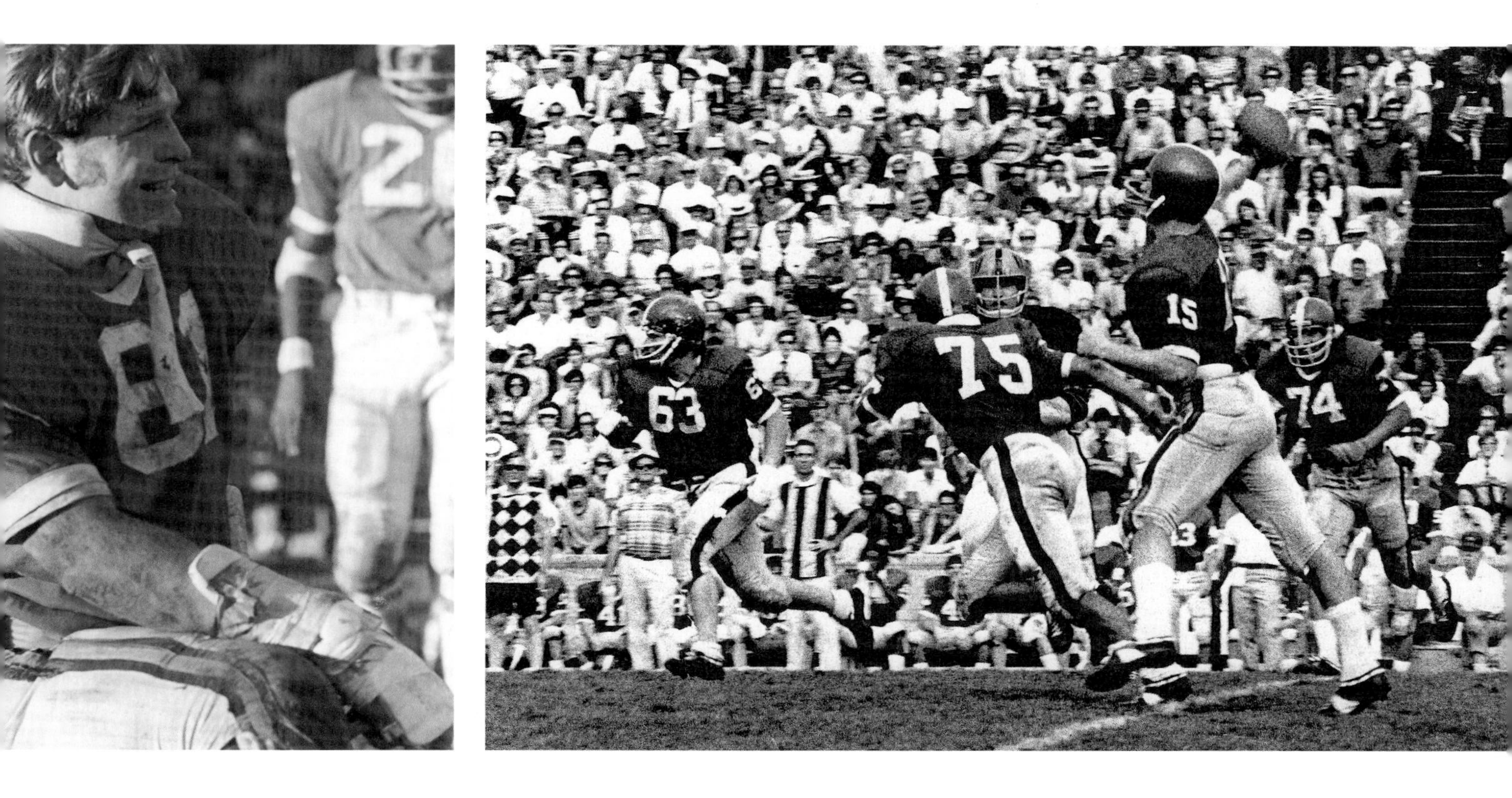

In a 1970 game, Rutgers guards Dave Rinehimer (#51) and Murray Bakst (#63) lead blocking for halfback Larry Robertson (#42), who takes a handoff from QB Mike Yancheff (#15). (Courtesy Mike Yancheff)

Jim Romanosky, put two TDs of its own on the board and was out in front of Rutgers 14 to 7 in the third period.

Scarlet soph sensation Larry Robertson knotted the score at 14-all when he scored on a 10-yard TD run. The game stayed stuck at 14 to 14 until late in the last period, when Scarlet safety Sam Chapman made a key interception.

Mike Yancheff came on at quarterback in place of Rich Policastro. Yancheff engineered a miraculous 57-yard march down the field and personally scored the winning touchdown with thirty-eight seconds left to go in the game.

Rutgers' centennial dream season became a nightmare against Delaware the following week. The Blue Hens shut out the Scarlet Knights and Rutgers' record dipped to 5 wins and 2 losses.

The Knights were still shell-shocked by their loss to Delaware when they met Connecticut the following week. The Huskies, under the guidance of their outstanding QB, Rich Robustelli, edged the Knights in a hard-fought contest.

Rutgers righted its gridiron ship and prepared for its final game of the season against Colgate. Holy Cross, originally scheduled for the week before Colgate, had to be cancelled. Holy Cross did not play any games in 1969. The entire team came down with hepatitis after drinking water from a contaminated pipe during preseason camp.

When Colgate came to New Jersey, Rutgers was ready to rumble. The Red Raiders of Colgate had a high-profile quarterback in Steve Goepel. Many experts consider Goepel to be one of Colgate's best QBs ever. He later played in the pro ranks with the Dallas Cowboys and the New England Patriots. Colgate's Steve Goepel against Rutgers' Rich Policastro promised to be a real aerial dogfight.

However, it was the Scarlet's Policastro, behind solid blocking by Jack Orrizzi, Murray Bakst, Mike Kizis, and John Bauer, who stole the thunder on the field. Rutgers scored the first 3 times it had the ball. Bruce Van Ness concluded his college career in spectacular fashion by scoring 3 times. Van Ness rushed for 2 touchdowns and caught a TD pass from Policastro. Superstar passer Rich Policastro had a record-setting final game performance. He fired 5 touchdown passes in the Colgate contest to establish a standard that stood for 30-plus years. Also catching touchdown tosses that afternoon were ends Randy Bokesch, Jim Fallon, and Jim Benedict, and fullback Steve Ferrughelli. Rutgers finished its centennial season with a 48 to 12 blasting of Colgate. The Scarlet Knights posted a very respectable 6 and 3 record to begin its second hundred years of football.

Defensive captain Lee Schneider received All-East honors and had a pro tryout with the New York Giants. He later became dean of students at Rutgers Cook College. Safety Sam Chapman had 5 interceptions in 1969. Defensive back John Miller made 8 interceptions that same year. Defensive end Mike Pellowski had 9 quarterback sacks.

On the offensive side, split end Jim Benedict was selected All-East. Benedict caught 48 passes for 650 yards and 3 TDs in 1969. During the course of his two-year career at Rutgers, Jim Benedict pulled in a total of 67 passes for 865 yards and 7 touchdowns. He briefly returned to Rutgers as an assistant coach under Terry Shea in the late 1990s. Offensive captain Bob Stonebraker concluded his Rutgers career with 44 catches for 544 yards and 7 touchdowns.

Bruce Van Ness was also All-East. He led the team in scoring with 48 points. Van Ness rushed for 375 yards on 105 carries and had 4 rushing touchdowns. He also caught 24 passes for 244 yards and 4 touchdowns. Bruce Van Ness had a total of 2,216 all-purpose yards during the course of his career. He played in the North-South All-Star game and was voted the MVP of that contest. Van Ness was a fifth-round draft choice for the Atlanta

Left: An opposing running back is surrounded by Rutgers tacklers John Miller (#20), Andy Malekoff (#67), and Mike Pellowski (#81). (Courtesy M. J. Pellowski)

Right: Rutgers rover back Larry Clymer (#41) upends a Boston University running back as linebacker Frank Zukas looks on. (Courtesy Frank Zukas)

Left: Scarlet Knights defensive back John Miller had 10 career interceptions, including 8 in 1969. (Courtesy John Miller)

Right: Larry Clymer, who had 3 interceptions against Colgate in 1970, was voted the Scarlet Knights' Most Valuable Player that same season. (From the personal collection of Larry Clymer/Courtesy Rutgers Athletic Communications)

Falcons. Van Ness later helped the Montreal Alouettes win a CFL Championship and was the league's Rookie of the Year.

Quarterback Rich Policastro was All-East and an Honorable Mention All-American. He was also the Scarlet's Most Valuable Player. In 1969 Policastro completed 149 passes in 258 attempts for 1,690 yards and 14 touchdowns. He threw only 6 interceptions. Over his career Policastro, completed a total of 212 passes in 380 attempts for 2,684 yards and 29 touchdowns. He misfired on a total of only 9 interceptions. He is the top-rated passer in Rutgers history. Rich Policastro played in the Blue-Gray All-Star game and later served as a color commentator on radio broadcasts of Rutgers football games.

The year following college football's centennial was a big one for New Jersey athletes playing football at other schools. Joe Theismann of South River, New Jersey, quarterbacked Notre Dame to a record of 10 wins and 1 loss in his senior year and ended up finishing second to Stanford quarterback Jim Plunkett in the Heisman Trophy race. Running back Ed Marinaro of New Milford, New Jersey, led the nation with 1,425 rushing yards in his junior year at Cornell. Fullback Franco Harris of Rancocas Valley, New Jersey, was Penn State's go-to guy. Harris had rushed for 643 yards and 10 touchdowns the year before. Years later, Franco Harris would star for the Super Bowl champion Pittsburgh Steelers.

Rutgers had a Pennsylvania connection of its own in 1970. The Scarlet had the backfield duet of co-captain and quarterback Mike Yancheff and halfback Larry Robertson. Yancheff and Robertson had played together in high school at Hummelstown, Pennsylvania.

In the backfield with Yancheff and Robertson were fullbacks Steve Ferrughelli, Rich Roby, and Bill Donaldson. The wideouts were speedy and sure-handed. They included Al Fenstemacher, Bob Carney, and Bruce Miller.

The defense, led by co-captain and defensive end Mike Pellowski, included end Andy Naporano, rover back Larry Clymer, and linebackers Sam Picketts, Andy Malekoff, Gary Martin, and Frank Zukas. The defensive backfield unit was built around John Miller, Sam Chapman, Hal Lippman, and Joe Epps.

The season opened with a convincing win over Lafayette. New kicker John Pesce had field goals of 30 and 35 yards and booted 5 extra points.

On the defensive side for Rutgers, linebacker Sam Picketts had an interception, a knocked-down pass, and 12 tackles.

The Princeton Tigers avenged their centennial loss by blasting the Scarlet Knights. Rutgers faced another tough Ivy opponent as it traveled to Boston for a game against Harvard in week three of the season. Harvard pinned another defeat on the Knights. The only highlight of the game for Scarlet fans was a Sam Picketts interception, which he returned 54 yards for a score.

Rutgers and Lehigh locked horns in a defensive contest in week four. Bob Zieniuk, Brill Bierle, and Roy Malinak got their first varsity starts on defense. Co-captain Mike Pellowski made 9 tackles and had 3 quarterback sacks in the contest, and senior flanker Al Fenstemacher caught 9 passes in the game. But Rutgers lost a heartbreaker 7 to 0.

Delaware then tagged downward-spiraling Rutgers with loss number four.

Columbia came next. The Columbia-Rutgers game of 1970 marked the one-hundredth anniversary of the schools' interstate rivalry. Rutgers had beaten Columbia 6 to 3 when the teams first played back in 1870. In 1970 Columbia returned the favor before twenty thousand screaming home fans. Rutgers suffered another defeat. With four games left to play, a complete collapse was possible. Seniors who had started on the great 1968 team and the very good 1969 team rallied troops.

For the game against Bucknell, the Rutgers offense made some changes. Bill Donaldson made his first start at halfback. Larry Christoff moved from guard to tight end. Christoff would excel at tight end and evolve into one of Rutgers' all-time greats. In addition, swift sophomore Bob Carney started at split end.

The revamped Scarlet offense clicked. Quarterback Mike Yancheff completed 13 of 19 passes for 111 yards and 1 TD. Larry Christoff hauled in 7 passes in his first game as a tight end. The defense was spearheaded by Jim Liguori and Andy Naporano, who combined to block and recover a Bucknell punt. Rutgers rebounded from the abyss with a well-earned win over Bucknell.

It was back to Boston in week eight for a gridiron battle against Boston University. The Scarlet defense barred the Beantowners' offense from the end zone, holding them to just a field goal on the

Rutgers assistant coach Bill Speranza (left) poses with three Scarlet Knight players and an unidentified Scarlet Knight. The players are, left to right, John Miller, Larry Christoff, and Frank Zukas. (Courtesy Frank Zukas)

Rutgers defenders Roy Malinak (#85) and Frank Zukas (#61) bring down a Tigers running back in the 1971 Princeton game. (Courtesy Frank Zukas)

day. Frank Zukas, Andy Malekoff, and Larry Walsh had big days on defense. Senior defensive end Mike Pellowski had a banner afternoon, registering 14 tackles and 2 quarterback sacks in the Rutgers win.

Quarterback and offensive captain Mike Yancheff rose to the occasion in the next game against Holy Cross. He completed 10 of 20 passes good for 4 touchdowns. Rutgers won for its third straight rebound victory.

The last game of the 1970 schedule was against Colgate at home. The Colgate contest was Rutgers rover back Larry Clymer's time to shine. In his final game as a Scarlet Knight, Clymer tied a record by making 3 interceptions in one game. Inspired by Clymer's fierce defensive play, Rutgers topped Colgate in the final contest of the year for the Scarlet squad. Rutgers finished the year with a record of 5 wins and 5 losses. It was only a .500 season, but there was more than just an average record to the story. A team that had lost 5 straight games righted the ship through self-determination and finished the year with 4 consecutive victories to salvage its self-respect.

In 1970 Larry Clymer made 100 tackles and had 4 interceptions. He had a total of 7 interceptions during his three-year career. He was named the team's Most Valuable Player and AP All-East. Sam Picketts made 108 tackles in 1970. He had 1 quarterback sack, 2 blocked kicks, and 1 interception. Picketts earned ECAC All-East honors.

Defensive co-captain Mike Pellowski had 61 tackles and 7 quarterback sacks in 1970. He had a total of 18 quarterback sacks in his three-year career. He won All-East Honorable Mention and went on to professional trials with the New England Patriots after graduation. Defensive halfback John Miller completed a great two-year career. He had 2 interceptions in 1970 to add to the 8 picks he had in 1969 for a career total of 10 interceptions. Safety Sam Chapman had 6 interceptions in 1970, bringing his career total to 11 interceptions.

Offensive tackle Mike Kizis earned All-East mention. Fullback Steve Ferrughelli had a tryout in the Canadian Football League. Flanker Al Fenstemacher completed his Rutgers career with a total of 71 receptions. QB MikeYancheff, who doubled as a punter, had 131 punts over his career for 4,711 yards. Yancheff went on to pro trials with the Los Angeles Rams.

In 1971 the University of Nebraska, coached by Bob Devaney, went 13 and 0 to capture the National Championship. Cornell's Ed Marinaro led the country in rushing for the second straight year with a total of 1,881 yards.

At Rutgers, Leo Gasienica was now the man calling signals behind center for the Scarlet. Tri-captains Sam Picketts, Bill Donaldson, and Larry Robertson had many new faces in both the offensive and defensive huddles. Twenty seniors, many of them multi-year starters, had moved on. The offense still had a strong nucleus with backs Bill Donaldson, Larry Robertson, Charley DiPonziano, Bruce Miller, Ron Shycko, and newcomer Jim "J. J." Jennings. Jennings was something special.

Rutgers baseball coach and former football coach Matt Bolger described Jim Jennings as "the prototype of the modern pro back. J. J. Jennings is big, fast, and strong. He can run past you, around you, or over you."

Jennings's first year as a varsity player was 1971. He would go on to become one of the greatest ground gainers in Rutgers history.

The 1971 Rutgers receiving corps was led by Bob Carney, Tom Sweeney, Bob Shutte, and Larry Christoff, the last of whom caught 8 touchdown passes as a tight end in 1970.

The strong point of the defense was its steady crew of head-hunting linebackers. Leading the pack was three-year starter Sam Picketts. Right behind him were John Witkowski, Frank Zukas, and Andy Malekoff.

Alan Bain led a defensive line that included Steve Allen, Bob Dillard, and Jack Salemi.

The secondary was an area of little concern to the coaches. It was aptly manned by Joe Epps, Gary Smolyn, and Ed Jones. Jones was destined to become one of Rutgers' all-time greats in the defensive secondary.

The Rutgers 1971 season began with a hard-to-swallow loss to Lafayette. The Scarlet Knights unleashed their rage on Princeton in game two. Rutgers clobbered the Tigers to even their record.

Up next was Cornell and the Big Red's star back Ed Marinaro. Rutgers quarterback Leo Gasienica unholstered his rifle arm and fired 20 completions in 30 attempts for more than 200 yards. Bob Carney caught 9 passes in the contest and Larry Christoff hauled in 6. The Scarlet aerial act was impressive, but not good enough, as Cornell's Ed Marinaro stole the spotlight. Cornell won. Successive defeats over the following five weeks dimmed the hopes of the Scarlet faithful as the season neared its end.

Scarlet Knights linebackers including Sam Picketts (#52) and Bob Wilusz pursue a Cornell running back. (Courtesy Frank Zukas)

Above: All-American running back Ed Marinaro of Cornell is stopped by Rutgers' Bob Shutte (#44) as the Knights' Alan Bain (#76) looks on. (Courtesy Frank Zukas)

Opposite: Andy Malekoff was defensive captain of the Scarlet Knights in 1972. His uncle Al "Boomy" Malekoff played for Rutgers in the late 1940s. (Courtesy Andy Malekoff)

Once again, the Rutgers players pulled together to terminate the slide. The team rebounded with a string of hard-fought wins to close out the year. Rutgers shaded Holy Cross 14 to 13 and beat Colgate 28 to 6. In the Urban Classic against Morgan State, Rutgers punctuated its mini winning streak with a shocking upset in its final game. Morgan State came into the contest with a record of 6 wins, 3 losses, and 1 tie. The Bears expected the Knights to be easy pickings for win number seven. They were wrong. The Rutgers offense picked apart the Morgan State defense for 27 points. The Rutgers defense held the Bears to a mere 8 points. The Scarlet Knights recorded their 4th win in 11 outings.

Tri-captain and linebacker Sam Picketts was selected ECAC and AP All-East. Picketts was also named the MVP of the 1971 Knights squad. He had 5 interceptions in 1971 and finished his career with a total of 7 interceptions.

Halfback and tri-captain Larry Robertson led the Scarlet Knights in rushing (405 yards) and scoring (42 points). Robertson tallied a total of 12 touchdowns in his career as a Rutgers player.

Jim "J. J." Jennings had 60 carries in 1971, good for a total of 320 yards. He had a 5.3-yard average per carry and scored 4 touchdowns. His best years were yet to come.

In 1972, flanker Johnny Rodgers of Nebraska won the Heisman Trophy. Defensive back Brad Van Pelt of Michigan State won the Maxwell Award. The University of Southern California, coached by John McKay, went 12 and 0 and won the National Championship.

Rutgers won back some of its faint-hearted football fans by reversing recent trends and posting a winning record in 1972. It was also the first year women students were admitted to Rutgers University. After one hundred–plus years Rutgers was finally coed.

Scarlet co-captains Andy Malekoff and Dave Rinehimer, with assistance from Ron Shyko, Jim Maloney, Len Boone, Tom Sweeny, Bill Bolash, Andy Farkas, and Tony Pawlik, helped steer Rutgers back onto the winning path.

Tony Pawlik would end up rated as one of Rutgers' best at pilfering opponents' passes. He helped fill a gaping void in the defensive secondary created when Ed Jones was unable to play. Tony Pawlik and Bill Bolash were former teammates at Manville High School in New Jersey. In 1972 the NCAA gave major colleges permission to use freshmen on their varsity football and basketball teams for the first time since 1950. Rutgers' first freshman starter was defensive end Dwight Lipscomb from Plainfield High School in New Jersey.

Senior signal caller Leo Gasienica confidently lined up behind a solid wall of offensive blockers that included Andy Tighe, Vic Lapkowicz, Scott Spencer, Bob Morton, Dale Sipos, and Bruce Montigney. The keys to the Rutgers offense of 1972 was the arm of QB Leo Gasienica and the legs of running back J. J. Jennings.

On the defensive side, linebackers Andy Mazer, John Witkowski, Andy Malekoff, and Frank Zukas were all seasoned players. The defensive line featured Bob Dillard, Marty Benante, Steve Allen, and Jack Salemi.

Pass defender Len Boone rounded out the secondary unit of Tony Pawlik and Gary Smolyn.

Coach John Bateman's 1972 Scarlet Knights started slow. Rutgers lost to Holy Cross and then bounced back to wallop Lehigh. The Lehigh victory was a good win. Lehigh was led by quarterback Kim McQuilken, one of the greatest and most prolific passers in Lehigh history. McQuilken passed for 6,996 yards and 37 touchdowns during his three-year stay at Lehigh. He ended up playing in the National Football League.

After Lehigh the Scarlet Knights endured a back-breaking loss to archrival Princeton. Princeton's Howie Baetjer scored with fifty-six seconds left in the game to enable the Tigers to top the Knights 7 to 6. Speedy Rutgers halfback Ron Shycko shone in the Princeton contest. Shycko gained 111 yards in 20 carries.

Left: Scarlet Knights John Witkowski (#55), Frank Zukas (#61), and Bob Shutte (#44) combine to make a stop in 1972. (Courtesy Frank Zukas)

Right: A swarming Rutgers defense buries All-American running back Ed Marinaro of Cornell. (Courtesy Frank Zukas)

Opposite: Rutgers' Tony Pawlik (#16) joins his Scarlet teammates in piling up on a Lehigh ball carrier in this 1972 gridiron contest. (Courtesy Frank Zukas)

A win over longtime opponent Lafayette was sandwiched between losses to Cornell and Army. After the Army defeat, the Rutgers offensive was machine driven by the powerful strides of Jim "J. J." Jennings.

Jennings put together consecutive 100-plus-yard rushing games against Columbia, Connecticut, and Boston University. Rutgers won all three contests. The team's record stood at 5 wins and 4 losses with 2 games still in the well.

The Scarlet Knights thrashed the Morgan State Bears. Speedy Tom Sweeney had a 97-yard kickoff return for a touchdown in that contest. In the final game of the season against Colgate, J. J. Jennings lugged the pigskin a record 40 times. Rutgers won 43 to 13 to finish the year with 7 wins and 4 losses.

Tight end Larry Christoff was selected All-East and was also named an Honorable Mention All-American. During his Rutgers career, Christoff caught a total of 68 passes for 8 touchdowns. He shared the Homer Hazel Award as the team's Most Valuable Player with J. J. Jennings. Christoff went on to try out with the Baltimore Colts in the NFL.

J. J. Jennings carried the ball 287 times in 1972 and gained 1,262 yards. He scored 9 touchdowns and averaged 4.4 yards per carry. Jennings was an All-East pick by the ECAC and the Associated Press.

Kicker John Pesce led the 1972 Scarlet Knights in scoring with a total of 56 points. Pesce was good on 16 of 29 field goals during his career for a .552 field goal percentage.

2
16

Above: Lehigh's Jack Rizzo attempts to escape Rutgers linebacker Frank Zukas in 1972 action between the two schools. (Courtesy Frank Zukas)

Opposite, top: An alert Gary Smolyn pounces on a loose pigskin in the 1972 Rutgers-BU contest. (Courtesy Frank Zukas)

Opposite, bottom: Tight end Larry Christoff bulls his way forward. The man with the pipe in the background is team doctor and surgeon Hyman Copleman. (Courtesy Larry Christoff)

Guard Andy Tighe was voted to the ECAC All-East team. Guard Dave Rinehimer was on the Associated Press All-East team. Quarterback Leo Gasienica was also mentioned on the AP All-East squad.

Gasienica completed 107 of 196 passes for 1,409 yards and 8 touchdowns in 1972. His career stats were equally impressive. Leo Gascienica completed a total of 230 of 448 passes for 2,801 yards and 16 touchdowns. He is one of Rutgers' top ten all-time passers.

At the conclusion of the 1972 season, head coach Dr. John Bateman stepped down from his position as the gridiron mentor of the Rutgers Scarlet Knights. Bateman was one of the most successful coaches in Rutgers history. He won 73 games, lost 51, and had 0 ties. Perhaps Bateman's teams never tied any contests because Dr. John always made the gutsy choice in close contests. He played to win.

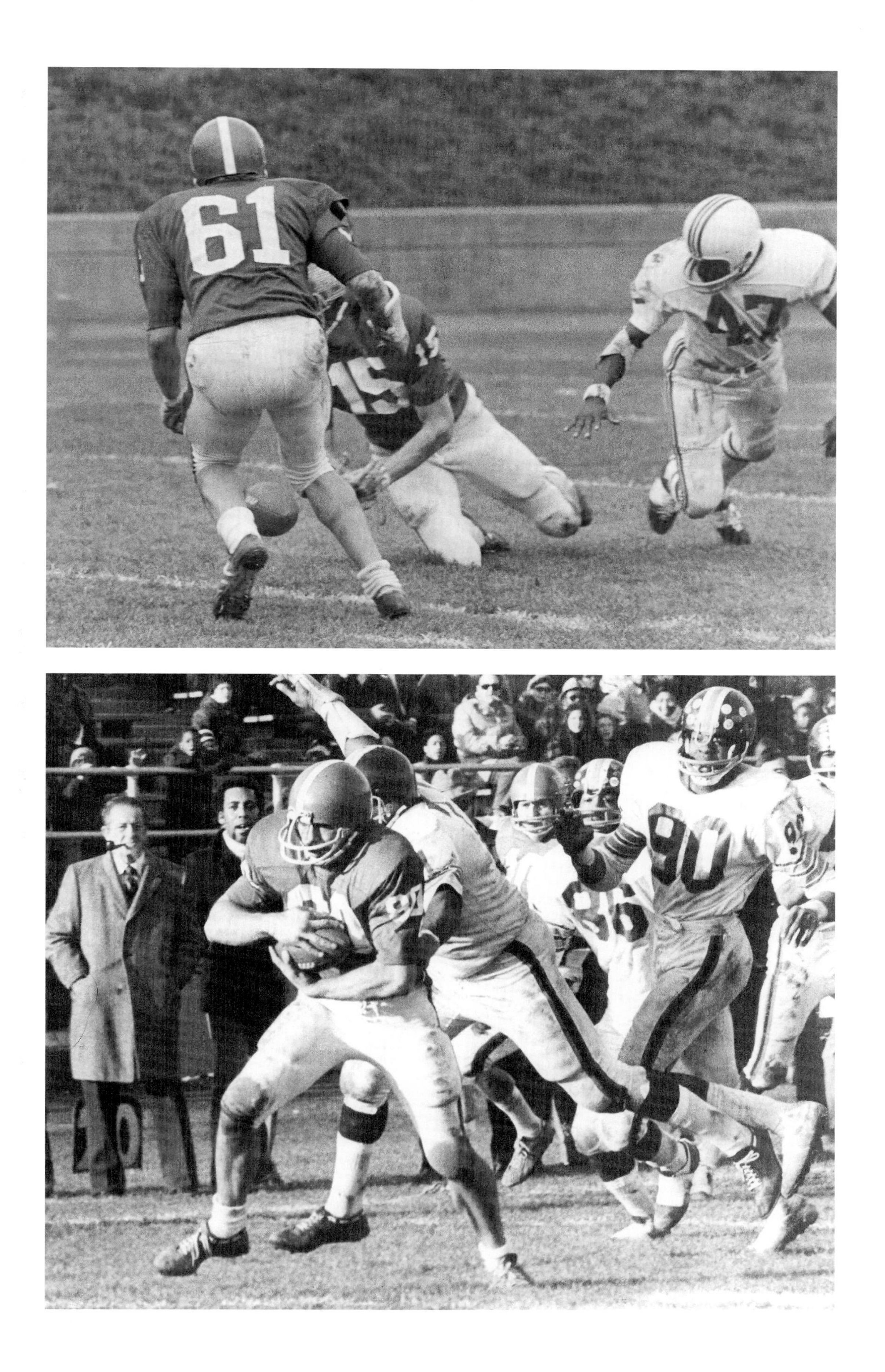
61
47
90

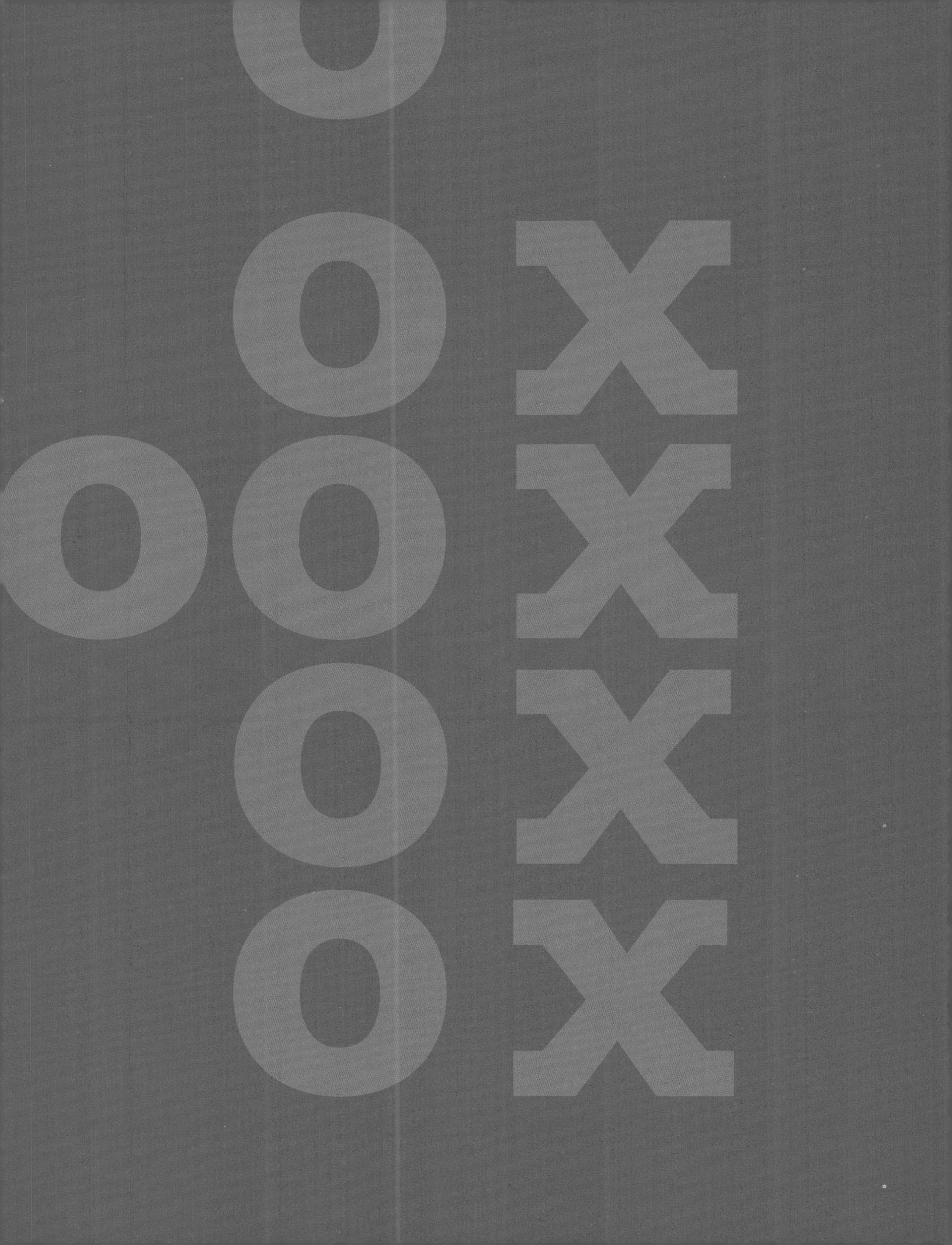

PART THREE 1973–2000

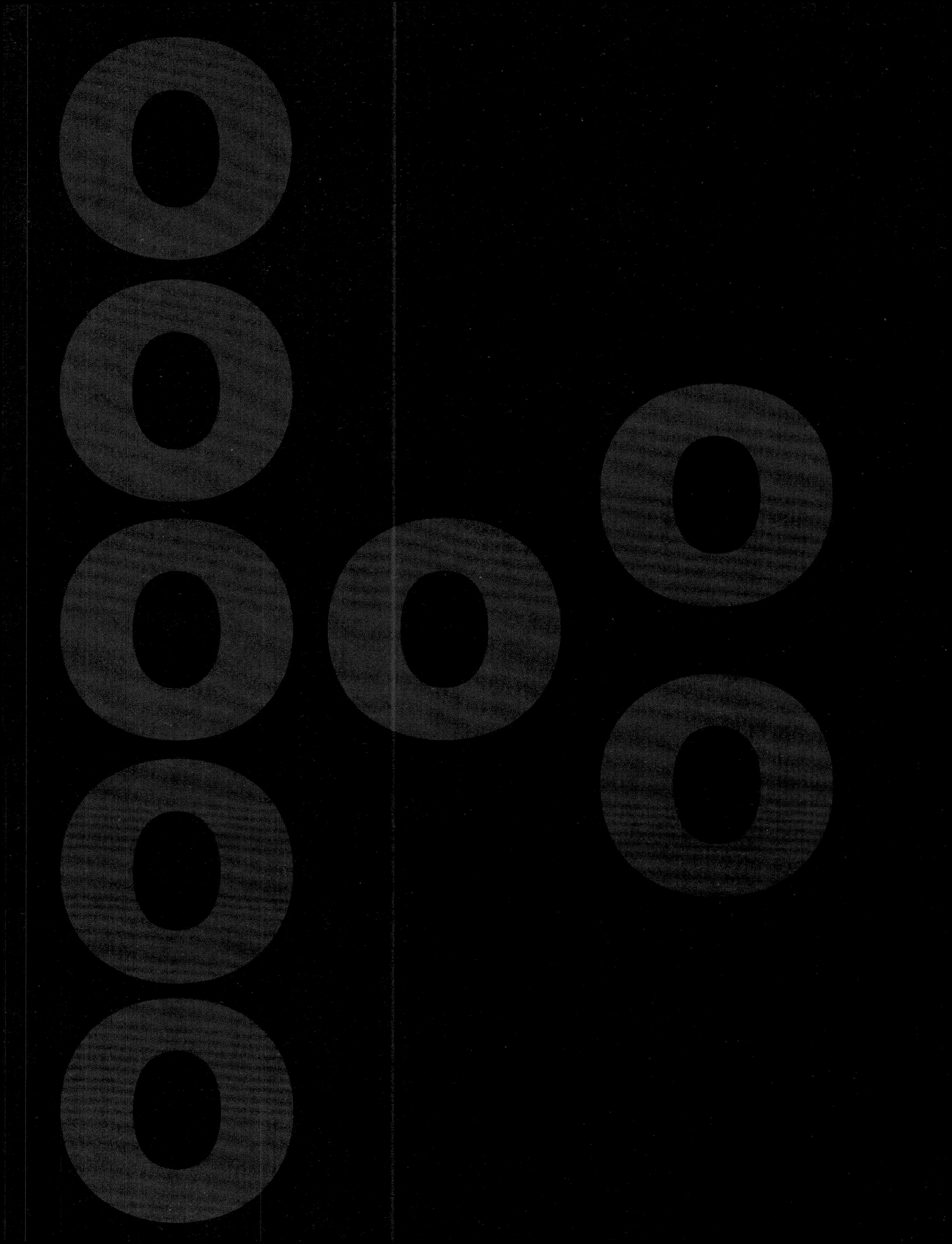

CHAPTER 9

A WINNING FORMULA

1973–1983

The University of Notre Dame, coached by Ara Parseghian, finished their 1973 season 11–0 and was ranked number 1 in the country. Penn State running back John Cappelletti won the Heisman Trophy in 1973 as college football's best player.

A player from one of football's oldest but less recognized colleges made a big splash on the national scene in 1973. Rutgers' Jim Jennings led the nation in scoring that season. Jim "J. J." Jennings's national scoring crown in 1973 signaled to football fans across the nation that things were changing at Rutgers.

Rutgers football came under new leadership in 1973. Longtime Rutgers athletic director Al Twitchell was replaced by Assistant Athletic Director Fred Gruninger. Legendary Rutgers quarterback and longtime associate coach Frank Burns took charge of a Scarlet Knights program seeking a new direction. "There's great talent in this state," Burns said at a press conference. "If we could just get the top ones to stay home we could compete with anybody. It would be a team of great state pride." Burns's coaching staff included former Rutgers players Jim Taigia, Mike Kizis, Pete Savino, Bob Naso, and Bill Speranza. Paul Moran and Ted Cottrell rounded out the staff. Cottrell was a former NFL linebacker.

At the same time a committee of prominent Rutgers alumni headed by David "Sonny" Werblin submitted a report recommending that Rutgers upgrade its sports programs. Werblin was also a member of the Rutgers Board of Governors. "The major fiscal need for our program if it is to be upgraded will be financial aid to athletes," new AD Fred Gruninger advised. At the time, the Barr Scholarship supported 15 to 20 football athletes per year. To go big-time Rutgers would need 25 to 30 scholarships per year. Rutgers planned to generate more sports revenue by playing name schools at the huge new Meadowlands Stadium in Hackensack, New Jersey. Rutgers also formed its Scarlet R Club to serve as a fundraiser for additional scholarships.

Plans were in place to go big-time. All Rutgers had to do now was win some football games. That task was left to the coaches and players. All-American running back J. J. Jennings would help make that possible. Co-captains Andy Tighe and John Witkowski would also contribute to the cause along with Bill Bolash, Ed Jones, Tom Sweeney, Ed Sessions, Paul Krasnavage, and Tony Pawlik.

Above: Former Rutgers star quarterback and offensive coordinator Frank Burns became the head coach of the Scarlet Knights in 1973. (Courtesy Rutgers Athletic Communications)

Below: Jim "J. J." Jennings of Rutgers led the nation in scoring in 1973. (Courtesy Rutgers Athletic Communications)

Rutgers faced two new gridiron opponents in 1973. On the schedule for the first time were Air Force and Tampa.

The Scarlet Knights suffered a tough loss even before they played their first game that year. Starting quarterback Gary Smolyn was injured in preseason and sidelined. Steve Havran stepped in behind center Bruce Montigney.

Up first for new head coach Frank Burns's squad was old rival Lehigh. Rutgers dominated a fine Lehigh squad that had already won two games. The Scarlet defense held Lehigh to just 98 yards rushing and intercepted 4 passes. J. J. Jennings lugged the pigskin 36 times for a total of 116 yards. Rutgers won 31 to 13.

A decisive win over Princeton followed the week after. Rutgers was 2–0 when the University of Massachusetts came to New Jersey and edged the Knights 25 to 22. Rutgers rebounded with an easy win over Lafayette. Safety Tony Pawlik had 3 interceptions in that contest.

With Steve Havran sharing quarterback duties with John Piccirillo, Rutgers continued to roll. The Knights posted back-to-back wins over Delaware and Columbia. J. J. Jennings had chalked up 6 consecutive 100-plus-yard rushing games. Rutgers was 5–1.

Prospects looked bright until Connecticut bested the Knights. Rutgers then jetted to Colorado and was shot down by Air Force. The Scarlet Knights were 6–3 after beating Holy Cross.

Colgate then came calling. The potent Red Raiders offense was spearheaded by two outstanding athletes. Quarterback Tom Parr was an All-America candidate. Fullback Mark Van Eeghen was a top pro prospect. He eventually became an offensive starter for the Oakland Raiders. At Oakland, Van Eeghen replaced another Colgate grad, Marv Hubbard, at fullback.

Colgate proved to be too tough for Rutgers, as did first-time foe Tampa. The Scarlet Knights skidded to a season record of 6 wins and 5 losses. Coach Frank Burns's maiden voyage as the Scarlet's gridiron master was a modest success.

Rutgers' Tony Pawlik had a big year in 1973. He intercepted 8 passes and returned them for 137 yards. Defensive back Ed Jones made the AP All-East team, as did defensive tackle Steve Allen. Guard Andy Tighe was named to the AP All-East team. Tighe went on to try out with the New York Jets.

Jim "J. J." Jennings led the nation in scoring in 1973 with a total of 128 points. He scored 21 touchdowns and 2 extra points for an average of 11.6 points per game. Jennings carried the ball 303 times for 1,353 yards. Over his three-year career J. J. Jennings carried the ball 650 times for 2,935 yards and 34 touchdowns. He averaged 4.5 yards per carry.

Jim "J. J." Jennings was an Honorable Mention All-American by the Associated Press. He was also AP and ECAC All-East. Jennings was voted the Scarlet Knights' MVP and played in the Hula Bowl. He was also a National Football Foundation Scholar-Athlete Award winner. J. J. Jennings tried out with the Kansas City Chiefs and later starred for the Memphis Southmen and the Philadelphia Bell of the World Football League.

Head coach Frank Burns of Rutgers continued to upgrade his program in 1974. Bert Kosup became the starting quarterback, and he was destined for greatness. Kosup was joined behind the line by two excellent young backs in Curt Edwards and Mike Fisher. Kosup's backup was Matt Allison. Before coming to Rutgers, Allison had played professional baseball in the Philadelphia Phillies organization.

Mark Twitty was now the top receiver. The offensive line was anchored by center and co-captain Andrew Zdobylak. Defense was a Scarlet strong point. It was led by co-captain Tony Pawlik, linebacker Tom Holmes, and defensive linemen Paul Krasnavage and Nate Toran.

Left: Running back Bill Bolash was a three-year letterman. Bolash was one of many athletes from Manville High School in New Jersey to play football at Rutgers. (From the personal collection of Bert Kosup/Courtesy Rutgers Athletic Communications)

Center: Dwight Lipscomb of Plainfield, New Jersey, was one of Rutgers' first football players to start as a freshman in the modern era. (Courtesy Dwight Lipscomb)

Right: Rutgers' Harold Golden (#80), Andy Mazer (#44), and Paul Krasnavage (#64) during the return of a blocked punt against Delaware. (Courtesy Paul Krasnavage)

Another new foe appeared on the Rutgers schedule in 1974. The Rainbow Warriors of Hawaii hosted the Scarlet Knights of New Jersey for the first time ever. Back on the schedule after a long absence was William and Mary. Rutgers had last played football against William and Mary back in 1957.

Rutgers opened the season with a close win over Bucknell. The following week, Tony Pawlik returned a punt 94 yards for a touchdown against Princeton, but the game ended in a 6 to 6 tie. Wins over Harvard and Lehigh came back to back. The Knights were 3–0–1 going into game four against William and Mary. William and Mary defeated Rutgers 28 to 15 in a hard-fought contest.

The next week, the Scarlet stepped it up in a Rutgers victory over Air Force. The Knights then dropped a heartbreaking 7 to 9 loss to Connecticut before scoring wins over Lafayette, Boston University, and Colgate. QB Bert Kosup of Rutgers had a 94-yard completion to receiver Mark Twitty in the Colgate win. The year concluded with a loss to Hawaii. Rutgers posted a season record of 7 wins, 3 losses, and 1 tie in 1974.

Rutgers center Andy Zdobylak was rewarded for his offensive line work by being named All-East. Tom Holmes and Paul Krasnavage were also selected to the All-East team.

Cornerback Ed Jones had 7 interceptions in 1974. He finished his Rutgers career with 14 total interceptions. Jones was named the team's Most Valuable Player and voted All-East by the ECAC and the *New York Times*. He played pro football after graduation for the

Above: Two great Rutgers defenders converge on a Connecticut ball carrier. Nate Toran is #77 and Paul Krasnavage is #64. (Courtesy Paul Krasnavage)

Right: Scarlet QB Bert Kosup (#11) pitches out to running back Mike Fisher (#24). (Courtesy Bert Kosup)

Dallas Cowboys and the Buffalo Bills in the NFL. Jones jumped to the Canadian Football League and starred for the Edmonton Eskimos and the British Columbia Lions. In 1980 he led the CFL with 11 interceptions.

Defensive end Nate Toran had 19 quarterback sacks in 1974 and earned All-East honors. Defensive tackle Paul Krasnavage also earned All-East honors. Linebacker Tom Holmes had 124 tackles in 1974 and was named ECAC and AP All-East.

Safety Tony Pawlik finished his Rutgers career with a total of 14 interceptions returned for 226 yards. He had 48 punt returns for 545 yards. Pawlik tried out with the New Orleans Saints in the NFL.

In 1975 Rutgers had a balanced offense guided by quarterback Bert Kosup. In the backfield were fullback Glen Kehler, speedster Mark Lassiter, and co-captain Curt Edwards. Fleet receiver Mark Twitty was the main target on passing downs. Guard Tony Ray was the top man on the offensive line.

On defense the Knights had end Nate Toran, tackle Dan Gray, and linebackers Tim Blanchard, Elvin Washington, and Jim Hughes. Co-captain Tom Holmes headed the hard-hitting unit.

The Scarlet Knights opened the 1975 season against Bucknell. Starting quarterback Bert Kosup was injured and needed surgery. Matt Allison was pressed into service as the Scarlet signal caller. Allison had a fine day, completing 15 of 20 passes for 145 yards. On defense, Dave Figueora picked off a Bucknell pass and returned the pigskin 64 yards. Rutgers rolled to an easy win.

Above: Tony Pawlik was one of the greatest pass defenders in Rutgers history. (From the personal collection of Bert Kosup/Courtesy Rutgers Athletic Communications)

Below: Rutgers defensive back Jim Teatom brings down an opposing ball carrier as Tom Mannon (#73), Elvin Washington (#56), and Paul Krasnavage pursue the play. (Courtesy Paul Krasnavage)

Rutgers' Paul Krasnavage bats down a pass against Harvard. (Courtesy Paul Krasnavage)

The Princeton Tigers clawed out a hard-fought win over Rutgers in game two. Next, Hawaii came to New Jersey and the Scarlet Knights edged the Rainbow Warriors 7 to 3. A loss to Lehigh followed.

Jeff Rebholz and Matt Allison began to share signal calling duties for the Scarlet. Consecutive wins over William and Mary, Columbia, Connecticut, Lafayette, Boston University, Colgate, and Syracuse made Rutgers fans believe the Knights were ready to step up to a bigger-time schedule. QB Jeff Rebholz and receiver Mark Twitty hooked up on a stunning 76-yard TD pass completion against Colgate. Fullback Curt Edwards had also stepped it up at the end of the season. He put together a string of 5 consecutive 100-plus-yard rushing games starting with the Connecticut contest.

Top left: Dwight Lipscomb (left) was a force on the defense for the Scarlet Knights from 1972 to 1975. (Courtesy Dwight Lipscomb)

Top right: Nick Sauter won three letters at offensive tackle for the Scarlet Knights. (From the personal collection of Bert Kosup/Courtesy Rutgers Athletic Communications)

Bottom left: Scarlet quarterback Matt Allison played professional baseball before playing college football for Rutgers. (Courtesy Matt Allison)

Bottom right: Running back Curt Edwards averaged 4.81 yards per carry in 1974 and 1975. He had 5 consecutive 100-yard games as a rusher for the Scarlet Knights. (From the personal collection of Bert Kosup/Courtesy Rutgers Athletic Communications)

Curt Edwards had a fantastic year in 1975. He rushed for 1,157 yards and tallied 9 rushing touchdowns. Edwards was the team's top scorer with 66 points. Over his two-year RU career, Curt Edwards ran for 2,046 yards on 425 carries for a 4.81-yard average per carry. The fleet fullback gained more than 100 yards in a game 9 times during his career. He also had one 200-plus-yard rushing game. Curt Edwards was named All-East by the Eastern College Athletic Association.

Wide receiver Mark Twitty pulled in a total of 7 touchdown passes that season. He had a career total of 12 touchdown catches. Offensive guard Tony Ray was named to the ECAC

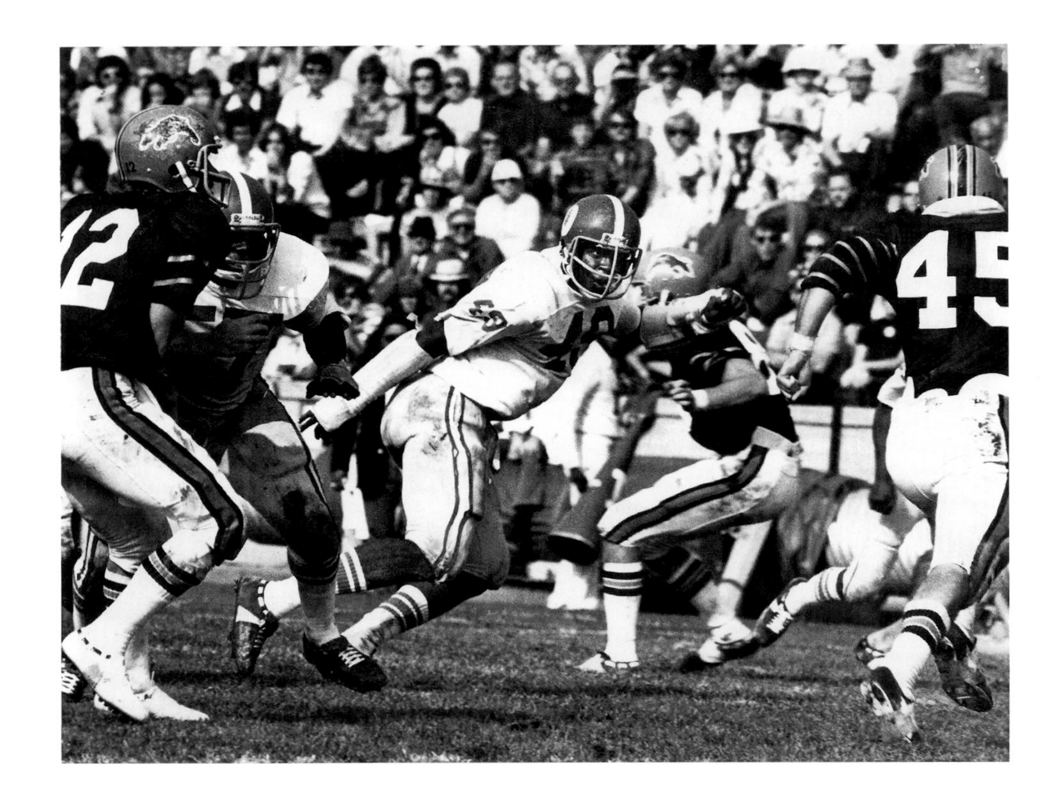

Above: Dwight Lipscomb (center) played both defensive end and linebacker during his four-year career at Rutgers. Lipscomb is seen here in action against Princeton in 1975. (Courtesy Dwight Lipscomb)

Below: Rutgers linebacker Tom Holmes led the Scarlet Knights with 96 tackles in 1975. (From the personal collection of Bert Kosup/Courtesy Rutgers Athletic Communications)

Opposite: All-America defensive end Nate Toran blocks a pass. (Courtesy Paul Krasnavage)

All-East. Punter Steve Simek finished his Rutgers career (1974–75) with 96 punts for 3,691 yards and a 38.4-yard-per-punt average.

There were many stars on defense in 1975. Tackle Dan Gray had 12 quarterback sacks. Linebacker and defensive end Dwight Lipscomb had 65 tackles, 4 QB sacks, and 3 fumble recoveries. Linebacker Tom Holmes was the top hitter with 96 tackles. He had a career total of 220 tackles. Defensive tackle Jim Alexander won All-East Honorable Mention from the Associated Press. Defensive back John Teatom was on the ECAC All-East team.

Scarlet Knight Nate Toran earned the highest accolades. The Associated Press named Toran a Third Team All-American for collecting 16 quarterback sacks. In addition, defensive end Nate Toran was voted All-East by the AP and ECAC. In his first three seasons as a Scarlet Knight, Toran had racked up an astonishing 35 quarterback sacks.

The Scarlet Knights' record of 9 wins and 2 losses was impressive. It was the first time Rutgers had posted 9 wins in a season since the undefeated team of 1961.

Coach Frank Burns's 1976 squad was loaded on both sides of the line of scrimmage. The offense was under the leadership of co-captain and offensive guard Dan Pfabe and quarterback Bert Kosup. Joining Pfabe on the offensive line were veterans John Gallo and Nick Sauter.

In the backfield with signal caller Bert Kosup were three backs of superstar caliber. The fullback was Glen Kehler, who would ramble for more than 2,500 yards before his Rutgers career was over. Kehler's running mates were Mark Lassiter and Mike Fisher. Lassiter and Fisher would total a combined 3,919 rushing yards and a combined 953 pass-receiving yards by the time their Scarlet careers ended.

Once again deep threat Mark Twitty was the go-to guy on passing downs.

Co-captain Nate Toran was the cornerstone of a defensive line that featured Dino Mangiero, John Alexander, and Dan Gray. Vicious tacklers Tim Blanchard, Jim Hughes, and Elvin Washington spearheaded the linebackers. The defensive secondary had ball hawks

Right: Bert Kosup, one of Rutgers' top-rated quarterbacks, gets great protection as he prepares to pass in 1976 action. (Courtesy Bert Kosup)

Below: Matt Allison, who filled in for an injured Bert Kosup in 1975, was Kosup's backup quarterback in 1976. (Courtesy Matt Allison)

Rutgers lineman John Alexander went on to a pro career in the NFL with the Miami Dolphins. (Courtesy Miami Dolphins)

Jim Teatom, Henry Jenkins, Don Harris, and Bob Hynoski, whose twin brother, Walt, was a wide receiver.

Other key performers on the talent-deep team were Jim O'Halloran, Jon Walling, Len Davis, Bob Davis, Sam Davis, Dennis Eckels, John Washington, John Bucci, Reggie Moultrie, and three-year letterman Dusty Bryan. Kicker Kennan Startzell was a new face and he would eventually boot his way into the Rutgers record book.

The Rutgers football squad of 1976 steamrolled to eleven straight wins. There were no really close contests or last-gasp trick plays to notch a victory. The dates and scores of Rutgers' fabulous undefeated season of 1976 are printed here:

9/11 Rutgers 13—Navy 3 (away)
9/18 Rutgers 19—Bucknell 7 (away)
9/25 Rutgers 17—Princeton 0 (away)
10/2 Rutgers 21—Cornell 14 (home)
10/9 Rutgers 38—Connecticut 0 (home)
10/16 Rutgers 28—Lehigh 21 (away)
10/23 Rutgers 47—Columbia 0 (Meadowlands)
10/30 Rutgers 24—Massachusetts 7 (home)
11/6 Rutgers 34—Louisville 0 (home)
11/13 Rutgers 29—Tulane 20 (away)
11/18 Rutgers 17—Colgate 9 (Meadowlands)

Rutgers' victory over Columbia in 1976 was the Scarlet Knights' first appearance at the Meadowlands. The game against Colgate at the Meadowlands was shown on ABC television.

Rutgers' offense scored a total of 287 points that year while its defense gave up a total of just 81 points to its opponents. The Scarlet Knights led the nation in total defense, rushing defense, and scoring defense. Rutgers won 18 games in a row over the 1975 and '76 seasons. The Scarlet Knights ended up ranked number 17 in the final AP poll of 1976. Rutgers had a better record than every other team in the Top 20 excluding Pittsburgh, the

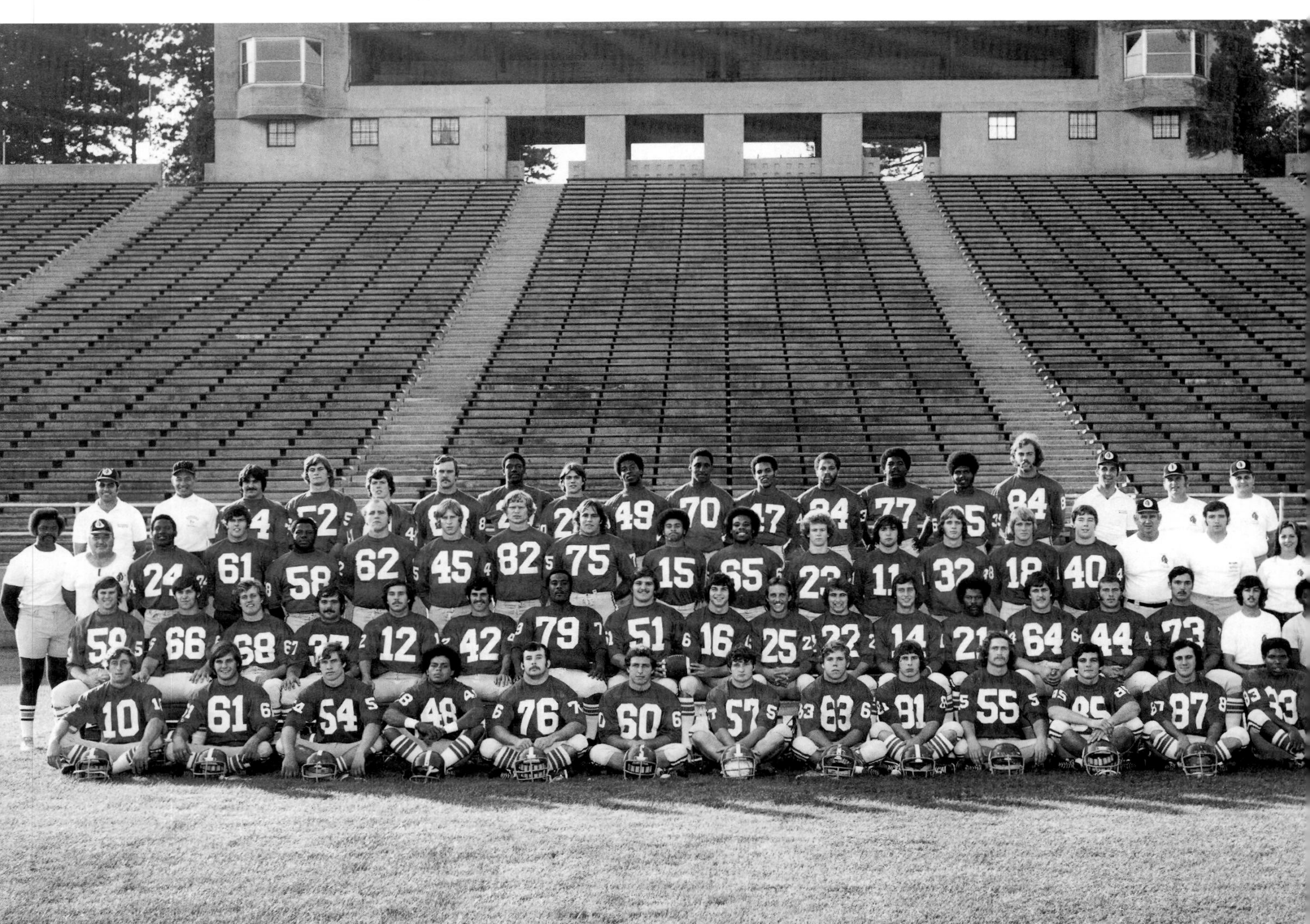

The 1976 Rutgers football team posted a perfect season record of 11–0 and finished the year ranked number 17 in the country. (From the personal collection of Bert Kosup/Courtesy Rutgers Athletic Communications)

Members of the 1976 Scarlet squad celebrate their undefeated season. (Courtesy Rutgers Athletic Communications)

only other undefeated team in the Top 20. Rutgers was invited to play in the new Independence Bowl in Shreveport, Louisiana. The team voted not to accept the bowl bid because the players felt they deserved to be invited to a more established bowl game.

In 1976 quarterback Bert Kosup completed 69 of 141 passes for 1,098 yards and 6 touchdowns. Running back Mark Lassiter scored 9 touchdowns in 1976. Kicker Kennan Startzell was the scoring champ with 65 points.

Defensive end Nate Toran had 17 more quarterback sacks in 1976. He completed his college pass-rushing career with a Rutgers-record 52 QB sacks. Toran was voted the team's Most Valuable Player. Defensive tackle Dan Gray had 10 quarterback sacks in 1976. He had a two-year total of 22 quarterback sacks. Linebacker Jim Hughes had 113 tackles and 5 interceptions. Safety Jim Teatom finished his Rutgers career with a total of 10 interceptions. Defensive back and return specialist Henry Jenkins concluded his Scarlet career with 50 punt returns for 726 yards.

Individual player honors were many. Wide receiver Mark Twitty was an AP and ECAC All-East. He was also an Honorable Mention All-American. Offensive tackle Nick Sauter was ECAC All-East.

Defensive tackle John Alexander was chosen All-East by the Eastern College Athletic Association and the Associated Press. He was also an AP Honorable Mention All-American and played in the East-West Shrine Bowl. Alexander continued his football career in the NFL with the Miami Dolphins. Defensive back Don Harris signed a pro contract with the Washington Redskins.

Linebacker Jim Hughes was selected to the All-East by the ECAC and the AP. In addition, he was an AP Honorable Mention All-American. Defensive back Henry Jenkins was an AP All-America Honorable Mention. Defensive back Jim Teatom won All-East mention from the ECAC.

Rutgers' Nate Toran was chosen All-East by the Associated Press and the Eastern College Athletic Association. He was a Second Team AP All-American. Nate Toran was also named a First Team Kodak All-American.

Above: Quarterback Bert Kosup, who guided Rutgers to an undefeated season in 1976, led Rutgers to a record of 8 wins and 3 losses in 1977. Kosup threw 25 touchdown passes during his college career. (From the personal collection of Bert Kosup/Courtesy Rutgers Athletic Communications)

Right: Matt Allison completed his Rutgers career in 1977. He was a gifted athlete who made several key starts as a Scarlet signal caller. (Courtesy Matt Allison)

Notre Dame went 11–1 in 1976 to win the National Championship. Running back Earl Campbell of Texas won the Heisman Trophy. Quarterback Doug Williams of Grambling finished fourth in the Heisman voting. Years later (in 1988), as a member of the Washington Redskins, Williams became the first African-American quarterback to start a Super Bowl game. He was named the MVP of Super Bowl XXII.

Rutgers' quarterback in 1977 was senior Bert Kosup. Kosup would put up the best numbers of his Rutgers career in 1977. Other senior leaders included defensive captain Jim Hughes and offensive captain Dan Pfabe. Pfabe was a two-time Rutgers captain.

The offensive squad of the preceding undefeated season was mainly still intact. New to the offense were receivers Tim Odell and Dave Dorn.

The Rutgers defense had lost many stars, but new ones were rising. They included Dino Mangiero, Ed Steward, and Bob Davis.

Rutgers opened the year against Penn State at Giants Stadium. The Nittany Lions mauled the Scarlet Knights and ended Rutgers' 18-game winning streak. Rutgers' lone touchdown in the game was scored by Lester Johnson of Somerville, New Jersey. After a bad loss to Colgate, some football fans thought that Rutgers was on a downward slide. They were wrong.

Field general Bert Kosup rallied his troops. The Scarlet Knights recorded consecutive victories over Bucknell, Princeton, Cornell, Connecticut, and Lehigh. The Knights were a respectable 5 and 2 going into their contest against William and Mary.

An unexpected turn of events caused concern to Rutgers' players, coaches, and fans. Head Coach Frank Burns suffered a mild heart attack before the game against William and Mary and had to sit out the remainder of the season. Defensive coordinator Bob Naso was pressed into emergency service as the head coach. The Scarlet Knights won 3 of their final 4 games. Rutgers finished with a record of 8 wins and 3 losses.

In 1977 team MVP Bert Kosup completed 82 of 157 passes for 1,445 yards and 10 touchdowns. In a losing effort to Temple, Kosup completed a 95-yard pass to George Carter. Over the course of his career as a Rutgers quarterback, Bert Kosup completed 214 passes in 448 attempts for 3,607 yards and 25 touchdowns.

Running back Mike Fisher tallied 9 rushing touchdowns in 1977. He was Rutgers' top scorer with 60 points. Over his Rutgers career Fisher rushed for 2,035 yards on 453 carries for an average of 4.49 yards per carry. He scored a total of 26 rushing touchdowns. He also caught 3 touchdown passes and scored 2 extra points for a grand total of 178 points in his career.

Mark Lassiter concluded his Rutgers career with a total of 1,884 rushing yards and 2,236 all-purpose yards.

Defensive back Bob Davis led the team with 121 tackles. Davis pilfered 12 passes over the span of his Rutgers career and returned the interceptions for a total of 177 yards. Star defensive tackle Dan Gray had 80 tackles and 7 quarterback sacks in 1977. Gray dropped opposing passers a total of 29 times over his career. Phil Parkins had a two-year total of 12 quarterback sacks. Senior linebacker Elvin Washington had 117 tackles and 2 sacks in 1977. He had a total of 290 tackles and 4 sacks in his career.

Safety Bob Davis was selected All-East by both the ECAC and AP. Defensive tackler Dan Gray was AP All-East. Gray continued his football career by trying out with the Detroit Lions.

Running back Billy Simms of Oklahoma was college football's best player in 1978. Simms won the Heisman Trophy. Quarterback Chuck Fusina of Penn State finished second in the Heisman, but won the Maxwell Trophy as college football's top performer. Alabama, coached by Paul "Bear" Bryant, was America's top college team. The Crimson Tide of Alabama won the national crown with an 11–1 record. Penn State and Alabama would figure in the fate of Rutgers' football success presently.

Coach Frank Burns recovered from his health problems and returned to the football sidelines for the 1978 season. Team captains Tim Blanchard and John Bucci welcomed him back for their senior seasons.

In 1978 competition for the quarterback slot was between Bob Hering and young Ed McMichael. Ted Blackwell and Dave Dorn provided offensive punch. John Gallo, John Bucci, and Kevin Kurdyla were counted on to beef up the offensive line. Fullback

Dino Mangiero had 26 quarterback sacks during his Rutgers career.
(Courtesy Rutgers Athletic Communications)

Glen Kehler, receiver Tim Odell, and place kicker Kennan Startzell were all offensive weapons.

On defense Tim Blanchard, Jim Hughes, Dino Mangiero, Ed Steward, Mike Rustemeyer, and Deron Cherry were key performers.

Rutgers opened the season with the toughest opponent on their schedule, Penn State. Led by their Heisman Trophy candidate, quarterback Chuck Fusina, the Nittany Lions went 11–1 in 1978 and ended up ranked 5th in the nation. After getting dumped by Penn State, Rutgers recovered to trash Princeton, Yale, Connecticut, and Villanova. The Scarlet Knights were 5–1 when they took on Columbia at Giants Stadium in their seventh game of the season. Speedster Dave Dorn had a 94-yard kickoff return against Columbia and the Knights walloped the Lions 69 to 0.

Wins over Massachusetts, Temple, and Holy Cross followed. Going into the final regular season game against Colgate, Rutgers was 9 and 1 with nine consecutive victories. Colgate played the spoiler and bested Rutgers 14 to 9. The Scarlet Knights ended their regular season with a loss, but there was still more football to come.

Rutgers went to its first bowl game. The Knights were invited to bash helmets against Arizona State in the Garden State Bowl. One year earlier, in 1977, the Sun Devils of Arizona State, coached by Frank Kush, had a 9–3 record and were ranked 18th in the nation.

The Scarlet Knights of Rutgers accepted the invitation and took on the Arizona State Sun Devils in postseason play. Rutgers opened the scoring in the Garden State Bowl. Dave

Dorn ran 47 yards for a touchdown in the first period. Kennan Startzell added the PAT. Rutgers played tough defense and Ed Steward recovered a fumble, which set up a 46-yard field goal by Startzell. Rutgers jumped out to a 10–0 lead.

Arizona State quarterback Mark Malone rallied his forces. However, a Malone pass was picked off by an alert Bob Hynoski. Hynoski headed for the opposing end zone and raced 36 yards before he was tackled on the Sun Devils' four-yard line. It appeared that Rutgers would coast to a 17–0 first half lead. However, looks can deceive. Rutgers' Dave Dorn suddenly fumbled the ball back to Arizona State.

The Sun Devils mounted a drive and QB Mark Malone connected with Bob Weathers for a 14-yard scoring strike before the half ended. Rutgers' lead was reduced to 10–7.

Momentum switched sides in the second half. Mark Malone threw 2 touchdown passes and ran for a score as Arizona State took a commanding 28 to 10 lead.

In the fourth period, Ted Blackwell of Rutgers plunged into the end zone for a touchdown and then added the 2-point conversion. The score was Sun Devils 28, Knights 18.

Kennan Startzell followed up the Rutgers score with a superb onside kick. The ball squirted here, bounced there, and skidded into the Sun Devils' end zone, where it was covered by Craig Nielsen of the Scarlet Knights for an apparent touchdown. The bizarre play would have made the score Arizona State 28 and Rutgers 24 with minutes to go in the game. However, Rutgers was called for offsides and the touchdown was a moot point. The ball went over to Arizona State. Quarterback Mark Malone added another score and Arizona State defeated Rutgers 34 to 18 in the 1978 Garden State Bowl. In the contest Rutgers' Ed Steward played like a one-man gang. Steward registered 15 tackles on the day.

Ed Steward had a breakout year in 1978. In addition to his great bowl-game performance, he dropped opposing passers 10 times during the regular season. Dino Mangiero also had a stellar season. Mangiero registered 98 tackles and 9 quarterback sacks. Bob Hynoski picked off 6 interceptions. Co-captain Jim Hughes finished his Rutgers career with 10 interceptions, which he returned for 222 yards. Linebacker Tim Blanchard was the Scarlet's top tackler in 1978. Blanchard had 122 tackles and 4 sacks. In his four years at Rutgers, Blanchard made a total of 312 tackles and 4 sacks.

Quarterback Bob Hering led Rutgers in passing with 1,193 yards. Kicker Kennan Startzell topped all scorers with 76 points.

Fullback Glen Kehler was the best ground gainer. Kehler rushed for 883 yards on 212 carries and 3 touchdowns. Glen Kehler rushed for 2,567 yards on 537 carries as a Scarlet Knight. He had a 4.8-yards-per-carry average and scored a total of 5 touchdowns.

Center John Bucci, tackle Kevin Kurdyla, and flanker Dave Dorn were AP All-East picks. Tackle John Gallo was selected All-East by United Press International and the Eastern College Athletic Association.

Deron Cherry's first year as a Scarlet defensive back and punter was 1978. Cherry became one of Rutgers' all-time great players. (Courtesy Kansas City Chiefs)

Defensive back Mark Freeman was AP All-East. Jim Hughes was ECAC All-East and AP All-East. Ed Steward was AP All-East and Honorable Mention All-American by the Associated Press.

In 1979 Ed McMichael grabbed the quarterback reigns for Rutgers. McMichael would get offensive support from Tim Odell, Dave Dorn, Ted Blackwell, and newcomer Albert Ray. Offensive captain Pete Honeyford was a respected team leader and was aided by Frank Naylor, Kevin Kurdyla, Jim Zurich, and tight end Steve Pfirman.

Defensive captain Dino Mangiero led by example. He was a hard tackler and a powerful pass rusher. Mangiero and Ed Steward joined forces with Bill Pickel and Mike Rustmeyer to form a fearsome foursome. Deron Cherry, Ken Smith, and Mark Freeman were outstanding in the defensive secondary. Jim Dumont and his twin brother Bob Dumont were great new additions to a rugged defensive outfit.

Rutgers opened its 1979 gridiron campaign with an easy shutout win over Holy Cross. In the second game Penn State continued its early dominance over the Knights and recorded a win. Rutgers then beat Bucknell and Princeton back to back. In the Princeton win, Rutgers' Ken Smith had an 84-yard punt return. A bad loss to a very good Temple team followed. The Scarlet Knights next bumped helmets with the Huskies of Connecticut. In Rutgers' victory over Connecticut, Kennan Startzell booted a 48-yard field goal.

Up next was William and Mary. An injury to a usual starter forced Albert Ray into action in the backfield. Ray jumped into his running shoes, scoring 2 touchdowns in the first half. He ran for 123 yards on 21 carries for the day. Rutgers won and had a 5 and 2 record as it prepared to take on its marquee foe of the season.

Rutgers traveled to Knoxville, Tennessee, to take on the University of Tennessee. More than eighty thousand fans jammed into the stadium expecting to see the Tennessee Volunteers wipe out no-name Rutgers. By the time the game was over, football fans in the state of Tennessee not only knew the name of the Rutgers Scarlet Knights, but also cursed the upstart gridiron team from New Jersey.

Tennessee came into the contest ranked 17th in the country. The Vols had not lost to a team from the East since 1941. The Volunteers started out like a house on fire. They burned the Rutgers defense and scored a touchdown five minutes after the opening kickoff. They had a fast 7 to 0 lead. It didn't last.

Rutgers' Ed Steward made a key interception. Scarlet quarterback Ed McMichael came in and connected with Dave Dorn for a 37-yard completion. McMichael then launched a rocket to wideout Tim Odell. Odell went up high to make the catch and came down in the end zone. He scored the touchdown, but was knocked out. When a groggy Tim Odell regained his senses in the locker room at the half, the score was 7 to 7.

In the second half, the Rutgers defense shone. Great plays by defensive back Mark Pineiro and tackle Dino Mangiero held Tennessee scoreless. Scarlet kicker Kennan Startzell booted two field goals. One was a 43-yarder and the other was a 32-yarder. Rutgers took a 13 to 7 lead and held it in a stranglehold.

Rutgers offensive tackle Tony Cella broke his leg in the game, but felt no pain as he was carried off the field by his victorious teammates. It was the Tennessee football players and fans who were in anguish that day. Rutgers beat Tennessee 13 to 7 to give Frank Burns his signature win of the season.

When asked about the upset victory, Burns replied, "It was the greatest of my career."

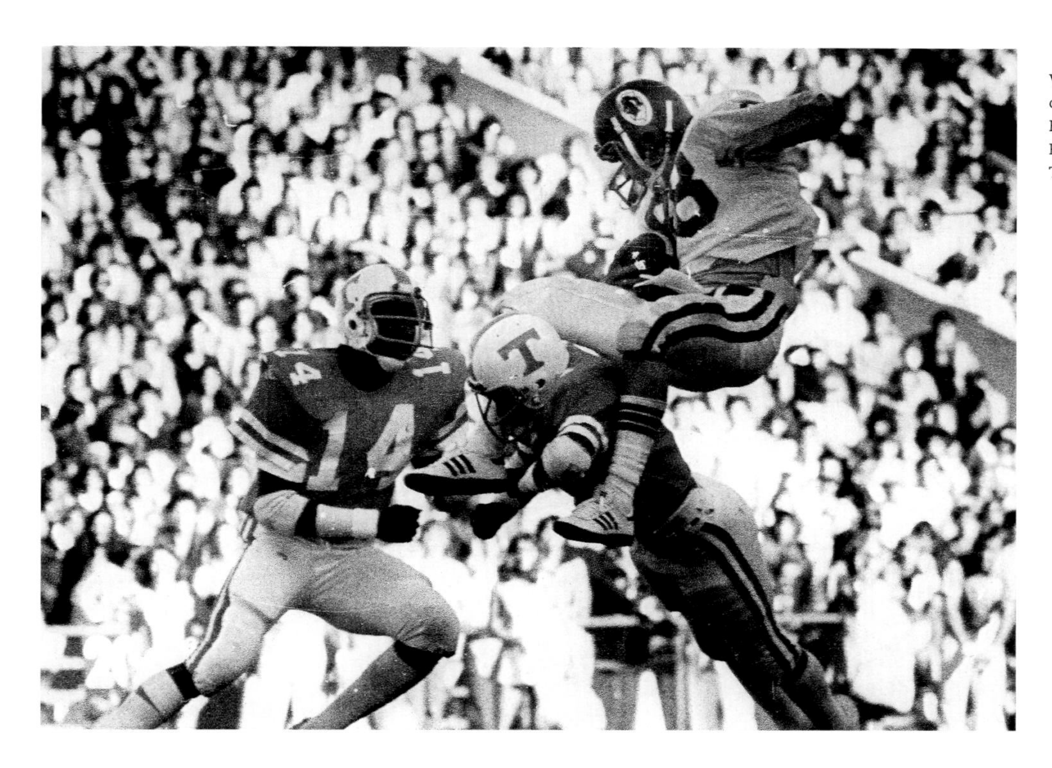

Wide receiver Tim Odell ranks as one of Rutgers' all-time great receivers. Here Odell makes a key catch in Rutgers' 13 to 7 upset victory over Tennessee in 1979. (Courtesy Tim Odell)

Rutgers AD Fred Gruninger said, "The victory over Tennessee will open doors that were difficult to open in the past. It will convince people of the quality of our program."

After the Tennessee game, Rutgers sandwiched a loss to Villanova between wins over Army and Louisville. The Scarlet Knights won 8 games and lost 3. It was another great year for Scarlet football in New Jersey.

In 1979 QB Ed McMichael completed 124 passes in 211 attempts for 1,529 yards and 7 touchdowns.

Dino Mangiero had 113 tackles and 14 quarterback sacks during the 1979 season. Mangiero's career totals of 288 tackles and 26 QB sacks were staggering stats. Dino Mangiero was named First Team All-East by the Associated Press and Third Team All-American. He later played pro football for the Kansas City Chiefs. Defensive back Mark Freeman had an NFL tryout with the New York Jets. Defensive back and punter Deron Cherry was voted the team's Most Valuable Player. He was also named AP All-East.

Kicker Kennan Startzell was a First Team AP All-East selection. He finished his Rutgers career with a total of 261 points on 46 field goals and 123 PATs. Offensive tackle Kevin Kurdyla and wide receiver Dave Dorn were AP All-East selections. Center Frank Naylor, QB Ed McMichael, receiver Tim Odell, and DB Ken Smith received All-East mention.

In 1980 an Alabama bear made a long trek to Giants Stadium in New Jersey to play football. Paul "Bear" Bryant and his Crimson Tide footballers were eager to wrestle with the Rutgers Scarlet Knights on the gridiron. A wrestling match was how Bear Bryant got his famous nickname. As a teenager, Paul Bryant wrestled a bear in a traveling show for a cash prize of a dollar a minute. According to Bryant he never got paid for his daring stunt. He did, however, get tagged with a famous nickname that stayed with him throughout his life.

The year 1980 was the first time in the long history of Rutgers that the team had four captains. Selected to lead the team were Ted Blackwell, Ed McMichael, Ken Smith, and Deron Cherry.

Back on offense in 1980 were receivers Tim Odell and Dave Dorn. Joining them as capable backups were David Palumbo and Brian Crockett. The tight end was Steve Pfirman. The offensive line boasted the blocking skills of Tony Cella, Kevin Kurdyla, Frank Naylor, Jeff George, and Rich Spitzer. Alex Falcinelli stepped into the kicking shoes left vacant by the departed Kennan Startzell.

The defense was talented. In addition to Smith and Cherry, Dan Errico and Mark Paneiro rounded out the secondary. The linebackers were Jeff Blanchard, Mike Knight, Andy Carino, and Keith Woetzel. The line consisted of Alan Schmid, Bill Pickel, Mike Rustemeyer, and Ed Steward. It was a veteran unit that played smash-mouth football.

Above: In 1980, the Scarlet Knights' David Palumbo (#19) makes a key catch in a 44 to 13 victory over Princeton. It was the final game between Rutgers and the Tigers. (Courtesy Dave Palumbo)

Below: Defensive back and punter Deron Cherry was co-captain of the 1980 team. (Courtesy Rutgers Athletic Communications)

Opposite: The program cover for the 1980 contest between Rutgers and Alabama featured Frank Burns and Paul "Bear" Bryant. (From the personal collection of M. J. Pellowski/Courtesy Rutgers Athletic Communications)

Temple University was Rutgers' first opponent of the 1980 season. Rutgers' defense held the Temple Owls offense to no touchdowns and Rutgers posted an easy victory. The Scarlet Knights next entertained the University of Cincinnati on the gridiron for the first time ever. The key play in the contest for the Rutgers Knights was a fake punt flawlessly pulled off by Deron Cherry and Ken Smith. Cherry, Rutgers punter and all-around athlete, took the snap and fired a strike to defensive back Ken Smith. Smith pulled in the pigskin and raced 31 yards for a touchdown. Rutgers won 24 to 7.

The game that followed put an end to college football's oldest rivalry. Rutgers and Princeton had moved in different gridiron directions after the first one hundred years of play. Princeton could not keep pace with Rutgers in term of the strides toward big-time sports Rutgers was taking. Princeton and Rutgers parted ways as football opponents. The 1980 game was the final one between the Tigers and the Scarlet Knights.

In the contest, it was the Knights, not the Tigers, who came out roaring. Scarlet quarterback Ed McMichael fired 4 touchdown passes that day. Receiver Dave Palumbo had some key receptions. Rutgers rolled to a 44–13 win.

Another Ivy League opponent was the next scheduled foe. Rutgers crushed Cornell for its fourth win in a row.

Paul "Bear" Bryant led the Alabama Crimson Tide into the Meadowlands of New Jersey to bump heads with Frank Burns's Scarlet Knights. Instead of bumping heads, the contest turned into a head-on collision. Alabama was the number-1-ranked team in the country at the time and heavily favored to win. The Rutgers players never bothered to read the odds against them. They just played their hearts out. Alabama squeaked by Rutgers 17 to 13 in a stunning test of gridiron wills. Alabama finished the season 10–2 and ranked sixth in the nation.

After the Giants Stadium gridiron clash, Bear Bryant said, "We didn't beat Rutgers. All I can say is we won."

The heartbreaking loss to Alabama drained some momentum out of the Scarlet squad, and consecutive losses to William and Mary and Syracuse followed.

In the game against Army at West Point, Rutgers' Ken Smith had a 97-yard kickoff return for a touchdown. Rutgers' record then stood at 5 wins and 3 losses. Wins over Virginia and Colgate were sandwiched around a loss to West Virginia.

RUTGERS
vs.
ALABAMA

GIANTS STADIUM
OCT. 11, 1980
$2.00

FOOTBALL
MAGAZINE

Top: The Scarlet Knights in action against West Virginia in 1980. On the field are Knights Bryant Moore (#39), and Dave Palumbo (#19). Rutgers players looking on are Dan Errico (#20), Mark Seger (#13), Jim Zurich (#56), Alan Andrews (#31), Bill Pickel (#62), Ralph Amiano (#72), and Joe Rafferty (#54). (Courtesy Dave Palumbo)

Bottom: Tight end Steve Pfirman (#89) of Rutgers prepares to block as wide receiver Dave Palumbo makes a catch against Army in 1980. (Courtesy Dave Palumbo)

Rutgers completed its 1980 schedule with a record of 7 wins and 4 losses. It was Frank Burns's eighth winning season in a row. Rutgers fans who hungered for big-time college football in New Jersey saw the streak as the light at the end of the tunnel.

At the end of the 1980 season, Rutgers bid farewell to an outstanding group of athletes. Quarterback Ed McMichael completed 146 passes in 229 attempts for 1,761 yards and 10 touchdowns in 1980. Over his career McMichael completed 292 passes on 474 attempts for 3,584 yards and 20 touchdowns. Ed McMichael was AP All-East and an Honorable Mention AP All-American. He went on to play pro ball for the New Jersey Generals of the United States Football League. Running back Ted Blackwell had a career total of 1,829 rushing yards, 476 receiving yards, 215 yards on punt returns, and 39 yards on kickoff returns for a grand total of 2,559 all-purpose yards. Ted Blackwell had NFL trials with the New York Jets.

Wide receiver Tim Odell caught 49 passes for 718 yards and 4 touchdowns in 1980. Over his career, Odell grabbed 112 passes for 1,702 yards and 9 touchdowns. He was AP All-East

In 1980 the Scarlet Knights posted a 37 to 21 win over Army at West Point. (Courtesy Dave Palumbo)

and Honorable Mention AP All-America. Tim Odell moved on to the NFL to try out with the Cincinnati Bengals.

David Dorn finished his Rutgers career with 851 rushing yards, 1,340 receiving yards, 353 punt return yards, and 764 kickoff return yards. He caught a total of 73 passes, including 11 touchdown passes, during his career. Dorn move on to play for the Oakland Raiders in the NFL after graduation.

Offensive tackle Kevin Kurdyla was named AP All-East for his spectacular line play. He was also Honorable Mention AP All-America and turned pro with the New York Giants.

Defensive back Ken Smith was named the team's Most Valuable Player. He finished his career with 384 yards in punt returns. He was AP All-East and Honorable Mention AP All-America. Smith tried out with the Detroit Lions in the NFL. Defensive back Bill Hill signed a pro contract with the Cleveland Browns.

Ed Steward finished his Rutgers career with 222 career tackles and 17 quarterback sacks. He tried out with the Denver Broncos in the NFL. Defensive back Dwayne Wilson played for the Philadelphia Stars in the USFL. Linebacker Jeff Blanchard turned pro and played for the Hamilton Tiger Cats in the CFL.

Deron Cherry won AP All-East and AP Honorable Mention All-America honors in 1980. He finished his punting career at Rutgers with 188 punts for 7,413 yards. He had a career average of 39.4 yards per punt. He was also an outstanding safety. Deron Cherry went on to star for many years as a player for the Kansas City Chiefs in the National Football League. He is a member of the Kansas City Chiefs Hall of Fame.

Rutgers had a large group of capable seniors on its squad in 1981. The veteran team was skippered by co-captains Andy Carino and Frank Naylor. Carino was a linebacker on defense and Naylor was an offensive center. Joining Naylor on the O line were Jeff George, Jim Zurich, Tony Cella, and Rich Spitzer. In the backfield were quarterbacks Ralph Leek and Jacque LaPrarie and star running back Albert Ray. The receiving corps featured seniors Steve Pfirman, Brian Crockett, and David Palumbo. Andrew "Shake & Bake" Baker was a newcomer. Baker got his nickname because of the shifty moves he executed during the running of pass patterns.

Left: Deron Cherry went on to have a long NFL career with the Kansas City Chiefs after he graduated from Rutgers. He made six appearances in the NFL Pro Bowl. (Courtesy Kansas City Chiefs)

Right: Eric "Rusty" Hochberg took over at quarterback for Rutgers in the 1980s. (Courtesy Rutgers Athletic Communications)

The seniors on the veteran defensive unit included Mike Rustemeyer, Mike Knight, and star tackle Bill Pickel.

The linebackers included experienced players like Keith Woetzel, Jim Dumont, and Jim's brother, Bob Dumont.

The season began with solid wins over Syracuse, Colgate, and Virginia. A bump in the road was a shutout loss at Cincinnati. The Scarlet recovered with well-earned victories over Cornell and Army. And then the wheels came off the Scarlet offense. Rutgers managed a slim total of only 25 points over the next four games. First Temple got the best of Rutgers at home. Next the Knights went south for a rematch with Coach Bear Bryant's Alabama squad. Rutgers contributed to Bryant's impressive total of career wins. Bryant would retire from college coaching after the 1982 season with a total of 323 wins, 85 losses, and 17 ties.

Unfortunately for the Scarlet, up next was Pittsburgh, coached by Jackie Sherrill. The Panthers, under the guidance of their star quarterback, Dan Marino, went 11–1 and ended up ranked fourth in the nation. Rutgers was one of Marino's many victims that season.

Things did not get any easier the following week. The Knights' next opponent was the West Virginia Mountaineers. Rutgers was tagged with a tough loss.

Last but not least on the schedule was Boston College. On the Eagles squad was a young quarterback named Doug Flutie. The Eagles clawed the Knights and a winning season flew out the window. Rutgers finished with a record of 5 wins and 6 losses. Scarlet head coach Frank Burns had his first losing year.

Albert Ray was Rutgers' leading rusher with 679 yards. Ray rushed for a total of 2,024 yards over his football playing career on the banks.

Offensive center Frank Naylor won the Homer Hazel award as the team's Most Valuable Player. Naylor was also an AP All-East choice. He tried out with the Seattle Seahawks.

Brian Crocket eventually became Rutgers' VP for external affairs.

Linebacker and co-captain Andy Carino turned pro and played for the New Jersey Generals of the USFL.

Linebacker Jim Dumont made 95 tackles and had 2 quarterback sacks in 1981. He was an All-East selection along with defensive linemen Bill Pickel and Mike Rustemeyer. Rustemeyer ended up with a total of 16 quarterback sacks in his four seasons as a Scarlet Knight pass rusher.

Rutgers' 1982 football schedule was brutal. It included Penn State, which went 11–1 that year to capture college football's National Championship. Also on the Scarlet schedule were Pittsburgh and West Virginia. Pittsburgh posted a record of 9–3 in 1982 and finished ranked number 10 in the country. West Virginia went 9–3 that same season and ended up ranked 19th in the nation.

Scarlet tri-captains Tony Cella, Rich Spitzer, and Bill Pickel did not shy away from the challenge. Neither did the members of a new, young offensive group headed by quarterbacks Eric "Rusty" Hochberg and Jacque LaPrarie. New running back Albert Smith showed plenty of promise. Sophomore tight end Alan Andrews was a big target on pass plays. The offense appeared more than capable.

On defense, tri-captain Bill Pickel was top dog among a vicious pack of punishing hitters that included Bill Beschner, Bob Dumont, and Tony Sagnella and defensive backs Bill Houston, Dan Errico, Carl Howard, and Harold Young.

The season got off to a tough start. The Knights were outgunned against Syracuse and Penn State. Rutgers rocked Temple, William and Mary, and Army to better its record to 3 wins and 2 losses. In the William and Mary win, Scarlet kicker Alex Falcinelli booted a 51-yard field goal.

A gut-wrenching 13 to 14 loss to Boston College and Doug Flutie proved to be the pivotal game of the season. In the Knights' game against the BC Eagles, Rutgers' Alex Falcinelli kicked a 50-yard field goal. The next week, Rutgers beat Colgate with some help from ball hawk Bill Houston. Houston picked off a Colgate pass and returned the interception 94 yards for a touchdown.

The Scarlet Knights also bested Richmond before being toppled by Auburn, West Virginia, and Pittsburgh. In the game against Pittsburgh, Rutgers kicker Alex Falcinelli made another successful 51-yard field goal.

The Knights' slim, 1-point loss to the Eagles of Boston College cost them a .500 season. Rutgers finished the year with 5 wins in 11 gridiron outings. Coach Frank Burns endured his second losing season in a row.

Individually, many players shone for the Scarlet Knights in 1982. Kicker Alex Falcinelli led the team in scoring with 52 points. Over his career, Falcinelli made 38 of 49 field goals for a .776 percentage. In 1982 Alex Falcinelli was named second team All-East by the AP and an Honorable Mention All-American. He tried out with the St. Louis Cardinals in the NFL.

Quarterback Jacque LaPrarie led Rutgers in passing with 1,164 yards.

Flanker Andrew Baker caught 30 passes for 472 yards and 2 touchdowns. Baker was named All-East by the Associated Press. Scarlet running back Bryant Moore was an AP All-East mention. Running back Joe Burke signed a pro contract with the Dallas Cowboys. Offensive tackle Rich Spitzer signed with the Seattle Seahawks of the NFL. Rutgers' other offensive tackle, Tony Cella, also signed to play pro football with the Seahawks.

Linebacker Jim Dumont had 133 tackles and 2 sacks in 1982. Dumont was awarded a berth on the AP All-East Team. He was also Honorable Mention on the Associated Press

Bill Pickel won a Super Bowl Championship with the Oakland Raiders. (Courtesy Rutgers Athletic Communications)

All-America squad. Defensive tackle Bill Beschner and defensive back Bill Houston were mentions on the AP All-East squad. Houston had a total of 6 interceptions in 1982.

Linebacker Keith Woetzel had 127 tackles and 1 QB sack in 1982. Woetzel was on the Associated Press All-East Team. Keith Woetzel totaled 363 tackles and had 1 quarterback sack in his four years as a Scarlet Knights defender. He signed a pro contract to play for the Miami Dolphins.

Defensive captain Bill Pickel concluded his football career at Rutgers with a total of 16 quarterback sacks. After graduation he had a brilliant NFL career with the Oakland Raiders. Bill Pickel was on the Raiders Super Bowl Championship team of 1984.

In 1983 Rutgers announced plans to raise six million dollars to improve its football facilities. "Rutgers football is well and it's going to get better," predicted university president Dr. Edward J. Bloustein.

Rutgers co-captains Jim Dumont and John Owens were committed to playing hard-nosed football. Their Rutgers teammates also dedicated themselves to the same goal. The offense was led by promising young quarterback Eric "Rusty" Hochberg. Running back Albert Smith was a rising star. Receivers Andrew Baker, Boris Pendergrass, and Alan Andrews could catch and ran good routes. Jim Keating, Clem Udovich, Joe DiGilio, John Owens, and Joe Pennucci were solid linemen.

The defense had twins Jim and Bob Dumont playing defensive end and linebacker. Other members of that defensive fraternity included newcomers Tyronne Stowe and Harry Swayne. Stowe and Swayne would develop into two of Rutgers' greatest defensive stars.

Rutgers opened with a thrashing of Connecticut. Losses to Boston College and Syracuse followed the opening day victory.

In the contest against Penn State in Giants Stadium, Rutgers quarterback Rusty Hochberg got off to a hot start. Hochberg completed 19 of 34 passes for 367 yards and 2 touchdowns. He connected with Andrew Baker for a 76-yard scoring strike. Suddenly, disaster struck for the Scarlet. Quarterback Rusty Hochberg suffered a knee injury in the game and was lost for the season. Before he wrecked his knee against the Nittany Lions, Hochberg had completed 19 of 34 passes for 367 yards. Rutgers' Jacque LaPrarie was pressed into service as the Rutgers signal caller.

Head Coach Frank Burns described the different athletic abilities of his two quarterbacks. "Eric [Hochberg] is more of a drop-back, classic passer," said Burns. "LaPrarie is more of a scrambler, an action pass type who is a better runner."

After the Penn State loss, the ball was in the hands of action-pass-type QB Jacque LaPrarie. The sudden switch at quarterback resulted in a tough loss to Army. Next on the schedule was Colgate. The Scarlet Knights rallied around LaPrarie. Running back Albert Smith had his first 100-plus-yard rushing game and scored a touchdown. Tight end Alan Andrews caught 4 passes. Andrew Baker snared 3 passes for 67 yards and 1 touchdown.

Despite individual Scarlet heroics, Rutgers found itself losing to Colgate after Len Bellezza tallied a Scarlet touchdown to make the score Rutgers 21 and Colgate 26.

With less than a minute and a half to go, Rutgers had the ball and was driving. Scarlet QB LaPrarie hit Andrew Baker with a pinpoint pass. Baker raced to the Red Raiders' 5-yard line, where he was tackled with time ticking down. Jacque LaPrarie took a loss on the next play. The Scarlet quarterback Frank Burns dubbed a "scrambler" then scooted into the end zone to make the score Rutgers 27 and Colgate 26. Jacque LaPrarie hit Andrew Baker with a 2-point play pass to increase the Scarlet lead to 29 to 26. A late Bill Houston interception iced the win for Rutgers.

The Scarlet Knights chalked up another strong outing the following week against William and Mary. Albert Smith gained 86 yards and scored 3 touchdowns. QB Jacque LaPrarie hit tight ends Scott Drake and Alan Andrews with touchdown passes. Rutgers won the contest.

Unfortunately, that was the last taste of victory for the Scarlet Knights in 1983. Losses to Tennessee, Cincinnati, West Virginia, and Temple followed. Rutgers won only 3 of its 11 games.

Tight end Alan Andrews caught 48 passes in 1983 and made AP All-East. Offensive lineman and co-captain John Owens was AP All-East and Honorable Mention All-America. Center Joe DiGilio was AP All-East.

Linebacker and co-captain Jim Dumont was voted the Most Valuable Player on the Rutgers squad for the second straight year. In 1983 Dumont made 154 tackles. His career total of 448 tackles and 5 QB sacks rates him as one of the Scarlet's all-time top tacklers. He was First Team AP All-East in 1983 and Third Team All-America. He went on to play for the Cleveland Browns in the NFL.

Bob Dumont recovered a total of 5 fumbles over his career. He was an AP All-East mention. Bob Dumont turned pro as a member of the Los Angeles Rams.

Defensive tackle Bill Beshner and defensive back Bill Houston received mentions on the AP All-East team. Houston had six interceptions in 1983.

The 1983 season turned out to be Frank Burns's last year as a Scarlet coach. Frank Burns, the ultimate Rutgers football icon, finished his Rutgers coaching career with 78 wins, 43 losses, and 1 tie.

CHAPTER 10

ROLLER-COASTER FOOTBALL 1984–1989

In 1984, New Jersey governor Tom Kean announced a three-million-dollar plan to upgrade the football facilities at Rutgers University. Half of the money would come from the state budget and half would come from the New Jersey Sports and Exposition Authority, which operated the Meadlowlands Sports Complex. "It is an investment in the future that will bring back more dollars than the state is giving," announced Governor Kean at a press conference.

The planned improvements thrilled those Rutgers fans who yearned to play big-time football. Rutgers' new head football coach, Dick Anderson, was pleased, but kept his enthusiasm under restraint. Anderson, a former assistant under Joe Paterno at Penn State, knew the leap into big-time football competition would take time. "It won't happen overnight," Anderson told reporters. "We've got to have a couple of good recruiting years." Anderson's task was to keep New Jersey athletes home.

"We seek the best student-athletes who will stay in our program and graduate," Rutgers AD Fred Gruninger told the press. "The competition for them is fierce."

Head Coach Dick Anderson's new Scarlet coaching staff included Wayne Moses, Pat Flaherty, Ed O'Neil, Jerry Petercuskie, Bob Slowik, Paul Kennedy, Otto Kneidinger, Tony Toto, Mel Caseiro, and Kevin Carty. Tony Toto and Mel Caseiro both had New Jersey

Rutgers began to upgrade its football facilities in the 1980s. (Courtesy Melanie J. Pellowski)

Improvements at Rutgers Stadium continued over the next few years. (Courtesy Melanie J. Pellowski)

connections. Toto was from East Brunswick, New Jersey. Caseiro had been born and raised in South River.

The 1984 Rutgers team had many outstanding athletes. Tight end Alan Andrews was the offensive captain. Linebacker Lionel Washington was the defensive captain.

Quarterback Eric “Rusty” Hochberg was the field general. In the backfield were runners Albert Smith, Dwayne Hooper, and Vernon Williams. Backing up Hochberg was Joe Gagliardi, a transfer from Tulane. Former quarterback Jacque LaPrarie had moved to the defensive secondary.

Lionel Washington’s defensive corps included cornerback John Cummins, linebacker Tyronne Stowe, nose guard George Pickel, and tackles Tony Sagnella and Harry Swayne.

Kicking was a Rutgers strong point. Tom Angstadt could boot field goals with the best in the nation and Gary Liska was one of the best punters in Scarlet history.

New head coach Dick Anderson had the talent to cope with a brutally tough schedule. The first test came early in the year. Anderson’s Scarlet Knights took the field against his former school, Penn State, in the opening game of the 1984 season. Dick Anderson had to match gridiron wits against his old football mentor, Joe Paterno.

A crowd of eighty-four thousand came out to watch the Nittany Lions host the Rutgers Scarlet Knights. Penn State was led by its star back, D. J. Dozier. Rutgers was in the game all the way, but could muster only 12 points. Penn State put 15 points on the scoreboard to edge the Knights in Dick Anderson’s debut as a head coach.

Dick Anderson, a former Lafayette and Penn State assistant, became the head coach at Rutgers in 1984. (Courtesy Lafayette College Archives)

The following week Rutgers edged Temple 10 to 9. In week three the Scarlet Knights traveled to Syracuse. After defensive tackle Barry Buchowski recovered a Syracuse fumble, Tom Angstadt kicked his first of 4 field goals on the day. Rutgers’ Albert Smith rushed for 121 yards on 23 carries and tallied a TD.

Jacque LaPrarie, who started his first game on defense in place of the injured Roger Pollard, had 12 tackles and an interception. Rutgers won 19 to zip and was 2 and 1 going into its contest against Cincinnati.

Rutgers’ Tom Angstadt booted 5 field goals against Cincinnati and Rutgers won easily.

Highly ranked Kentucky handed Rutgers a defeat the following week. Wins over Army and Louisville followed. In the Louisville game, Scarlet quarterback Rusty Hochberg completed 26 of 37 passes for 358 yards.

The Boston College Eagles were the red team's next foe. Rutgers' Dan McHarris had a dazzling 44-yard punt return for a touchdown, but the game proved to be a battle of arm strength between the Knights' Rusty Hochberg and the Eagles' Doug Flutie. Hochberg completed 23 of 51 passes for 249 yards and 1 touchdown. It was an amazing effort against a Top 5 team, but it wasn't enough.

Doug Flutie threw for 318 yards and 3 touchdowns to lead Boston College to a 35 to 23 win over Rutgers.

After the Rutgers–Boston College dogfight, the Knights took on the Mountaineers of West Virginia at Giants Stadium. West Virginia was ranked in the Top 20, and scouts from the Gator Bowl, the Peach Bowl, and the Citrus Bowl watched as Rutgers leveled the Mountaineers.

The Scarlet Knights' Albert Smith ran for 2 touchdowns. Rusty Hochberg hit Andrew Baker with a 36-yard scoring strike. Tom Angstadt kicked a booming 50-yard field goal. Rutgers won 23 to 19.

In the final game of the year, Rutgers dumped Colgate to finish with a season record of 7 wins and 3 losses. Two of those losses were to ranked teams. One win was over a ranked team. Nevertheless, Rutgers did not go bowling in 1984. However, the team did seem ready to take the leap to big-time football.

In 1984 Andrew Baker led all receivers with 583 yards. Baker was the first Rutgers receiver to lead the squad in receiving yards for four straight years. Andrew Baker pulled in 42 passes for 3 touchdowns in 1984. Over his Rutgers career, Baker made 127 catches for a total of 2,268 yards and 11 touchdowns. The MVP of the team, he was named an Honorable Mention All-American and AP All-East. Baker also had an NFL tryout with Pittsburgh.

Tight end Alan Andrews had 106 career receptions for 9 touchdowns. He was First Team AP All-East and a Second Team AP All-American. Andrews played in the East-West Shrine All-Star game. Alan Andrews later played for the Pittsburgh Steelers in the NFL.

Rutgers split end Boris Pendergrass signed a pro football contract with the Washington Redskins.

Defensive back Harold Young received Honorable Mention All-America honors from the *Sporting News*. He was also AP All-East. Young was signed to a professional contract by the Oakland Raiders. Linebacker Tyronne Stowe, center Joe DiGilio, running back Albert Smith, and defensive tackle George Pickel were on the Associated Press All-East Second Team.

Rutgers' schedule increased in difficulty in 1985. In addition to brutal games against Boston College, Pittsburgh, and Syracuse, Rutgers had to play Florida, Tennessee, and Penn State.

Offensive guard Clem Udovich and defensive tackle George Pickel were co-captains of a Scarlet squad that was not intimidated by the challenge of schedule. The Knights who gave Rutgers fans a valiant effort week after week included Lee Getz, Kevin Spitzer, Tom Keating,

Clem Udovich (left) and George Pickel were co-captains of the 1985 Scarlet Knights. (Courtesy Clem Udovich)

Albert Smith, Curt Stephens, Scott Drake, and wideout Eric Young, a New Brunswick, New Jersey, native who excelled in baseball as well as football.

The Rutgers defense was granite solid. Tyronne Stowe, Harry Swayne, Doug Kokoskie, Steve Twamley, Tony Sagnella, and George Pickel rocked opposing ball carriers whenever they met.

Coach Dick Anderson marched his Scarlet squad south to take on the University of Florida in the opening game of the 1985 season.

The Florida Gators had their way with the Rutgers Scarlet Knights until the middle of the third period. Florida had a comfortable 28 to 7 lead when the game got dicey. More than seventy thousand football fans in Florida watched in awe as Rutgers linebacker Todd McIver intercepted a Gator pass and returned it 48 yards for a touchdown. McIver's outstanding play made the score 28 to 14 in favor of Florida.

Eric Young of New Brunswick, New Jersey, was a star wide receiver in football at Rutgers and a star second baseman for the Dodgers. (Courtesy L.A. Dodgers)

Scarlet linebacker Tyronne Stowe then pounced on a Gator fumble. Dick Anderson decided to shake up the Rutgers offense by inserting Joe Gagliardi at quarterback in place of Eric Hochberg. Gagliardi guided the Knights to the Gators' 1-yard line, where Albert Smith plunged into the end zone for the score. The Gators' lead was cut to 28 to 20 after a missed 2-point try.

Rutgers got the ball back after a fine defensive stand. Joe Gagliardi again moved Rutgers the length of the field. Gagliardi capped off the drive by hitting tight end Bruce Campbell with a 16-yard touchdown pass. Fullback Curtis Stephens then made the big play of the day. He hauled in a Gagliardi pass on the 2-point play to tie the score at 28-all.

Rutgers next executed a perfect onside kick, but time ran out. The Knights tied the Gators and ended Florida's ten-game winning streak.

Rutgers didn't lose, nor did they win. The team came close to pulling off one of the most stunning upsets in Scarlet history. It was almost a great victory. In fact, the 1985 season was the year of "almost" for Rutgers. The following week, Rutgers lost to unranked Army by 4 points.

"That's been the story with Rutgers," Dick Anderson explained to the press. "Up and down like a roller coaster." After that, Penn State, the number 3 team in the country, beat the Knights by a touchdown. Rutgers then lost to Temple by a single point. The Knights topped Richmond and Colgate to finish the year with a record of 2 wins, 8 losses, and 1 tie. It was a tough season that could have been much better with a little gridiron luck. It became apparent that Coach Dick Anderson was no miracle worker.

Joe Gagliardi led the Scarlet in passing in 1985 with 1,273 yards. Eric Hochberg completed 79 of 169 passes for 752 yards and 4 touchdowns. Hochberg had a career total of 337 completions in 634 attempts for 3,825 yards and 18 touchdowns.

In 1985 Albert Smith had 112 carries for 362 yards and 5 touchdowns. He led the Scarlet Knights in rushing (362 yards), scoring (42 points), and receiving yards (244). He was the first Scarlet Knight to win the offensive triple crown. Over his career, Albert Smith had

542 carries for 2,269 yards and 23 touchdowns. He was Honorable Mention AP All-East and turned pro with the New York Giants.

Offensive guard Lee Getz was selected All-East by the Associated Press. Running back Vernon Williams signed a pro contract with the Chicago Bears.

Linebacker Tyronne Stowe made 157 tackles and had 3 QB sacks in 1985. He was voted the Most Valuable Player. Stowe also earned Honorable Mention AP All-America honors and AP All-East honors. Defensive teammates Jean Austin, George Pickel, and Steve Twamley were also All-East mentions. Defensive tackler Tony Sagnella was signed to a pro contract by the Washington Redskins.

Rutgers started back up the gridiron roller coaster in 1986 with an opening victory over Boston College. Co-captains Tyronne Stowe and Lee Getz were backed by a strong group of veterans and newcomers. Joe Gagliardi was the starting quarterback, but was being pressured by new signal caller Scott Erney.

Two-sport star Eric Young was a swift receiver with great hands. Bruce Campbell, Tyronne McQueen, and Brian Cobb were also good pass-catching targets. Running back Curt Stephens was joined by Mark Prescott.

Going into the second game of the season against Kentucky, Coach Dick Anderson knew defense was his squad's strong point. Veterans Tyronne Stowe, Harry Swayne, Jean Austin, Alec Hoke, and Paul Halada were joined by newcomers Pat Udovich and Darrin Czellecz.

Rutgers played stubborn defense in game two and ended up deadlocked with Kentucky 16–16 at game's end. Wins over Cincinnati and Syracuse came back to back.

The Scarlet Knights played their hearts out against a Penn State team that ended up as the number 1 squad in the country, but suffered a 13 to 6 loss. A 15 to 3 loss to Florida followed. The Knights racked up solid wins over Army and Louisville before dropping another gridiron contest to West Virginia. Tyronne Stowe had a remarkable 27 tackles against West Virginia. Rutgers ended its season with defeats at the hands of Pittsburgh and Temple. The Temple Owls were paced by their great running back Paul Palmer. Palmer led the nation in rushing with 1,866 yards and finished second in the Heisman Trophy race to QB Vinnie Testaverde of Miami.

Rutgers finished the year with a 5–5–1 record. Scarlet QB Joe Gagliardi had 218 completions in 359 attempts for 2,197 yards and 13 touchdowns over his career. Scott Erney began his Rutgers quarterbacking career with 96 completions in 190 attempts for 1,180 yards and 6 TDs.

Rutgers center Mike Dillon was picked All-East by the Associated Press. Scarlet guard Lee Getz earned ECAC All-East honors. Getz played in the East-West Shrine Game and signed a pro contract with the Pittsburgh Steelers.

Linebacker Matt Bachman was an Honorable Mention All-East selection by the Associated Press. The New York Jets signed Bachman to a pro contract. Defensive tackle Harry Swayne was ECAC and AP All-East. He signed a pro contract with the Tampa Bay Buccaneers. Swayne played for fifteen years in the National Football League with the Denver Broncos, the Baltimore Ravens, the Miami Dolphins, and the San Diego Chargers. Harry Swayne won two Super Bowl rings with the Broncos and one with the Ravens.

Linebacker Tyronne Stowe had 150 tackles in 1986. Stowe totaled 533 tackles and 5 quarterback sacks over his career. He is Rutgers' all-time leading tackler. Tyronne Stowe was the MVP of the Rutgers team in 1986 for the second straight year. Stowe was an Honorable Mention AP All-American and First Team AP and ECAC All-East selection. He played

Rutgers' Harry Swayne had a long NFL career after his graduation from Rutgers. Swayne played with the Tampa Bay Buccaneers, the San Diego Chargers, the Denver Broncos, and the Baltimore Ravens. (Courtesy the Allens, No. Miami Beach, Florida)

in the Hula Bowl All-Star Game and the Blue-Gray Football Classic. Tyronne Stowe signed with the Pittsburgh Steelers and played ten seasons in the National Football League.

Scarlet co-captains Jean Austin and Curtis Stephens prepared for an opening day contest against the Bearcats of Cincinnati in 1987. Fullback Stephens was now taking handoffs from quarterback Scott Erney.

Targets for Scott Erney's passes were receivers Eric Young, Brian Cobb, and newcomer James Jenkins. The offensive line was built around Steve Tardy and Jeff Erickson.

The defense had a ferocious group of linebackers including Pat Udovich, Chris Evans, Bob Spiedel, and Darrin Czellecz. The line was anchored by George Bankos, Alec Hoke, and Carter Giles. Jean Austin and Sean Washington were leaders in the secondary.

Rutgers topped Cincinnati in the season opener. In game two, Syracuse, under the guidance of quarterback Don McPherson, bested Rutgers.

Rutgers quarterback Scott Erney engineered a fantastic 19 to 18 win over Kentucky the following week in Giants Stadium. Rutgers returned to Meadowlands the very next week for a game against the Duke Blue Devils. The Scarlet Knights burned the Blue Devils for their third win of the early season. Penn State proved too tough the following week and slipped by Rutgers 35 to 21. Good wins over Boston College and Army made the Knights 5–2 with four games remaining against Vanderbilt, Pittsburgh, West Virginia, and Temple. Unfortunately, the wheels on the Rutgers gridiron machine wobbled and the Knights managed only one more win, which came in their final game against the Temple Owls. Coach Dick Anderson's club finished with 6 wins and 5 losses.

Above: In 1987 Coach Dick Anderson's Scarlet Knights counted wins over Kentucky, Duke, and Boston College among their six season victories. (Courtesy Lafayette College Archives)

Below: Linebacker Chris Evans had an outstanding game against Kentucky in 1987. Evans won Rutgers' Upstream Award for academic achievement that same season. (Courtesy Chris Evans)

Quarterback Scott Erney won the Homer Hazel Award as the team's Most Valuable Player. Fullback Curtis Stephens and running back Henry Henderson, who led the Scarlet Knights with 846 rushing yards, were AP All-East mentions.

Wide receiver Bruce Campbell finished his Rutgers career with a total of 75 receptions.

Receiver and kick return specialist Brian Cobb was an Honorable Mention AP All-America selection and an AP All-East choice. Cobb had 24 kickoff returns for 524 yards in 1987. He had a career total of 1,121 yards in kickoff returns. Brian Cobb signed to play football in the NFL with the Pittsburgh Steelers.

On the defensive side of the ball, Bob Speidel made 128 tackles in 1987. Defensive end Alec Hoke was named an Honorable Mention on the AP All-America squad. He was also AP All-East. Defensive backs Jean Austin and Sean Washington won All-East mentions. Sean Washington signed to play pro football with the Dallas Cowboys.

The Scarlet Knights set their sights on Michigan State as the 1988 season opened. Tri-captains Derek Baker, George Bankos, and Bill Dubiel, along with their Knight teammates, were confident the Spartans could be cut down on opening day. Rutgers superstar

Rutgers' Eric Young went on to play major league baseball for many years. (Courtesy L.A. Dodgers)

quarterback Scott Erney had Eric Young, Brett Mersola, and James Jenkins to throw to. Mike Botti and Jim Cann were capable runners.

On defense, Head Coach Dick Anderson had linebackers Pat Udovich and Darrin Czellecz, defensive linemen George Bankos and Doug Kokoskie, and back Dan McHarris.

Gridiron experts were shocked when Rutgers put the kibosh on Michigan State on opening day. The Scarlet Knights' 17 to 13 victory over the Spartans made football fans nationwide take notice of Rutgers. The victory was as important to the program as the victory over Tennessee years earlier. However, the very next week the Scarlet Knights once again skidded off the track. Vanderbilt edged Rutgers 31 to 30 at Giants Stadium. Scarlet QB Scott Erney completed 35 of 55 passes for 436 yards and 2 touchdowns. Wide receiver Eric Young caught 13 passes in the closely contested battle. Next up for the Knights was Penn State, one of the top-ranked teams in the country. Going into the final minutes of the contest, Rutgers was clinging to a hard-earned 21 to 16 lead over the heavily favored Nittany Lions. Penn State was camped on the Rutgers 3-yard line with four chances to punch the pigskin into the end zone for the go-ahead score. A stubborn Rutgers defense refused to wilt under the pressure. Penn State was denied once, twice, and three times. On the fourth and final attempt to smash into the end zone, the Nittany Lions' Gary Brown grabbed the handoff and headed up and over. Rutgers linebacker Pat Udovich turned out to be the Nittany Lion killer. Udovich met Brown in midair and drove him back with a crushing tackle. The Scarlet Knights defense held and Rutgers stunned the nation by thumping Penn State 21 to 16 for an impressive and important win.

Cincinnati was the Knights' next victim. Rutgers beat the Bearcats. The Orange of Syracuse then put the crush on the Scarlet. Rutgers bounced back with a win over Boston College.

Once again, the Rutgers roller coaster took a disastrous dip late in the season. Close losses to Army, Temple, Pittsburgh, and West Virginia followed. The Knights topped Colgate in the season finale to finish the year with 5 wins in 11 outings.

Although the season record doesn't reflect it, Rutgers had a good year in 1988. Sports experts seemed to understand that fact, as five Rutgers Scarlet Knights were rewarded with Honorable Mention on the AP All-America squad. Defensive tackle George Bankos, offensive lineman Steve Tardy, punter Matt O'Connell, wide receiver Eric Young, and quarterback Scott Erney were all so honored.

For the second straight year, Scott Erney was named the team's Most Valuable Player. In 1988 Erney completed 188 of 339 passes for 2,123 yards and 13 touchdowns. Receiver Brett Mersola was Honorable Mention All-East.

Flanker Eric Young had 48 catches for 592 yards and 3 touchdowns in 1988. Over his Scarlet career, Young caught 109 passes for 1,522 yards and 9 touchdowns. In addition, Eric Young had 79 rushing yards, 24 yards on punt returns, and 1,445 yards on kickoff returns. Young's total of 2,928 all-purpose yards ranks as one of Rutgers' best efforts. Eric Young signed to play pro baseball after graduation. He became a star second baseman for the Los Angeles Dodgers and played in the major leagues for many years with several different teams.

In 1988 running back Mike Botti led Rutgers in rushing with 715 yards. Kicker Carmen Sclafani led in scoring with 78 total points. Sclafani was Honorable Mention AP All-East. He kicked a total of 29 field goals over his career.

Coach Dick Anderson guided the Scarlet Knights to their first modern-era victory over Penn State in 1988. (Courtesy Lafayette College Archives)

Punter Matt O'Connell concluded his Rutgers career with 237 points for a total of 9,469 yards. O'Connell was AP All-East.

Defensive tackle George Bankos was ECAC All-East. Fellow defensive lineman Carter Giles was Honorable Mention AP All-East. Tackle Doug Kokoskie went on to become an associate director of athletics operations at Rutgers.

Rutgers captains Pat Udovich, Darrin Czellecz, Jeff Erickson, and Scott Erney prepared for a trip to Ireland at the end of the 1989 season. The Scarlet Knights were scheduled to play the Pittsburgh Panthers in Dublin in the Emerald Isle Classic. The final game of the year would be a tough test for the Knights. Pittsburgh was a Top 20 team. But before the flight to the Emerald Isle, Rutgers had ten other games to play.

Quarterback Scott Erney was entering his final season as a Scarlet Knight. New wide receiver Jim Guarantano would make his presence known before the year was out.

Once again, Coach Dick Anderson's defense was impressive. Helping with the defense was graduate assistant Greg Schiano, a former linebacker at Bucknell. Linebackers Pat Udovich, Darrin Czellecz, and new arrival Shawn Williams were all eager hitters. New return man Marshall Roberts was also ready to make his mark at Rutgers.

Rutgers opened the season with ties in games against both Cincinnati and Ball State. Ball State was a first-time Scarlet foe. Wins over Boston College and Northwestern piqued Scarlet fans' hopes for a successful season. In the Northwestern contest, Scarlet quarterback Scott Erney and receiver Randy Johnson teamed up for two of Rutgers' all-time great pass completions. Erney completed both an 83-yard and a 90-yard pass to Johnson.

After the Northwestern victory, the Rutgers gridiron roller coaster took a horrible plunge. The Knights finished the year without another win.

One of the few high points was a 63-yard punt return for a touchdown by Marshall Roberts against West Virginia.

Scarlet kicker Doug Giesler completed his Rutgers career by being named All-East by the ECAC and the AP. Giesler made a total of 27 field goals. Offensive lineman Jeff Erickson earned All-East mention. Erickson played in the Blue-Gray All-Star Classic. Tackle Steve Tardy was a National Football Foundation Scholar-Athlete. Tardy was also a Second Team All-American. Running back Jim Cann led his Scarlet team in rushing (429 yards), receiving (507 yards), and scoring (66 pts). Cann received All-East mention from the Associated

Washington Redskins

88 JAMES JENKINS
TIGHT END

Press. Special-teams star Gary Melton also received AP All-East honors. Tyronne McQueen finished his Rutgers career with a total of 95 catches.

Quarterback Scott Erney was the Knights' Most Valuable Player for the third year in a row. In 1989, Erney completed 208 passes in 374 attempts for 2,536 yards and 15 touchdowns. Over his four-year Scarlet career, Scott Erney completed 614 of 1,128 passes for 7,198 yards and 41 touchdowns. Erney went on to star as a quarterback for the Barcelona (Spain) Dragons in the World Football League.

Linebacker Pat Udovich led the Scarlet in tackles in 1989. Udovich had 140 tackles and 2 quarterback sacks. Udovich played in the Blue-Gray All-Star Classic. Over his Rutgers career, Pat Udovich had a total of 363 tackles and 5 sacks. Linebacker Darrin Czellecz had 89 tackles and 1 QB sack in the 1989 season. Over his Rutgers career, Czellecz totaled 289 tackles and 3 quarterback sacks. Czellecz later became a Secret Service agent. He was the second Rutgers footballer to serve the nation in that way. Center Jack Orrizzi, who played on the 1969 Scarlet squad, also worked as a Secret Service agent after his graduation.

Jim Guarantano began his fine Rutgers receiving career in 1989. (Courtesy Rutgers Athletic Communications)

Dick Anderson was dismissed at the end of the 1989 football season. The roller coaster ride came to a screeching halt. Anderson's career record totaled 27 wins, 34 losses, and 4 ties.

James Jenkins was a four-year letter-winner at Rutgers (1987, 1988, 1989, 1990). He was one in a long line of great tight ends who played football for the Scarlet Knights. (Courtesy Washington Redskins)

CHAPTER 11

A GROUP OF STAR PLAYERS

1990–1995

Rutgers football finally seemed to be on its way to big-time recognition. The Scarlet Knights now played nationally ranked opponents like Alabama, Tennessee, Michigan State, Auburn, Kentucky, Vanderbilt, Florida, and others. On the future schedule were gridiron clashes against top teams like Notre Dame, Miami, and Texas.

Rutgers had slowly but steadily improved its football facilities. The Knights had a practice bubble that was one of the nation's largest fully air-supported facilities. The bubble housed a spectacular 120-yard tract of artificial turf. For years, Rutgers was forced to schedule its biggest games at Giants Stadium in the Meadowlands because its home field was too small. In the near future, the stadium would be refurbished and its seating capacity increased to 41,500. Along with the stadium upgrade would come the completion of Rutgers football's offices and training facility, the Hale Center.

Rutgers had other upgrades in the works. Now the Knights needed the right coach to guide its football squad. When Doug Graber was announced as the new head coach, Rutgers fans, alumni, and players were confident Graber was that guy. Doug Graber had been the head coach at Montana State. He was also a veteran NFL coach who'd coached with the Kansas City Chiefs and had served as the defensive coordinator of the Tampa Bay Buccaneers. Graber was well respected and knew the game of football. He quickly assembled a talented staff, which included Arnold Jeter, Rich Rachel, Scott Lustig, Pat Flaherty, Phil Zacharias, Marty Barrett, Mark Deal, Ed O'Neil, Rock Gullickson, Mose Rison, and Dick Jamieson. Jamieson had played professional football with the Houston Oilers and the Baltimore Colts, and pro baseball in the Pittsburgh Pirates organization.

New Rutgers University president Dr. Francis L. Lawrence was confident Doug Graber would guide the Scarlet football program into the national limelight. It would not be an easy task. Rutgers' 1990 schedule included contests against Kentucky, Michigan State, and Penn State.

The 1990 edition of the Scarlet Knights was headed by co-captains James Jenkins and Marty Mayes. Running backs Craig Mitter, Bill Bailey, and Tekay Dorsey were solid performers who carried the pigskin with authority.

Rutgers tight end James Jenkins was the Scarlet Knights' offensive captain in 1990. (Courtesy Washington Redskins)

Rutgers had capable receivers in Jim Guarantano and Chris Brantley. Tight ends James Jenkins and Tim Pernetti were reliable pass targets. The quarterback was athletic Tom Tarver, who could run and throw. Protection for Tarver was provided by Ken Dammann, Doug Kavulich, and Travis Broadbent.

The defense included hard hitters Elnardo Webster, Andrew Beckett, Glen Nave, Jay Bellamy, and Malik Jackson.

Doug Graber notched his first Rutgers win on opening day against Kentucky at Giants Stadium. Win number two came against Colgate.

Rutgers then traveled to Penn State. Joe Paterno's Nittany Lions got the best of the Knights. The Michigan State Spartans, coached by George Perles, also topped Doug Graber's Scarlet Knights. Rutgers' only other victory of the year came against Akron at home. In a tight contest against Boston College, Rutgers' David Dunne had a 75-yard punt. In a losing effort against Syracuse, Doug Giesler had a 50-yard field goal. John Benestad had a 55-yard field goal against West Virginia.

Tekay Dorsey was Rutgers' rushing leader with 505 yards, and was named Second Team AP All-East. Offensive tackle Alan Mitchell was also Second Team AP All-East. Back Bill Bailey was an AP All-East mention. Tight end James Jenkins was named the Scarlet's Most Valuable Player. James Jenkins signed with the Washington Redskins and played in Super Bowl XXVI.

Rutgers kick-return specialist Ron Allen was voted First Team All-East by the AP and ECAC.

Defensive lineman Scott Miller was First Team ECAC All-East and Second Team AP All-East. He played in the Blue-Gray All-Star Classic. Scott Miller also played pro football for the London Monarchs of the World Football League and the New Jersey Red Dogs of the Arena Football League.

In 1991 Rutgers made a giant stride toward big-time football. The Scarlet Knights joined the Big East Conference. Numbered among the Big East's football-playing schools at the time were Miami, Boston College, Pittsburgh, Syracuse, West Virginia, Temple, and Virginia Tech. "From the standpoint of perception, recognition, and national exposure this is the best thing that could possibly happen to us," Doug Graber told writers. Also on Rutgers' schedule in 1991 were Duke, Northwestern, Michigan State, Penn State, and Army.

Co-captain Tim Christ and center Travis Broadbent provided leadership on offense for Rutgers in 1991. Defensive co-captain Elnardo Webster was surrounded by talented teammates who included Shawn Williams, Doug Adkins, Kory Kozak, and Jamil Jackson.

Marshall Roberts's 42-yard punt return against Boston College on opening day helped the Scarlet Knights top the Eagles for win number one. After a bitter loss to Duke, Rutgers rebounded against Northwestern. Gary Melton's 96-yard kickoff return in that game helped the Scarlet Knights chalk up their second victory in three outings. Another win the following week at Michigan State had Rutgers fans singing the praises of second-year head coach Doug Graber. When the Scarlet Knights traveled up the New Jersey Turnpike to Giants Stadium, visiting Army went down to defeat. Linebacker Shawn Williams had 16 tackles in that victory. After Rutgers bested the University of Maine the following week, the Knights had an impressive record of 5 wins and only 1 loss.

Once again, Penn State burst the Knights' bubble and handed Rutgers its second defeat of the year. The Scarlet's next opponent was Syracuse. Head coach Paul Pasqualoni's team also bested Rutgers. West Virginia and Pittsburgh did the same. The Scarlet concluded the

James Jenkins moved on to the NFL after his Rutgers football career ended. Jenkins was a member of the Washington Redskins squad that won Super Bowl XXVI. (Courtesy Washington Redskins)

season with a convincing shutout of Temple. Rutgers' record of 6 wins and 5 losses wasn't spectacular, but it did make for a winning year.

Scarlet quarterback Tom Tarver had an outstanding season in 1991. Tarver completed a total of 164 of 307 passes for 1,969 yards and 10 touchdowns. Tarver totaled 285 completions in 518 attempts for 3,607 yards and 20 TDs over his career. Center Travis Broadbent, who snapped the pigskin to Tarver, was named First Team AP and ECAC All-East.

Wide receiver Jim Guarantano was named Second Team All-East. In 1991, Gary Melton had 433 receiving yards and 435 yards on kickoff returns. He had a career total of 1,018 yards on kickoff returns. Melton signed to play pro football with the Washington Redskins.

Rutgers quarterback Bryan Fortay gets a hug from tight end Tim Pernetti after Fortay scored a touchdown against Navy in 1992. (Courtesy Tim Pernetti)

Offensive guard and co-captain Tim Christ signed an NFL contract with the Philadelphia Eagles.

Marshall Roberts was First Team ECAC All-East and Second Team AP All-East. Defensive backs Jay Bellamy and Malik Jackson were Second Team AP All-East. Ron Allen was Honorable Mention ECAC All-East, and he finished his career at Rutgers with 1,283 yards in kickoff returns. Linebacker Shawn Williams made 79 tackles and 12 quarterback sacks in the 1991 season. Co-captain Elnardo Webster made 81 tackles. Webster was selected to the ECAC and AP All-East First Team.

Elnardo Webster and Malik Jackson were also named to the All–Big East Conference. They were the first Scarlet Knights to be so honored. Moving on to a pro career was Elnardo Webster, who had a total of 15 QB sacks over his Scarlet career. Webster signed with the Pittsburgh Steelers.

In 1992 New Jersey governor Jim Florio authorized legislation that in part, called for expanding the seating capacity of Rutgers Stadium to forty-five thousand. The governor said the expansion would bring Rutgers Stadium up to the standards of the Big East Football Conference.

Rutgers players were also moving up to Big East Conference standards in 1992. The Knights had two skilled quarterbacks on the roster that season. They were Bryan Fortay and Ray Lucas. Fortay had been a star at East Brunswick High School in New Jersey, where he'd been named the Coca-Cola High School Player of the Year. Originally, Bryan Fortay had gone to the University of Miami, but later transferred to Rutgers. Ray Lucas was a promising redshirt freshman signal caller from Harrison, New Jersey.

Joining the offensive backfield that season was a rugged running back from Highland Park, New Jersey, named Bruce Presley. Presley played high school football for Coach Joe Policastro. Joe Policastro was the older brother of former Rutgers star quarterback Rich Policastro. Craig Mitter, Tekay Dorsey, and Bruce Presley provided Rutgers with a potent ground game. Tri-captains Travis Broadbent, Jim Guarantano, and Shawn Williams were leaders of a veteran squad. The offense featured Chris Brantley, Mario Henry, and tight ends Marco Battaglia and Tim Pernetti.

The defense was led by Glen Nave, Mike Spitzer, Mark Washington, and Jason Curry.

Doug Graber was optimistic about the team's chances. "I think we have enough physical talent coming back to not make a bowl appearance a wild and crazy dream," predicted the Scarlet coach.

However, the Eagles of Boston College, coached by Tom Coughlin, surprised Rutgers on opening day. The next week, the Scarlet evened their record with a win over Colgate. Marshall Roberts had an 85-yard punt return for a touchdown against Colgate. A second win followed when Rutgers topped a very good Pittsburgh team in the first night game ever played at Rutgers Stadium. The next week the Knights torpedoed Navy for their third consecutive victory.

Rutgers and Navy have a long gridiron history: the first Rutgers-Navy battle took place in 1891. (Courtesy U.S. Naval Academy)

Right: Defensive back Jay Bellamy (#9) was Second Team All-East in 1992. Wide receiver Jim Guarantano (#18) was First Team All-East that same year. (Courtesy Rutgers Athletic Communications)

Opposite: Marco Battaglia started as a freshman for Rutgers and began a tremendous career as a Scarlet tight end. (Courtesy Rutgers Athletic Communications)

Penn State and Syracuse saddled Rutgers with back-to-back losses to even the Knights' record at 3 wins and 3 losses. Coach Doug Graber's Knights then recorded back-to-back victories over Army and Virginia Tech. In the Virginia Tech game, Rutgers' Chris Brantley scored 4 touchdowns. Quarterback Brian Fortay passed for 338 yards as Rutgers slipped past Virginia Tech 50 to 49 in a classic thriller. On the Scarlet defensive side, Malik Jackson intercepted 3 Virginia Tech passes to tie a Rutgers record.

The following week against Cincinnati, Rutgers signal caller Brian Fortay connected with Bruce Presley for a long 84-yard pass completion. Unfortunately, the Knights came up short on the scoreboard and the Bearcats won. Impressive Scarlet victories over West Virginia and Temple concluded a very fine 7–4 season.

Quarterback Brian Fortay was Rutgers' top passer in 1992 with 1,608 yards. Ray Lucas completed 61 of 105 passes for 836 yards and 4 TDs in 1992. Chris Brantley pulled in 40 passes for 559 yards and 6 touchdowns. Senior Jim Guarantano made 56 receptions for 755 yards and 6 TDs. Over his four-year career, Guarantano caught 158 passes for 2,065 yards and 11 touchdowns. Jim Guarantano was named AP Honorable Mention All-American for his gridiron work in 1992. He was also First Team AP All-East and First Team All–Big East.

Rutgers running back Bruce Presley rushed for 817 yards and 7 touchdowns in 1992. Presley was voted a Second Team Freshman All-American by the *Sporting News*. In addition, Bruce Presley was the ECAC and Big East Rookie of the Year. Running back Craig Mitter finished his Rutgers career with five 100-plus-yard rushing games. Mitter was an All–Big East choice. Mitter signed to play pro with the New York Giants. Center Travis Broadbent was an All-East choice by the ECAC and the AP.

Defensive back Jay Bellamy was an All-East choice on the Associated Press team. Defensive back Malik Jackson was ECAC All-East.

Shawn Williams had 69 tackles in 1992. He sacked opposing quarterbacks a total of 21 times over his Rutgers career. Williams was First Team ECAC and AP All-East. Shawn

N.J.
Rutgers
BIG
EAST

Williams played in the East-West Shrine Game and the Blue-Gray Classic. He signed to play pro football with the New York Jets.

Marshall Roberts, who returned punts for a total of 1,018 yards at Rutgers, signed to play Arena Football. Roberts played professionally for the Sacramento Gold Miners and the Orlando Predators.

The 1993 Scarlet Knights had no home games. The new Rutgers football stadium was under construction and would not be ready for use until the following year. The Scarlet Knights were forced to play five away games and six games at Giants Stadium. The severity of the schedule was also a concern. Rutgers played five teams ranked in the Top 25 in 1993.

Scarlet co-captains Bill Bailey and Andrew Beckett prepped their squad to meet the challenge. Rutgers had the offensive potential to put up lots of points. Quarterbacks Ray Lucas and Brian Fortay were back. Bruce Presley had a dazzling new running mate in Terrell Willis. Kicker John Benestad, who led the team in scoring with 71 points the year before, was on hand and ready with foot. Senior pass-receiving sensation Chris Brantley could be counted on to make clutch catches. Tight end Marco Battaglia was on the verge of stardom. Defensive leaders were Mike Spitzer, Alcides Catanho, and Brian Sheridan.

The Scarlet Knights beat Colgate at Giants Stadium to open the season. The next week it was back to the Meadowlands for an exciting 39 to 38 win over Duke. A trip to Penn State proved fruitless. The Nittany Lions won.

After the defeat, Rutgers returned to Giants Stadium and toppled Temple. The Knights were a very respectable 3–1 at that point.

Suddenly the season started to go sour. Coach Tom Coughlin's Boston College Eagles visited Giants Stadium and exited with a win over Rutgers.

A contest against Army at West Point resulted in win number four for Rutgers. Sadly, that was the final victory the Knights would savor that season.

Coach Frank Beamer's Virginia Tech squad beat Rutgers. Coach Don Nehlen's West Virginia club also defeated the Knights. Coach Dennis Erickson's Miami team chalked up a win at Rutgers' expense. In the game against the Miami Hurricanes, Rutgers kicker John

Bruce Presley (#44) scored 20 touchdowns for Rutgers from 1992 to 1995 and played in the East-West Shrine Bowl. (Courtesy Rutgers Athletic Communications)

Benestad booted a 51-yard field goal. Pittsburgh and Syracuse also got the best of the Scarlet Knights that year.

Individually, several Rutgers players sparkled in 1993. Quarterback Ray Lucas completed 109 passes in 188 attempts for 1,011 yards and 7 touchdowns. Signal caller Brian Fortay completed 59 of 107 passes for 766 yards and 9 touchdowns. Over his career, Fortay had 174 completions in 337 attempts for 2,374 yards and 25 TDs.

Kicker John Benestad completed his Scarlet career with a total of 191 points.

Running back Terrell Willis scored 80 points in 1993 to lead all Rutgers scorers. Willis carried the pigskin 195 times for 1,261 yards and 13 touchdowns in his rookie season. He was voted the Most Valuable Player of the team and named a First Team Freshman All-American by the *Football News*. Terrell Willis was also an Honorable Mention AP All-American. The ECAC named Rutgers' Terrell Willis their Rookie of the Year. In addition, he was the Big East Rookie of the Year.

Receiver Chris Brantley was a First Team All–Big East choice. Brantley caught 56 passes for 589 yards and 7 touchdowns in 1993. His career totals were 144 receptions for 1,914 yards and 17 touchdowns. Chris Brantley was later a fourth-round draft pick of the NFL's Los Angeles Rams.

Wide receiver Mario Henry inked a pro contract with the New England Patriots. Offensive tackle Scott Vaughn was All–Big East and signed a pro deal with the Denver Broncos.

Rutgers' Jim Guarantano concluded his Scarlet football career with a total of 158 pass receptions. (Courtesy Rutgers Athletic Communications)

Malik Jackson finished his Rutgers career with a total of 11 interceptions. He later played arena football for the New Jersey Red Dogs.

Jay Bellamy signed a contract with the Seattle Seahawks to play in the NFL. Bellamy, Malik Jackson, and Chris Brantley all played in the Blue-Gray Classic all-star game. Malik Jackson was the defensive MVP of the contest.

Defensive captain Andrew Beckett was First Team ECAC All-East and Second Team All–Big East. The Cincinnati Bengals signed Andrew Beckett to a pro contract.

Rutgers quarterback Brian Fortay played in the Hula Bowl. He continued his football career as a pro signal caller for the Frankfurt Galaxy in the World Football League. Fortay also played arena football for the Miami Hooters.

Rutgers tight end Tim Pernetti embarked upon a radio and television career after graduation. Eventually, Pernetti became the color commentator for radio broadcasts of Rutgers football games.

The new forty-two-thousand-seat Rutgers stadium opened for business at the start of the 1994 season. Kent State christened the Scarlet's new turf on opening day.

Ray Lucas was now calling the signals at quarterback. Bruce Presley and Terrell Willis kept him company in the backfield. Tight end Marco Battaglia was the go-to guy in crucial passing situations. Reggie Funderburk and Steve Harper were also prime pass-catchers.

Captain Ken Dammann and Andy Gaebele anchored a steady offensive line.

Alcides Catanho captained a stubborn defensive unit that consisted of Bob Sneathen, Brian Sheridan, Mark Washington, and Keif Bryant.

Scarlet Knights receiver Tim Pernetti enjoyed a successful career in television and radio after graduation. In 2006 Pernetti was the color analyst for Rutgers radio broadcasts. (Courtesy Tim Pernetti)

The Scarlet Knights won the first coin toss in their new home. Coach Doug Graber's squad performed well from that moment on.

Scarlet quarterback Ray Lucas tallied the first touchdown. It came on an 8-yard TD run. Rutgers receiver Steven Harper caught the first touchdown pass. It was a beautiful 50-yard bomb from Ray Lucas. The final score was Rutgers 28 and Kent State 6.

The Scarlet Knights notched another win in week two. West Virginia was the victim. In game three, Syracuse slipped by Rutgers in a 37 to 36 nail-biter. Up next was Penn State.

Penn State quarterback Kerry Collins was coached by Dick Anderson, the former Rutgers head coach. All-American Kerry Collins would eventually win a Maxwell Award as America's top footballer. Kerry Collins led Penn State past Rutgers in a good game.

The following week, Rutgers had a tough trip south. The Scarlet Knights lost to sixth-ranked Miami. Rutgers went 3 up and 3 down for the rest of the season with wins over Army, Cincinnati, and Temple. Rutgers' Terrell Willis rushed for 232 yards in the Temple victory. In a loss to Virginia Tech, quarterback Ray Lucas passed for 374 yards. Rutgers finished with a record of 5 wins, 5 losses, and 1 tie in 1994. The tie was a 7 to 7 deadlock against Boston College. In the future, college football ties would become obsolete. An overtime system was developed and implemented to eliminate tie games.

In 1994 Ray Lucas completed 156 of 268 passes for 1,869 yards and 16 touchdowns. Marco Battaglia caught 53 passes for 779 yards and 4 touchdowns. As a reward for his outstanding effort, Battaglia was named an Honorable Mention All-American by United Press International. Battaglia was also a Second Team All–Big East choice and team MVP.

Running back Terrell Willis was First Team All–Big East and an Honorable Mention All-American by UPI. In 1994 Willis had 216 carries for 1,080 yards and 5 touchdowns. He was the first Rutgers back since Jim "J. J." Jennings to have back-to-back 1,000-plus-yard rushing seasons.

Reggie Funderburk caught 55 passes for 751 yards and 8 touchdowns. Funderburk was the team's top scorer with 48 points.

Offensive tackle Ken Dammann and defensive tackle Keif Bryant were ECAC All-East selections. Dammann was also an All–Big East choice and played in the East-West Shrine Bowl. Defensive end Bob Sneathen played in the Blue-Gray Classic.

Mark Washington was the top hitter for the Scarlet with 97 tackles and made All–Big East.

Five Rutgers football players moved on to NFL teams. Keif Bryant was a seventh-round selection of the Seattle Seahawks in the NFL draft. Linebacker Alcides Catanho signed with the New England Patriots. The Philadelphia Eagles inked Bob Sneathen to a contract. Ken Dammann signed with the Washington Redskins. Fullback Wes Bridges was signed by the Philadelphia Eagles.

Coach Doug Graber's football squad was stocked with talented athletes in 1995. Some of Rutgers' players were as good as the most heralded footballers in the nation. However, Rutgers still did not have the depth most big-time college football squads had. It was a

Rutgers fans celebrated home victories over Kent State and West Virginia in 1994. (Courtesy Joe Camporeale/Rutgers Athletic Communications)

problem that would be resolved eventually. In 1995 Rutgers star players had to suffer through another tough season.

Ray Lucas, Marco Battaglia, Brian Sheridan, and Mark Washington were stars at their positions. Lucas, Battaglia, Sheridan, and Washington were the Scarlet Knights' captains in 1995.

A talent-packed offense led by Terrell Willis, Bruce Presley, Steve Harper, Bill Powell, and Chad Bosch was primed and ready for action. Defensive stars were Rashod Swinger, Rahsaan Giddings, Jim Guarnera, and Aaron Brady.

Rutgers had tons of individual talent in 1995, but lacked a potent team punch. The Knights just could not mesh all of their unique individual abilities. Another stumbling block was the fact that the Scarlet played four teams ranked in the Top 20.

Coach Doug Graber's Scarlet squad lost to Duke and beat Navy out of the starting gate. Against a Penn State club that ended up ranked 13th in the country, Rutgers' Marco Battaglia showed off his talents on national television. Battaglia caught 13 passes for 184 yards and 3 TDs in a losing cause.

Rutgers then came up short in contests against Syracuse, Miami, and Virginia Tech.

A good win against Pittsburgh perked up the Knights. Rutgers' Paul Rivers scooped up a goal-line fumble and ran 100 yards with the pigskin to set an NCAA record. After a loss to West Virginia, Rutgers topped both Tulane and Temple. The Scarlet Knights closed out their season against Boston College. In a loss to the BC Eagles, rifle-armed Ray Lucas passed for a total of 327 yards.

Rutgers finished the year with 4 wins in 11 gridiron outings.

All-American Marco Battaglia went on to enjoy an NFL career with the Cincinnati Bengals. (Courtesy Rutgers Athletic Communications)

Rutgers' Ray Lucas completed 188 passes in 347 attempts for 2,180 yards and 16 touchdowns in 1995. Lucas had 514 completions in 908 attempts for 5,896 yards and 43 touchdowns for his Rutgers career. Bruce Presley carried the pigskin 147 times for 678 yards and 6 touchdowns in 1995. Over four years, Presley had 552 carries for 2,792 yards and 20 TDs. Bruce Presley had ten 100-plus-yard rushing games in his days at Rutgers.

Presley's running mate Terrell Willis had 177 carries for 773 yards and 2 touchdowns that season. In his career, Willis also had 10 100-plus-yard rushing games. In all, Terrell Willis had 586 carries for 3,114 yards and 20 touchdowns.

Linebacker Brian Sheridan topped the Scarlet in tackles in 1995 with 135 hits. Receiver Steve Harper hauled in 7 touchdown passes. Tight end Marco Battaglia was the leading scorer with 62 points. He was also named Rutgers' Most Valuable Player. Battaglia caught

69 passes for 894 yards and 10 touchdowns that season. Over his career, Marco Battaglia snared 171 passes good for 2,221 receiving yards and 16 touchdowns.

Marco Battaglia was named a consensus All-American. He was selected First Team All-America by the Associated Press, Walter Camp, the American Football Coaches Association, *Football News*, United Press International, the Football Writers, and *Pro College Football News*.

Marco Battaglia and Bruce Presley both played in the East-West Shrine Bowl. In addition, Presley played in the Blue-Gray Classic.

Running back Terrell Willis was ECAC All-East and All–Big East. Defensive lineman Jim Guarnera was ECAC All-East. Offensive lineman Robert Barr was All–Big East. He, too, was selected to play in the Blue-Gray Classic. Offensive lineman Chris Kennedy was Second Team All–Big East.

In 1995 Rutgers had more of its players signed to professional football contracts than in any year in its history. In all, fourteen Scarlet Knights inked NFL or CFL contracts. Listed below are the players who turned pro and the team each signed with.

OT Robert Barr: Seattle Seahawks (third-round draft pick)
TE Marco Battaglia: Cincinnati Bengals (second-round draft pick)
OG Matt Brown: San Diego Chargers
LB Rahsaan Giddings: Montreal Alouettes (CFL)
DE Jim Guarnera: San Francisco 49ers
QB Rob Higgins: San Diego Chargers
RB Ezra Johnson: New York Jets
OG Chris Kennedy: New York Giants
TE Dan Latore: Detroit Lions
QB Ray Lucas: New York Jets and New England Patriots
RB Bruce Presley: Indianapolis Colts
DE Rudy Smith: Dallas Cowboys
DB Mark Washington: New York Giants
RB Terrell Willis: New York Jets

Ray Lucas went on to play in the NFL for many years with the New York Jets and the New England Patriots. He later became a football analyst and color commentator on television.

Marco Battaglia was the thirty-ninth player selected in the NFL draft that year. He was a second-round pick of the Cincinnati Bengals and played for many years in the National Football League.

At the conclusion of the 1995 season, Head Coach Doug Graber and Rutgers football parted company. Doug Graber concluded his career at Rutgers with 29 wins, 36 losses, and 1 tie. In 2003 Doug Graber coached Frankfurt to the World Bowl Championship in NFL Europa. He now works as a TV sports broadcaster.

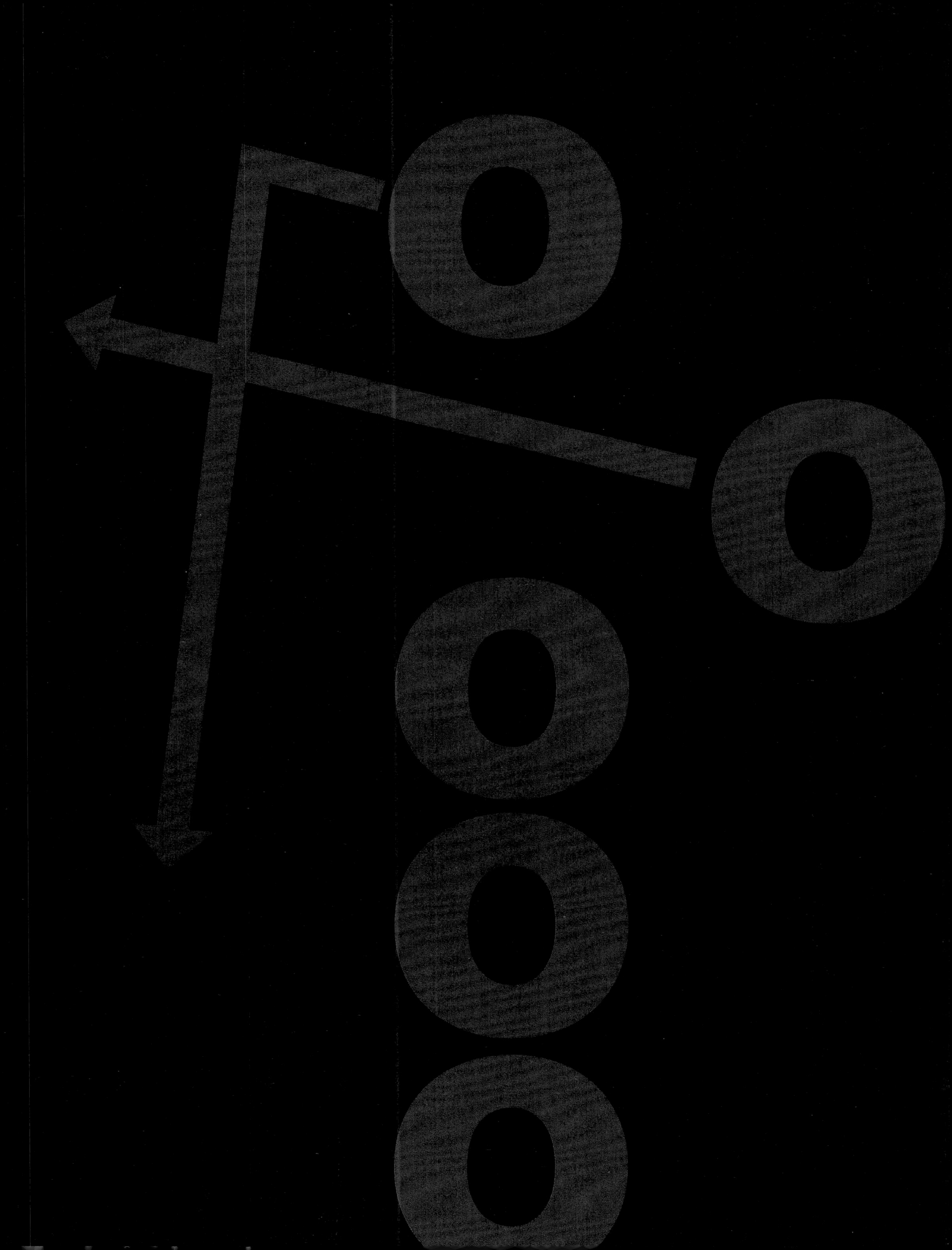

CHAPTER 12

BIG PLAYS AND FUMBLES 1996–2000

Once again, the hunt was on for a new head football coach at Rutgers. University president Francis Lawrence was determined to improve the football program at Rutgers. After numerous candidates were interviewed, Terry Shea, a coach with West Coast roots, was hired to resurrect Rutgers football. Shea had been the head coach at San Jose State and he'd worked with San Francisco 49ers coach Bill Walsh at Stanford. Terry Shea had an outstanding pigskin pedigree.

"Terry Shea has a superior mind for the game of football," pro coach Mike Holmgren said when he heard of Rutgers' choice.

Coach Shea was anxious to get Rutgers back on the winning path. "This can't be a year of transition for Rutgers because I won't allow it to be," Shea told the press after he was hired. Rutgers fans had one big question about Shea. Could a California coach bring a New Jersey football program in out of the cold?

Coach Shea was faced with a number of challenges from the start. First off, he installed a new offense that put a great deal of pressure on the team's signal caller. Rutgers had recently graduated its two top QBs. The new signal callers for the Knights were veteran Mike Stephans, newcomer Corey Valentine, and junior Ralph Sacca. Shea had to break in a new offensive system with a new field general.

Another potential pothole was the Scarlet Knights' 1996 schedule. It included four ranked teams and Coach Lou Holtz's Fighting Irish of Notre Dame. The Rutgers–Notre Dame clash would be the first gridiron meeting between the schools since Knute Rocke was the Irish's head coach way back in 1921.

Terry Shea's Scarlet club did have potential. Tri-captains Chad Bosch, Rob Seeger, and Rashod Swinger were hard workers who led by example. New arrival Jacki Crooks had the makings of an outstanding running back. Dennis Thomas was a talented ball carrier. Pass-catchers Andy Holland, Walt King, and Steve Harper ran good routes. The offensive line had T. J. Spizzo, Pete Donnelly, Matt Fleming, Ben French, and Rob Seeger.

On defense Chris Cebula, Shawn Devlin, and Rusty Swartz spearheaded a steadfast unit.

Terry Shea was the head coach at San Jose State before he became Rutgers' coach in 1996. (Courtesy San Jose State Athletic Communications)

Right: Mike Stephans became the starting quarterback at Rutgers in 1996. (Courtesy Mike Stephans)

Opposite: Rutgers' 1996 schedule included games against Miami, Virginia Tech, and Notre Dame. (Courtesy Mike Stephans)

Also on the squad was a young defensive lineman from Hillsborough High School in New Jersey who would eventually make his mark on the offensive line. Shaun O'Hara had made the Scarlet Knights squad as a walk-on in his freshman year. He later earned a football scholarship through hard work and determination.

Coach Terry Shea's Rutgers debut was a success. The Scarlet Knights topped Villanova on opening day. Rutgers' Nick Mike-Mayer booted a 48-yard field goal in that game. In week two of the season, Coach Shea's new offensive machine backfired and Navy scuttled the Scarlet. After the Navy loss, the Knights' run-and-shoot offense started to fire blanks. Rutgers dropped games to four nationally ranked teams—Miami, Virginia Tech, Syracuse, and a resurgent Army club coached by Bob Sutton. Corey Valentine, who began the year as Rutgers' starting quarterback, was replaced by Mike Stephans. After another loss, Rutgers

BIG
EAST

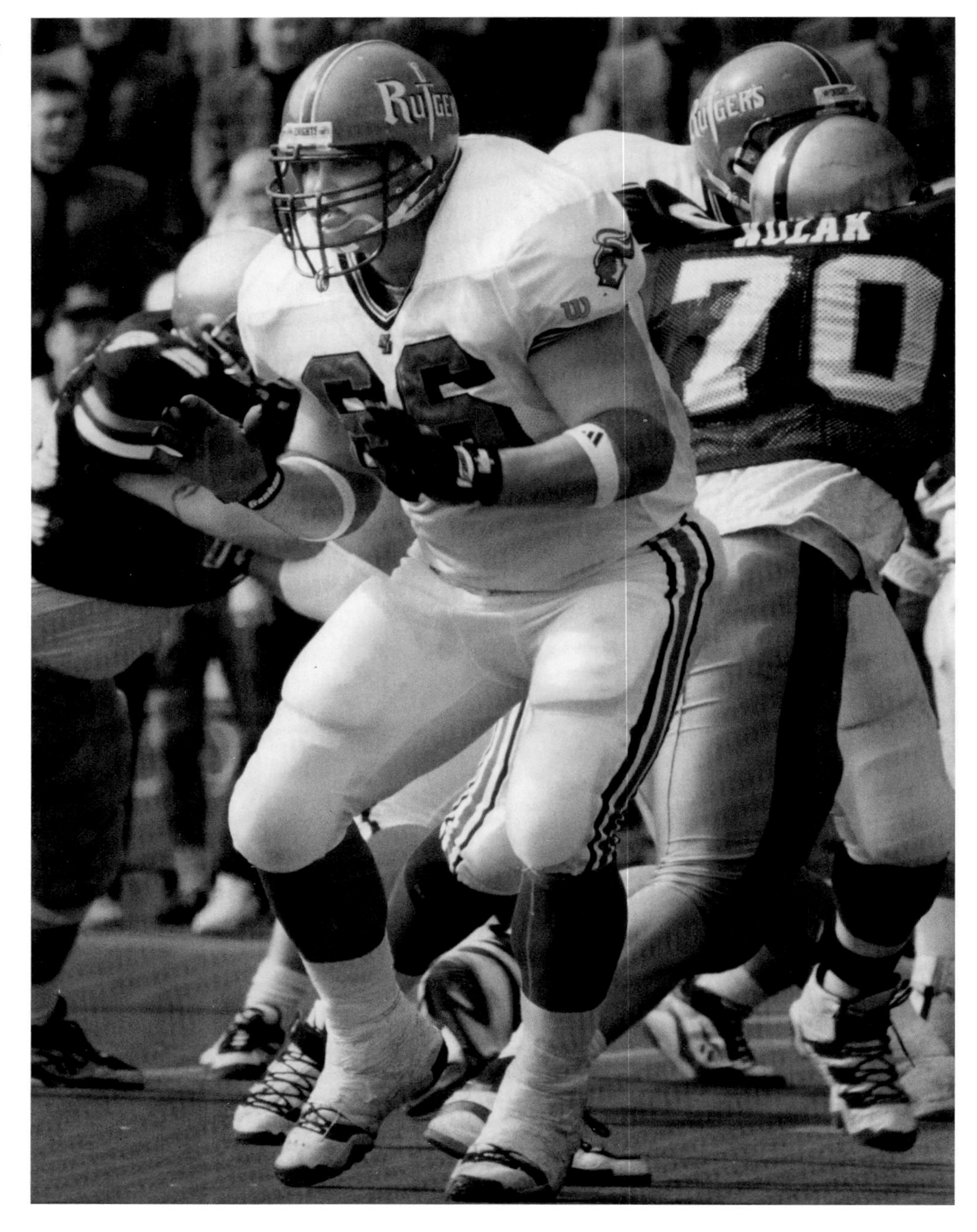

Shaun O'Hara began his playing career at Rutgers in 1997. He later played in the NFL for the Cleveland Browns and the New York Giants. (Courtesy Rutgers Athletic Communications)

rebounded with a solid win over Temple. Scarlet halfback Chad Bosch had a 90-yard run against the Temple Owls.

Rutgers proved to be no match for Notre Dame and finished the year without another win. The team, which had been ravaged by graduation, managed to record only one Big East Conference win and two victories overall.

Quarterback Mike Stephans led Rutgers in passing with 918 yards. Chad Bosch was the rushing leader with 523 yards.

Senior defensive lineman Rashod Swinger earned ECAC All-East honors. Rashod inked a pro contract with the San Diego Chargers of the NFL.

Jack McKiernan and Brian Sheridan were the co-captains of a 1997 Scarlet squad that featured Mike McMahon at quarterback, Jacki Crooks at running back, and Reggie

Funderburk at wide receiver. Dennis Thomas and Joe Diggs provided some extra pop at the backfield positions. Speedster Reggie Stephens returned kicks and also played defense.

Up front the offensive line boasted some big bodies with the likes of Clint Hunt, Shaun O'Hara, and center Jack McKiernan. The defense was led by Brian Sheridan, Dax Strohmeyer, Wayne Hampton, Aaron Brady, and Chris Cebula.

After an opening-day loss to Virginia Tech, the Rutgers defense was severely tested in game two of the season against Texas. The Scarlet D faced running back Ricky Williams, who led the nation in rushing that year. The Longhorns gored the Knights and easily won the contest. Rutgers then dropped back-to-back games to Navy and Boston College. In the game against Boston College, the Scarlet's Bill Powell connected with Walter King for an 81-yard pass completion. The losses piled up. In a defeat by Army, the Knights' new young quarterback, Mike McMahon, completed 26 of 42 passes for 386 yards and 1 touchdown.

The 1997 football season was a dark one for Rutgers fans, but brighter days were ahead. (Courtesy Rutgers Athletic Communications)

Reggie Stephens returned a kickoff 94 yards for a touchdown against Miami in a losing cause.

Despite some outstanding individual efforts, Coach Terry Shea's Scarlet Knights finished the 1997 season winless.

Rutgers receiver Reggie Funderburk caught 11 passes for 136 yards and 1 TD in 1997. Funderburk made 123 receptions for 1,464 yards and 10 touchdowns during his career at Rutgers. He also returned 59 punts for a total of 440 yards. Receiver Steven Harper finished his career with a total of 10 touchdown catches. Rutgers punter Jared Slovan finished his career with 252 punts for 9,756 yards. Slovan was named to the All–Big East and signed an NFL contract with the Washington Redskins.

Brian Sheridan collected 109 tackles and 1 sack that same season. He had a career total of 389 tackles and 1 QB sack. Sheridan was selected Second Team All–Big East and named Rutgers' Most Valuable Player. Scarlet defensive tackle Wayne Hampton made First Team ECAC All-East. Rashod Swinger was picked to participate in the Blue-Gray All-Star Classic.

Rutgers welcomed a new athletic director in 1998. Robert "Bob" Mulcahy was the choice of Governor Christine Todd Whitman. Mulcahy had run the New Jersey Sports Authority since 1979.

Bob Mulcahy was an expert in marketing. When he was hired, Mulcahy said his goal at Rutgers was to develop "a model athletic program that will be a focal point of campus life and a centerpiece of state pride."

Coach Terry Shea's squads improved in 1998. Quarterback Mike McMahon and running back Jacki Crooks ignited some much-needed offensive spark while co-captains Aaron Brady and Bill Powell demonstrated outstanding leadership qualities. The Scarlet offense also featured the talents of Andy Holland and Dennis Thomas. Top linemen were Pete Donnelly, Rich Mazza, Clint Hunt, and Randy Smith. Steve Barone was the place kicker and Mike Barr was the punter.

Quarterback Mike McMahon guided Rutgers to an exciting 7 to 6 win over Richmond on opening day. Bitter losses to Boston College and Syracuse came back to back in weeks two and three. Rutgers then bounced back and forth between wins and losses. The Scarlet Knights tasted victory against Army, but gagged on defeat against Miami. Pittsburgh was a win while Tulane was a loss.

Mike McMahon, shown here later as a Minnesota Viking, took over the signal calling at Rutgers in 1997. (Courtesy Rick A. Kolodziej/Minnesota Vikings)

Starting with the next week against Temple, Rutgers running back Jacki Crooks stepped it up. Crooks had four games in a row in which he rushed for 100 yards or more. In those contests, Rutgers recorded wins against Temple and Navy but lost to West Virginia and Virginia Tech. The Scarlet Knights concluded their 1998 football campaign with a record of 5 wins and 6 losses. Rutgers posted a Big East Conference record of 2 wins and 5 losses. Terry Shea was rewarded for breathing new life into the Rutgers program by being named the Big East Coach of the Year.

Jacki Crooks personally revived the Rutgers running game. Crooks carried the ball 159 times for 821 yards and 1 TD in 1998.

On defense, Aaron Brady made 136 tackles and 4.5 sacks as a Scarlet Knights linebacker. He was selected All–Big East by the *Football News* and went on to play for the New York Giants in the NFL.

Defensive back Reggie Stephens was named the winner of the Homer Hazel Award as the team's Most Valuable Player. Stephens was All–Big East and played in the East-West Shrine Bowl. He later inked a pro contract with the New York Giants. Wayne Hampton, Shaun O'Hara, and specialist Tosh Tiddick were all Second Team All–Big East. Wide receiver Bill Powell signed with the Dallas Cowboys to play pro football. Tight end Billy Woodward signed an NFL deal with the Seattle Seahawks.

Rutgers stumbled through a depressing season in 1999 despite the fine efforts of tri-captains Shaun O'Hara, Dax Strohmeyer, and Wayne Hampton. Jacki Crooks, Dennis Thomas, Walter King, and Mike McMahon all played hard and fast on offense. Newcomer L. J. Smith, a star athlete from Highland Park High School in New Jersey, made his gridiron presence known. Errol Johnson and Aaron Martin added depth to the receiving corps.

The defense featured Raheem Orr, Jabari Moore, Julian Ross, and Roger Wingate.

Rutgers traveled across the United States to play the University of California in its first game of the 1999 season. California won, but Rutgers found a fantastic tight end. L. J. Smith went into the game and the first pass he caught in his college career was for a touchdown. It was the Scarlet Knights' lone score of the day.

Rutgers' second game of the season attracted 41,511 fans. Texas came calling and returned to the Lone Star state victorious. Boston College, Wake Forest, Virginia Tech, and West Virginia also toppled Rutgers. In the West Virginia game, the Scarlet Knights' Mike Jones had an 80-yard pass completion to Walter King. Losses to Pittsburgh, Temple, and Navy added to the frustration felt by Rutgers players, coaches, and fans.

Finally, Rutgers redeemed itself with a win over Syracuse. The moment of gridiron joy was short-lived as Miami bested the Scarlet Knights the following week.

Jacki Crooks had a good season at running back during a bad year. Crooks carried the ball 161 times for 587 yards and 3 touchdowns. Over his four-year career, Jacki Crooks lugged the pigskin 570 times and gained a total of 2,434 yards. He tallied 5 rushing touchdowns. He also had 480 receiving yards.

On the defensive side of the ball, Wayne Hampton was Second Team ECAC All-East and Second Team All–Big East. He played in the Blue-Gray Classic and then signed a pro

Left: Gary Brackett starred at middle linebacker for the Scarlet Knights beginning in 1999. (Courtesy Rutgers Athletic Communications)

Right: Wide receiver Aaron Martin of Rutgers went on to enjoy a pro career in the NFL. (Courtesy Rutgers Athletic Communications)

Left: Middle linebacker Gary Brackett was one of the Scarlet Knights' top tacklers in 2000. Brackett won four varsity letters at Rutgers, and went on to play for the Indianapolis Colts. (Courtesy Indianapolis Colts)

Right: Scarlet quarterback Mike McMahon passed for more than 6,000 yards during his Rutgers career. McMahon played for several NFL teams, including the Minnesota Vikings, the Detroit Lions, and the Philadelphia Eagles. (Courtesy Rick A. Kolodziej/Minnesota Vikings)

contract with the San Diego Chargers. Linebacker Dax Strohmeyer was ECAC All-East. He continued his football career as a pro with the New York Jets. Rutgers punter Lee McDonald later played arena football for the Norfolk Nighthawks.

Offensive lineman Shaun O'Hara, who came to Rutgers as a walk-on player, made First Team All–Big East. O'Hara was signed as a free agent by the Cleveland Browns. He worked and battled his way into the Browns' starting lineup. Shaun O'Hara then moved to the New York Giants and became their starting center. He enjoyed a long and illustrious career in the pro ranks. O'Hara is a prime example of a determined athlete who refuses to give up.

The University of Notre Dame football team was scheduled for its first-ever visit to Rutgers Stadium in 2000. The rest of the usual football suspects rounded out the Scarlet schedule.

The preseason predictions rated Rutgers as sinking fast in the Big East. It would be up to the Scarlet co-captains Mike Jones and Garrett Shea to keep the squad's hopes for a successful year afloat. Defensive back Garrett Shea was in a unique position for a player. Terry Shea was his father. For the first time in Rutgers history, a Rutgers team captain was the son of a Rutgers head coach.

In order for Rutgers to achieve gridiron respectability in 2000, quarterback Mike McMahon and running back Dennis Thomas needed to have banner years. Scarlet players on both sides of the ball would be tested week after week. To the credit of each and every member of the 2000 team, the Scarlet Knights put forth Herculean efforts game after game. Those diehard loyal sons of Rutgers included Wesley Martin, Julian Ross, Tom Petko, Marty Pyszczymuka, Greg Pyszczymuka, Chad Schwenk, and Errol Johnson.

Supreme efforts came from future pro stars L. J. Smith at tight end and Gary Brackett at linebacker.

The Scarlet Knights charged out of the starting gate and scored 93 points while giving up just 21 in their first two games. Rutgers beat Villanova and thumped the University of Buffalo. A string of four losses followed before Rutgers battled back to a victory over Navy. A 24 to 31 overtime loss to West Virginia was a heartbreaker. The very next week, Coach Bob Davie brought his Notre Dame squad into Rutgers Stadium. Fans flooded the gates and filled 40,011 seats. Notre Dame posted a win, but Rutgers played with pride. The Scarlet Knights endured a year-ending loss to Syracuse to post a dismal 3–8 record. The 2000 season was a bitter disappointment, but gridiron redemption was only a few short years away. Unfortunately, Terry Shea would not be the man to resurrect Rutgers. Coach Shea left Rutgers with a career record of 11 wins and 44 losses.

Quarterback Mike McMahon couldn't be faulted for the subpar outcome of the season. McMahon completed 169 of 340 passes for 2,157 yards and 18 touchdowns. Over his career, Mike McMahon had 482 completions in 974 attempts for 6,608 yards and 41 touchdowns. He was the offensive MVP of the Blue-Gray Classic and also played in the East-West Shrine Bowl. McMahon was a fifth-round draft pick of the Detroit Lions in the NFL draft. Mike McMahon played for the Lions, the Minnesota Vikings, and the Philadelphia Eagles.

Dennis Thomas was the team's leading rusher with 587 yards. He was also the team's Most Valuable Player. Wide receiver Walter King totaled 10 touchdown catches over the course of his Rutgers career and signed to play with the New York Jets. Offensive lineman Rich Mazza was named All–Big East. Mazza signed a pro contract with the Detroit Lions. Defensive lineman Wesley Robertson was also All–Big East. In 2000 he led Rutgers by making 83 tackles. Robertson tried out with the Kansas City Chiefs.

At the conclusion of the 2000 season the Scarlet Knights were again in the market for a new head coach. Finding the right man was proving to be an endless quest for an elusive gridiron grail. The right guy had to be out there, but where?

Left: Nate Jones was a true scholar-athlete at Rutgers. He excelled in the classroom and on the gridiron as a defensive back and return specialist. (Courtesy Rutgers Athletic Communications)

Right: Tight end L. J. Smith caught a total of 60 passes for Rutgers in 1999 and 2000. (Courtesy Rutgers Athletic Communications)

PART FOUR 2001–2006

CHAPTER 13
A JERSEY GUY
2001–2004

Rutgers was a football team looking to rebuild its credibility. The Scarlet Knights had chalked up more than 550 victories over the years, but had suffered through a severe gridiron slump in recent seasons. Athletic Director Bob Mulcahy was determined to correct that downward swing. Before Mulcahy introduced Rutgers' new head coach, he gathered a group of key high-school football coaches from all over New Jersey. "For twenty-five years," Mulcahy told them, "I've kept hearing that you wanted one of your own. Now I'm giving you one, and now you guys have to deliver." Bob Mulcahy's remarks referred to the fact that New Jersey high school coaches longed for a head coach at Rutgers with Garden State roots. Rutgers was getting such a man in Greg Schiano. It was now up to New Jersey high school programs to steer their top players toward Rutgers.

Greg Schiano was from Wykoff, New Jersey, and had played high school football in the Garden State. Schiano attended Bucknell in Pennsylvania, where he was an All-Conference linebacker and team captain. When his dream of playing pro didn't materialize, he turned to coaching. In 1988 Schiano worked as an assistant coach at Ramapo High School in New Jersey. Schiano moved on to Rutgers, where he was a graduate assistant coach in 1989. In 1990 Greg Schiano was a grad assistant coach at Penn State. Schiano became the coach of defensive backs at Penn State in 1991 and remained there until 1996. He then worked as a coach in the National Football League with the Chicago Bears from 1996 to 1998. From 1999 to 2000 Greg Schiano was the defensive coordinator at the University of Miami.

Rutgers athletic director Bob Mulcahy (left) presents Greg Schiano as the new head coach of the Scarlet Knights in 2001. (Courtesy Rutgers Athletic Communications)

Coach Schiano's journey to the banks of the old Raritan was more like a return trip home than a move to a new job. Greg Schiano was a Jersey guy. Right from the start, he stated that his mission was to attract top New Jersey football players, who had a history of leaving the state for more celebrated programs. Schiano had the gridiron charisma to achieve that mission.

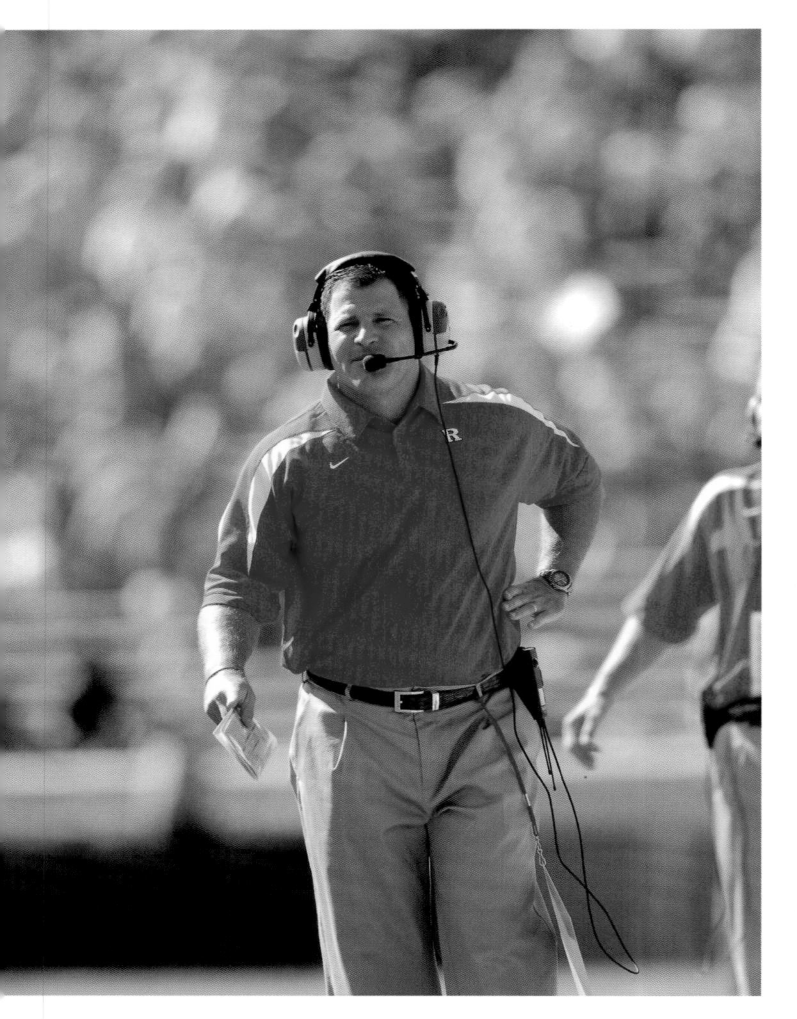

Former Rutgers tight end Tim Pernetti had known Greg Schiano for many years and loudly praised his choice as the Scarlet coach: "Greg Schiano is a man of great faith and strong will. Throughout his life he has illustrated a commitment and a passion as an athlete, coach, father, and husband. He's the type of man you want to take care of your son as they live the student-athlete experience at Rutgers."

However, Rutgers' first year under new head coach Schiano was not a miraculous turnaround. Building a successful big-time football program takes time. Attending Rutgers was not yet in vogue, though it would be soon enough. Schiano's 2001 Scarlet club had some very talented football players, including captains Gary Brackett, L. J. Smith, Mike Esposito, and Shawn Seabrooks. Quarterback Ryan Cubit and running back Dennis Thomas were capable offensive weapons. Aaron Martin could catch and run. Nate Jones was a spectacular special-teams threat. Other key performers were Trohn Carswell, Alfred Peterson, Brian Duffy, Ben Martin, and Antoine Lovelace.

Coach Greg Schiano's first Rutgers victory came on opening day of the 2001 season. Rutgers defeated the University of Buffalo 31 to 15. In the contest, Rutgers' Shawn Seabrooks had an interception, which he returned 73 yards for a score. Losses against Miami, Virginia Tech, Connecticut, Syracuse, and Temple followed. The team's second win was over Navy. In that game, Scarlet quarterback Ryan Cubit completed a 91-yard pass to Aaron Martin, and followed it up later with an 80-yard pass to the same receiver.

Above: Greg Schiano is a New Jersey native; Rutgers is the State University of New Jersey. The combination is a football match made in heaven. (Courtesy Grant Halverson/Rutgers Athletic Communications)

Below: Wide receiver Chris Baker began his Rutgers football career in 2001. (Courtesy San Francisco 49ers)

The Scarlet Knights then stumbled against West Virginia, Pittsburgh, and Boston College. In the BC loss, Nate Jones of the Scarlet Knights picked off a pass and returned the interception 70 yards for a Rutgers touchdown. Rutgers closed out Greg Schiano's first year as the Rutgers head coach with a defeat at the hands of California. A record of 2 wins and 9 losses sounds like a tough start, but consider that 4 of those losses were to Top 25 teams. Miami, coached by Larry Coker, went 12–0 that season and won the National Championship. Syracuse, coached by Paul Pasqualoni, ended up ranked 14th in the country. Coach Frank Beamer's Virginia Tech team was ranked 18th in the nation. Boston College, guided by Coach Tom O'Brien, ended the year ranked number 21.

Individually, several Rutgers players excelled. Quarterback Ryan Cubit had 1,432 passing yards that season. Running back Dennis Thomas rushed for 371 yards. Over his Rutgers career, Thomas gained a total of 1,139 yards. Dennis Thomas also had a total of 440 receiving yards and 1,173 yards on kickoff returns. He signed a pro contract with the Kansas City Chiefs.

Linebacker Gary Brackett won the Homer Hazel Award as the team's Most Valuable Player. Defensive end Alfred Peterson was named a Third Team All-American by the *Sporting News*.

Nate Jones led Rutgers in all-purpose yards in 2001 with 747 yards. (Courtesy Rutgers Athletic Communications)

Left: Nate Jones, shown here as a pro with the Dallas Cowboys, was an Academic All-American in 2002 and 2003. (Courtesy James D. Smith/ Dallas Cowboys)

Right: Gary Brackett won the Homer Hazel Award as Rutgers' Most Valuable Player in 2001 and 2002. He went on to play in the NFL for Indianapolis. (Courtesy Indianapolis Colts)

Tight end L. J. Smith was selected All-East by the ECAC and was Second Team All–Big East. In 2001, Smith caught 30 passes for 282 yards and 3 touchdowns.

The next season, Gary Brackett, Shawn Seabrooks, and L. J. Smith repeated as captains of the Scarlet Knights. It was the first time three players were so honored. Two talented quarterbacks shared signal-calling chores in 2002. They were Ted Trump and Ryan Hart. Hart was destined to become Rutgers' all-time leading passer.

Markis Facyson was Rutgers' featured runner. Newcomer Shawn Tucker joined a talented group of receivers. Speedy specialist Nate Jones, who was also a standout on defense, returned. Rutgers managed only 1 win in 2002. That lone victory was a 44 to 0 rout of Army.

Nate Jones provided some spectacular Scarlet moments in a number of losing efforts. Jones had a 100-yard kickoff return for a touchdown against Tennessee. He added another 100-yard kickoff return for a touchdown against Syracuse. Nate Jones returned 26 kickoffs for 736 yards in 2002. He was named ECAC All-East and All–Big East. The Big

East Conference also named Jones one of their special-teams players of the year. In addition, he was honored as a Second Team Academic All-American.

Rutgers' Mike Barr had 92 punts for 3,707 yards in 2002. Barr turned pro and went on to kick for the Pittsburgh Steelers and the NFL Europe champion Frankfurt Galaxy.

Wideout Aaron Martin signed a pro contract with the Dallas Cowboys and played in the NFL for several years. Tight end L. J. Smith was on the receiving end of 32 passes good for 384 yards and 3 touchdowns in 2002. Smith totaled 122 catches for 1,458 yards and 10 touchdowns as a Scarlet Knight. L. J. Smith was selected to play in the Senior Bowl, but an injury kept him out of action. Smith was a second-round draft pick of the Philadelphia Eagles and became a star receiver in the National Football League.

Rutgers' Shawn Seabrooks won All-East honors.

Rutgers captain Gary Brackett was an ECAC All-East choice. He was also team MVP for the second straight year. Brackett made 130 tackles in 2002. He signed to play pro football for the Indianapolis Colts. Gary Brackett's accomplishments as an athlete and as an individual are truly an inspiration. Brackett was an undersized linebacker who starred at Glassboro High School. He was considered too small to play big-time football and was ignored by many college recruiters. Brackett went to Rutgers and made the team as a walk-on. He not only earned a starting berth, but became a two-time captain.

After leaving Rutgers, Gary Brackett made the Indianapolis Colts as a free agent linebacker. The guy who was too small to play big-time college football played on special teams for two years in the National Football League. Brackett's dedication, determination, and hard work earned him a job as the Colts' starting middle linebacker in 2005. In 2006 Brackett was a starter on the Indianapolis Colts team led by quarterback Peyton Manning that won the Super Bowl.

Another member of the Colts' Super Bowl squad that season was reserve wide receiver Ricky Proehl. Proehl had starred as a pass catcher in the NFL for many years and had won Super Bowl rings with other teams.

Ricky Proehl is a graduate of Hillsborough High School in New Jersey, the same school that spawned former Rutgers stars Steve Tardy and Shaun O'Hara. Rutgers assistant coach Jay Butler and Scarlet lineman Mo Lange are also Hillsborough High School alums.

Coach Greg Schiano's rebuilding process was showing signs of improvement. More and more New Jersey football prospects were staying home and committing to Rutgers. The Scarlet coaches were also recruiting many top players from Florida, where Schiano was well known from his days as the University of Miami defensive coordinator. In fact, Rutgers had many alumni connections in Florida and had begun to recruit there back in the mid-1960s.

In 2003 Raheem Orr and Marty Pyszczymuka captained a Rutgers team primed to inflict some big-time football punishment on its foes. Ryan Hart was the starting quarterback. His receivers were Shawn Tucker, Tres Moses, and tough tight end Clark Harris. In the backfield was a powerful runner named Brian Leonard who could do it all. Nate Jones and Willie Foster were skilled and swift special-team players. On defense the Knights had Ryan Neill, Brandon Haw, and Jarvis Johnson. Rutgers looked ready to rumble.

Rutgers opened the season with a win over Buffalo. Tres Moses contributed to the Scarlet success on opening day with a 66-yard punt return. The following week, the Scarlet Knights were outdueled by the Spartans of Michigan State. Rutgers' Brandon Haw had an interception in the contest, which he returned 61 yards for a touchdown. Back-to-back wins over Army and Navy gave Rutgers a gridiron battle record of 3 and 1 going

Above: Ryan Neill was a standout at the defensive end position for Rutgers. (Courtesy Rutgers Athletic Communications)

Opposite: Fullback Brian Leonard was "Mr. Everything" on offense for the Scarlet Knights. (Courtesy Jim O'Connor/ Rutgers Athletic Communications)

into the start of its Big East Conference schedule. Unfortunately, the Knights came up short against Virginia Tech, West Virginia, and Pittsburgh. In a losing effort against the Pittsburgh Panthers, Scarlet QB Ryan Hart completed 27 of 52 passes for 384 yards and 2 touchdowns. The next week the Knights toppled Temple to even their season record at 4 wins and 4 losses. Connecticut, Boston College, and Miami managed to get the best of Rutgers over the next few weeks. Rutgers closed out the year with a solid win over Syracuse. Eddie Grimes had an interception and a 51-yard return for Rutgers in that game.

Rutgers finished the year with a record of 5 wins and 7 losses. It was an improvement. The Scarlet Knights had a core of key players on that squad who were about to awaken the sleeping giant on the banks of the old Raritan. Rutgers' long football hibernation was about to end.

Quarterback Ryan Hart completed 234 of 398 passes for 2,714 yards and 15 TDs in 2003. Shawn Tucker caught 50 passes for 726 yards and 2 touchdowns. Fullback Brian Leonard snared 53 passes for 488 yards and 5 TDs. Leonard carried the ball 213 times for 880 yards and 9 touchdowns. He was also the team's leading scorer with 86 points. Brian Leonard was selected a Freshman All-American by *College Football News*.

Kick return specialist Nate Jones concluded his Rutgers career with 82 kickoff returns for 1,902 yards. Jones was ECAC All-East and Second Team All–Big East. Nate Jones epitomized the Rutgers scholar-athlete. Jones won the Big East/Aeropostale Football Scholar Athlete of the Year Award in 2003. He was also a National Football Foundation

SCHUTT
BIG EAST
23

Left: Nate Jones won awards at Rutgers on the field and in the classroom. (Courtesy James D. Smith/ Dallas Cowboys)

Right: Scarlet quarterback Ryan Hart completed 295 passes during the 2004 football season. (Courtesy Jim O'Connor/ Rutgers Athletic Communications)

College Football Hall of Fame Scholar-Athlete. Nate Jones signed a pro contract with the Dallas Cowboys.

Jarvis Johnson led the Scarlet defense with 97 tackles in 2003 and was named ECAC All-East. Raheem Orr was voted Rutgers' Most Valuable Player. Orr registered a total of 18 quarterback sacks during his Rutgers career as a defensive end. Orr was ECAC All-East and All–Big East Conference. He played in the Blue-Gray Football Classic. Raheem Orr was a seventh-round pick in the NFL draft by the Houston Texans. He also played for the New York Giants. Defensive back Brandon Haw inked a pro contract with the Philadelphia Eagles and also played for the Frankfurt Galaxy in the NFL Europe league.

Games against Michigan State, Kent State, and Vanderbilt added spice to the steady Scarlet diet of Big East rivals in 2004. The Big East Conference was in a state of flux. Miami and Virginia Tech had left to join the Atlantic Coast Conference. Boston College and Temple would also soon be gone. A new Big East Conference was about to be formed.

Rutgers' 2004 squad was led by three outstanding captains. They were Ray Pilch, Tres Moses, and Jarvis Johnson. Pilch and Johnson had lettered for four straight years. Moses would also become a four-year letterman.

The offensive huddle looked like a who's who of future Scarlet record setters. Ryan Hart, Brian Leonard, Clark Harris, and Shawn Tucker were all back. Kicker Jeremy Ito was now part of the potent Scarlet scoring mix.

The offensive line had Jeremy Zuttah, John Glass, Cam Stephenson, and Corey Hyman.

On defense, Coach Schiano had Quintero Frierson, Gary Gibson, David Hurley, J'vonne Parker, Ramel Meekins, Ryan Neill, and Val Barnaby. Meekins, Neill, and Barnaby were the scourge of opposing quarterbacks because of their fearsome pass-rushing abilities.

Rutgers started the year with a great win over Michigan State. New Scarlet place kicker Jeremy Ito booted four field goals in that contest. Just when hopes for a big year were rising, the Scarlet Knights were upset by New Hampshire in game two. Kent State was a check mark in the win column as the Knights recorded their second victory of the year. In a tough loss to Syracuse, Scarlet tight end Clark Harris caught 5 passes for 51 yards and 2 touchdowns. Rutgers rebounded with a solid victory over Vanderbilt. Rutgers' "Mr. Everything" on offense, Brian Leonard, had a big day. Leonard ran for 150 yards and pulled in 9 passes for 64 yards. He scored 4 touchdowns. The following week Rutgers grounded the Temple Owls for win number four. Scarlet defensive back Ron Girault had 13 tackles and a key interception against Temple.

Pittsburgh topped Rutgers the following game. Boston College and Navy also got the better of Rutgers.

West Virginia and Connecticut were too much for the Knights to handle, and Rutgers finished the year with a total of 4 wins.

In the final game of the year against Connecticut, Terrence Shawell of Rutgers had a dazzling 87-yard pass completion to Tres Moses. Tres Moses was named Rutgers' Most Valuable Player at the end of the season. Moses pulled in 81 passes for 1,056 yards and 5 touchdowns in 2004.

Tight end Clark Harris caught 53 passes for 725 yards and 5 touchdowns. Brian Leonard caught 61 passes for 518 yards and 2 touchdowns. Leonard carried the ball 199 times for 732 yards and 7 touchdowns. Scarlet signal caller Ryan Hart completed 295 of 453 passes

Val Barnaby and Ryan Neill were a killer combination as Scarlet defensive ends. (Courtesy Jim O'Connor/Rutgers Athletic Communications)

Top: Tight end Clark Harris was a Scarlet fan favorite. Harris had 53 pass receptions in 2004. (Courtesy Rutgers Athletic Communications)

Bottom: Tres Moses made 81 pass receptions during the 2004 football season. (Courtesy Rutgers Athletic Communications)

Rutgers defeated Michigan State in 2004. (Courtesy Rutgers Athletic Communications)

for 3,154 yards and 17 touchdowns. The Rutgers scoring machine was now shifting into gear. Kicker Jeremy Ito was the top point producer. Ito tallied a total of 73 points in 2004.

Jeremy Ito was a First Team Freshman All-American on the squad selected by the *Sporting News*. Brian Leonard was picked a First Team All-American by *Football Weekly*. Clark Harris was selected ECAC All-East and All–Big East. Tres Moses was voted First Team ECAC All-East and First Team All–Big East.

On defense, Jarvis Johnson had 75 tackles to lead all hitters and ball hawks. Johnson signed to play in the NFL with the Baltimore Ravens. Pass-rush phenom Ryan Neill was named a First Team Big East All-Star. He was also Second Team ECAC All-East.

Rutgers stars had begun to shine on both offense and defense. The Scarlet glow was about to increase in intensity.

Head Coach Greg Schiano put it best when he said, "This is where college football began. Right here. It's important to keep that tradition alive." Football was once again alive and well on the banks of the old Raritan.

CHAPTER 14
"JUST KEEP CHOPPING!" 2005

Prior to the start of the 2005 season, the football scene at Rutgers University was electric. Scarlet supporters were charged with renewed enthusiasm and excitement. Fans were eager to see the new crop of Rutgers footballers Coach Greg Schiano had carefully cultivated from recruiting fields around the country.

New York running back Brian Leonard had passed up Penn State, Notre Dame, and Syracuse to follow his older brother Nate to the New Brunswick campus.

Offensive lineman Cam Stephenson, who was Australian by birth and Tongan on his mother's side, came to New Jersey from Harbor Junior College in Inglewood, California.

Quintero Frierson grew up a stone's throw from the University of Miami campus. Frierson came to Rutgers. Eric Foster, who played high school football in South Florida, made Rutgers his football destination.

Jamaal Westerman traveled in the opposite direction. Westerman left Canada to play football for Rutgers.

New Jersey native Ryan Neill, whose dad had played in the NFL, picked Rutgers.

Joe Porter and Val Barnaby had a short journey from Franklin to Rutgers.

Linebackers Brandon Renkart and Devraun Thompson from Piscataway, New Jersey, stayed home. Ramel Meekins came from Westwood, New Jersey. Jeremy Zuttah was from Edison, New Jersey. Kenny Britt came from Bayonne, New Jersey. Rutgers had finally begun to harvest the Garden State's gridiron talent.

Courtney Greene and Ray Rice took a roundabout path to Rutgers from New Rochelle, New York. Greene and Rice played together in high school and both originally committed to play college football for Coach Paul Pasqualoni at Syracuse. When Pasqualoni left Syracuse at the end of the 2004 season, both Courtney Greene and Ray Rice headed to Rutgers. The story is part of an ongoing tale of excellent recruitment and fine work by Coach Greg Schiano and his staff. Rutgers began to stockpile more and more quality student-athletes. Academic assistance and tutoring programs helped keep athletes in school and eligible. Rutgers' graduation rate for athletes was among the best in the nation. The talent depth problem that had plagued Rutgers for so many years was finally being rectified.

BIG EAST
RUTGERS

The Scarlet Knights were a new type of team in 2005 and the Big East was a new type of conference. Joining the Big East for the 2005 season were the University of Cincinnati, the University of Louisville, and the University of South Florida. The newcomers combined with old Big East rivals Rutgers, Pittsburgh, West Virginia, Syracuse, and Connecticut to form the new Big East Football Conference under the expert guidance of Commissioner Michael A. Tranghese.

Rutgers had a veteran club with several important new players in key positions. Newcomer Ray Rice joined Brian Leonard in the backfield. Rice was an explosive runner. He was built low to the ground, which made him tough to tackle. Ryan Hart was the senior signal caller, but he was being pressured by backup QB Mike Teel. The offensive line included Darnell Stapleton, Jeremy Zuttah, Pedro Sosa, Cameron Stephenson, John Glass, Mike Fladell, Sameeh McDonald, and Mike Gilmartin. The tight ends were potential All-American Clark Harris and super subs Sam Johnson and Anthony Cali.

Receiver Tres Moses was one of the tri-captains along with Will Gilkison and Ryan Neill.

Chris Baker, Tiquan Underwood, and Marcus Daniels were prime pass targets. Willie Foster was an opponent's nightmare on kickoff and punt returns.

The defensive line had Jamaal Westerman, Val Barnaby, Eric Foster, William Beckford, and Ryan Neill. The linebackers and defensive backs included Brandon Renkart, Devraun Thompson, Ron Girault, Derrick Roberson, Corey Barns, Jason Nugent, and Manny Collins.

Last but not least, Rutgers had a topnotch pair of kickers in Jeremy Ito and punter Joe Radigan.

Opposite: Ray Rice joined Brian Leonard in the Rutgers backfield in 2005 to form one of the best rushing combinations in the country. (Courtesy Jim O'Connor/Rutgers Athletic Communications)

Above: Rutgers' Chris Brown was an exceptional pass receiver. (Courtesy San Francisco 49ers)

Rutgers opened its 2005 gridiron campaign with a road game against the University of Illinois. Like Rutgers, Illinois is a school steeped in football tradition. It was where Harold "Red" Grange, the famous Galloping Ghost, and monster middle linebacker Dick Butkus played college football. The Scarlet Knights drew first blood with a 21-yard field goal by Jeremy Ito. Illinois battled back. Tim Brasic, the Illinois quarterback, fired a 6-yard TD pass to Jody Ellis. Illinois led 7 to 3 at the end of the first period. Rutgers' offense began to roll in the second period and the Scarlet defense stiffened.

Ryan Hart rifled a 55-yard touchdown bullet to Rutgers wide receiver Marcus Daniels. A short time later, Jeremy Ito added another field goal. This time Ito's boot was a 25-yarder, which made the score Rutgers 13 and Illinois 7. Brian Leonard then reeled in a 19-yard touchdown toss from QB Ryan Hart. Rutgers led 20 to 7 at the half.

In the third period, Brian Leonard invented a running move which from that day on became known as the "Leonard Leap." Leonard jumped over a would-be Illinois tackler on his way to scoring a spectacular 83-yard touchdown. The scoreboard read Rutgers 27 and Illinois 7 when fickle momentum changed sides. Illinois fought back and scored 20 unanswered points in the third and fourth periods. The game was tied 27 to 27 at the end of regulation time. The teams went into overtime.

Rutgers' Jeremy Ito kicked a 40-yard field goal, but Illinois scored the winning touchdown on a 2-yard run by Pierre Thomas. Illinois won 33 to 30. Rutgers had squandered a big lead and lost. Victory had slipped through the Scarlet's fingers. It was a bitter defeat. In a stone-silent locker room after a disappointing loss, Coach Greg Schiano addressed

Brian Leonard vaults over a tackler. The unique maneuver became known as the "Leonard Leap." (Courtesy Jim O'Connor/Rutgers Athletic Communications)

Opposite, top: Rutgers suffered a heartbreaking 30 to 33 overtime loss to Illinois in the opening game of the 2005 season. (Courtesy University of Illinois Division of Intercollegiate Athletics)

Opposite, bottom: After a loss to Illinois on opening day in 2005, Rutgers head coach Greg Schiano told his Scarlet team to "keep chopping!" (Courtesy Grant Halverson/Rutgers Athletic Communications)

his forlorn footballers. Schiano told his team the situation they were in was like being in a dark forest surrounded by trees. He said his players had two choices. They could curl up and cry or start chopping. The team rallied around their coach's words of woody wisdom and chose to chop! The result was the start of a new winning attitude. The Scarlet Knights began to chop their way through opponents.

The first cut of the chop came on the opening kickoff of the Scarlet's home contest against Villanova. Rutgers' Willie Foster fielded the first kick and raced 93 yards for a Scarlet score. The Villanova Wildcats came back to even the score on a Marvin Burrough pass to John Dieser. Rutgers blocked the extra point kick and the chop-a-thon began in earnest. Brian Leonard scored on a 2-yard run. Jeremy Ito boomed a 40-yard field goal. Ray Rice reached the end zone after an 11-yard scamper. Clark Harris grabbed a 15-yard TD toss from Ryan Hart. Leonard capped off Rutgers' scoring with a 2-yard touchdown run in the fourth period. The Scarlet Knights earned a 38 to 6 victory over Villanova.

In game three of the season, fullback Brian Leonard rushed for 121 yards on 24 carries and Shawn Tucker caught 3 passes for 48 yards and 1 touchdown in leading the Knights to a 17 to 3 win over the University of Buffalo.

NUGENT
91
41
E. FOSTER
56
Riddell
55
Telex
RadioCom

Left: Willie Foster had a 93-yard kickoff return for a touchdown in Rutgers' 2005 victory over Villanova. (Courtesy Rutgers Athletic Communications)

Right: Jeremy Ito kicked three field goals in Rutgers' victory over Pittsburgh in 2005. (Courtesy Chuck LeClaire/ Rutgers Athletic Communications)

The Pittsburgh Panthers took on the Scarlet Knights in game four. The Knights jumped out to a 17 to 0 lead in the first quarter. Brian Leonard pulled in a 33-yard pass from Ryan Hart and plunged into the end zone early in the contest. Kicker Jeremy Ito added the extra point and a 22-yard field goal. Willie Foster then flashed his speed in the faces of stunned Panther defenders by fielding a Pittsburgh punt and racing 71 yards to pay dirt.

In the second period Rutgers added 10 more points. Jeremy Ito booted a 26-yard field goal and Brian Leonard caught an 11-yard touchdown strike from Ryan Hart. Rutgers led 27 to 0 at the half.

Pittsburgh's talented QB Tyler Palko brought the Panthers back and outscored the Knights 14 to 7 in the third period and 15 to 3 in the fourth. In the third period, Rutgers' Tres Moses snared a 25-yard scoring pass from Ryan Hart, and in the fourth Jeremy Ito kicked a 42-yard field goal. A timely interception by Scarlet linebacker Brandon Renkart helped preserve a 37 to 29 Rutgers victory. In the win, quarterback Ryan Hart completed 12 of 25 passes for 207 yards and 2 touchdowns. Ray Rice ran for 114 yards on 15 carries.

The tall timber in the mountains of West Virginia proved to be a tough chop, and the Mountaineers edged the Knights 27 to 14 in game five.

In game six Coach Greg Schiano's gridiron ax was a lot sharper. The Knights started slow, but methodically sliced through a stubborn Syracuse defense to score 31 points in

3 quarters of play. Jeremy Ito accounted for 3 points in the first quarter on a successful 51-yard field goal. The Rutgers defense sparkled and the second score was the direct result of a defensive gem: Manny Collins blocked a Syracuse punt, then defensive back Corey Barnes pounced on the pigskin and returned it 16 yards for a touchdown.

Quarterback Mike Teel was in command of the Scarlet offense in place of Ryan Hart. In the second quarter, Teel hit Tres Moses with a 37-yard touchdown pass.

In the third, Rutgers continued to pile up points. Teel hit tight end Sam Johnson with a pass completion good for 24 yards and a touchdown.

Rutgers' Corey Barnes continued to dazzle the Scarlet fans on defense. Barnes scooped up a Syracuse fumble and dashed 26 yards for his second TD of the day. Rutgers led 31 to 0 before Syracuse put any points on the board. Syracuse kicked three field goals to close out the scoring. The Scarlet Knights bested Syracuse 31 to 9 to win their fourth game in six gridiron contests.

Game seven of the 2005 season was a nip-and-tuck battle against a tough Connecticut team. It was the game in which Rutgers rookie runner Ray Rice stepped into the spotlight.

The opening quarter came to a close with Rutgers out in front 3 to 0 thanks to a 44-yard field goal by Jeremy Ito. Connecticut regrouped and added a touchdown and a field goal. The Huskies led the Knights 10 to 3 at the break.

In the third quarter QB Ryan Hart, who was back behind center for Rutgers, completed a pass to Brian Leonard. Leonard made the catch and rumbled 19 yards into the end zone to knot the score at 10-all. Connecticut answered with a touchdown to reclaim the lead. Rutgers' Ryan Hart then connected with Tres Moses for a 31-yard completion and a touchdown. It was 17-all when the swarming Scarlet defense made a big play. A safety credited to the team provided a 2-point buffer for Rutgers.

Above: Rutgers quarterback Mike Teel threw 2 touchdown passes in a 2005 victory over Syracuse. (Courtesy Chuck LeClaire/Rutgers Athletic Communications)

Left: The Scarlet Knights' victory over Syracuse gave Rutgers their fourth win of the 2005 season. (Courtesy Syracuse Athletics)

RUTGERS
8
RUTGERS
23

Scarlet tight end Sam Johnson then caught a 15-yard touchdown toss from Ryan Hart. Rutgers' lead was a comfortable 26 to 17. However, that comfort zone soon eroded. Connecticut QB Dennis Brown threw a 15-yard touchdown pass to Jason Williams to make it a 26 to 24 game in favor of Rutgers with time winding down. The Scarlet defense stepped up once again. Rutgers' Ron Girault made a key interception to ice the Scarlet victory. Ray Rice was the star on offense for Rutgers. Rice carried the ball 27 times for a total of 215 yards!

Up next was Navy. Rutgers' Brian Leonard cruised into the end zone on a 7-yard run to score the game's first touchdown. Leonard added a 1-yard dive in the second to make Rutgers' lead 14 to 0. Midshipman Reggie Campbell then raced 60 yards with the pigskin to score a Navy touchdown. Rutgers answered. Ray Rice had a 3-yard TD plunge, which gave the Scarlet Knights a 21 to 7 lead at the half.

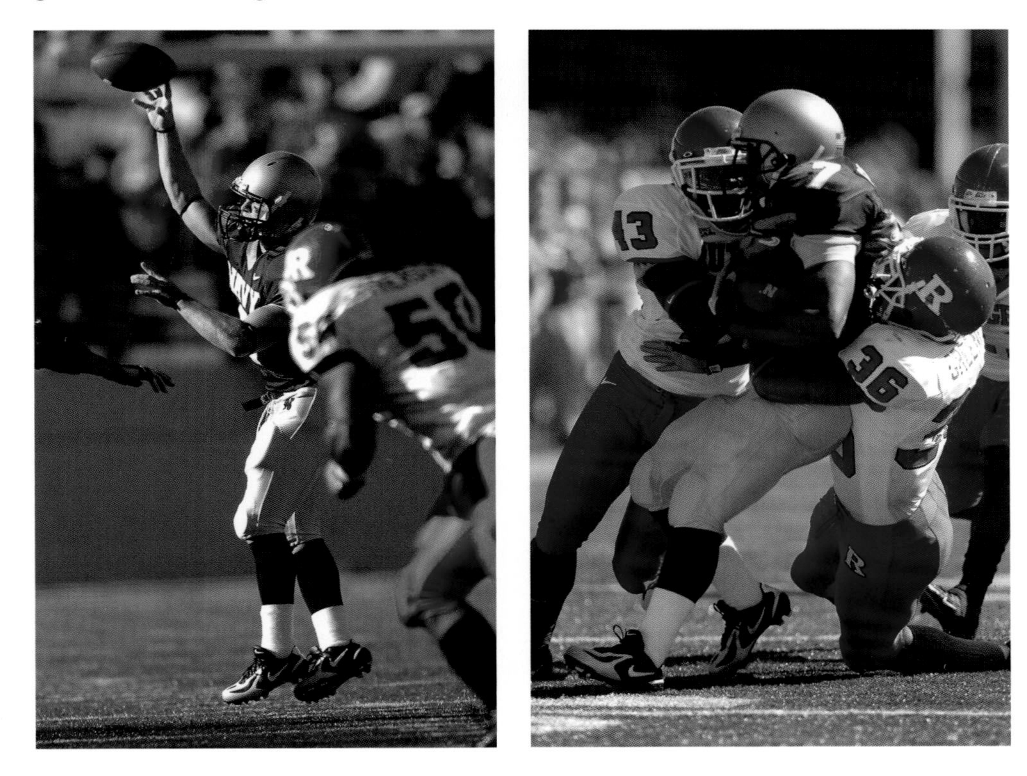

Opposite: Tres Moses catches a 31-yard touchdown pass in Rutgers' win over Connecticut during the 2005 season. (Courtesy Rutgers Athletic Communications)

Left: Rutgers' wins over Navy in 2005 and 2006 made the Scarlet Knights bowl eligible two years in a row. (Courtesy U.S. Naval Academy Communications)

Right: Rutgers defense shut down a potent Navy offense in 2005 and 2006. (Courtesy Tomasso DeRosa/Rutgers Athletic Communications)

Navy tallied a touchdown to open the third quarter. Jeremy Ito's 18-yard field goal made the score Rutgers 24 and Navy 14 as the third quarter came to a close. In the fourth, Navy scored a touchdown, but once again Rutgers' Ray Rice had a quick reply. Rice bulled his way into the end zone from 2 yards out to make the final score Rutgers 31 and Navy 21. Rice carried the ball 21 times for 80 yards and 2 touchdowns against Navy. Defensive back Ron Girault had an outstanding day against Navy. Girault recorded ten tackles. He also had a fumble recovery and an interception.

Game nine against South Florida turned into an offensive shootout. The South Florida Bulls gored the Rutgers defense for 21 points in the opening period. The Rutgers offense was penned up and held out of the end zone. South Florida led 21 to zip going into the second period of play.

Scarlet fullback Brian Leonard broke the ice when he caught a 3-yard touchdown pass from Ryan Hart. Unfortunately for Rutgers, South Florida replied by scoring a touchdown

Right: Darnell Stapleton (#53) was a member of a tough offensive line that blocked well on running and passing plays. (Courtesy Patti Banks/Rutgers Athletic Communications)

Below: Quarterback Ryan Hart passes his way into the Rutgers record books in 2005. (Courtesy Rutgers Athletic Communications)

of its own. Ryan Hart drove the Scarlet offense down the field and capped the march with a 3-yard touchdown toss to Tres Moses.

South Florida kicker Kyle Bronson added another 3 points for the Bulls. The score at the half was South Florida 31 and Rutgers 14.

Jeremy Ito's 29-yard chip-shot field goal early in the third period made the count South Florida 31 and Rutgers 17. Once again, the Bulls answered with a touchdown. Rutgers' Brian Leonard then bullied his way into the South Florida end zone from the 1-yard stripe to cut the lead to 13 points. Clark Harris's 4-yard touchdown reception in the fourth narrowed the Bulls' scoreboard bulge. It was South Florida 37 and Rutgers 31 with still time to play. With less than two minutes left, South Florida iced the game with a touchdown and a successful 2-point play. The Bulls beat the Scarlet Knights 45 to 31.

Ray Rice rushed for 158 yards against South Florida and Devraun Thompson had 13 tackles on defense.

Rutgers traveled to Kentucky to play Louisville, in its next game. Louisville, guided by its outstanding quarterback, Brian Brohm, got the better of Rutgers in that gridiron outing. The only points Rutgers could muster were a Jeremy Ito field goal and a safety that came after Manny Collins blocked a Louisville punt and the ball bounced out of the end zone.

Rutgers entered its final game of the season against Cincinnati with a record of 6 wins and 4 losses. The Scarlet Knights were already bowl eligible, but wanted another win to impress bowl scouts.

The Rutgers Scarlet Knights left nothing to doubt in their final contest. The Knights poured it on against the Bearcats. Jeremy Ito booted a 32-yard field goal. Brian Leonard scored a touchdown on a 12-yard run. Rutgers raced out to a 10–0 lead by the end of the first quarter. Cincinnati battled back to score 3 points on a Kevin Lovell field goal in the second quarter.

Field general Ryan Hart rallied his Scarlet troopers. Hart hit tight end Clark Harris with a 24-yard touchdown pass. Jeremy Ito blasted field goals of 31 yards and 41 yards. Rutgers led 23 to 3 at halftime.

Ray Rice ran wild for Rutgers in the third period. Rice tallied a touchdown on a dazzling 58-yard dash, and added another touchdown on an 11-yard scamper.

Cincinnati came back to score a touchdown in the fourth period, but the game was already out of reach. Rutgers' Brian Leonard added a 1-yard run for an insurance touchdown to end the scoring. Rutgers won big-time and recorded a 44 to 9 victory. Ray Rice totaled 195 rushing yards on the day. Ryan Hart completed 16 of 26 passes for 237 yards and 1 touchdown. Rutgers had chopped its way to an impressive season record of 7 wins and 4 losses. The big news was that the Scarlet Knights were going bowling for the first time since 1978, when Rutgers had played Arizona State in the Garden State Bowl. Rutgers was invited to play in the Insight Bowl in Arizona. In an amazing coincidence, Rutgers' opponent in the Insight Bowl was . . . Arizona State!

Rutgers' first trip to a major bowl in almost thirty years became a major sports story all across the nation. More than three hundred articles in a variety of newspapers large and small traced Rutgers' miracle journey from the brink of college football oblivion back to its current bowl-worthy accomplishments. Coach Greg Schiano and his Scarlet squad had chopped through a petrified forest of obstacles to obtain well-deserved national notoriety. America's oldest college football program had suddenly become America's newest Cinderella squad.

Rutgers sold more than seven thousand tickets to the Insight Bowl as fans flocked to Arizona in support of their Scarlet Knights. One Rutgers loyal son, award-winning actor

Coach Greg Schiano guided the Scarlet Knights to a 7–4 record in 2005, which earned Rutgers an invitation to play in the Insight Bowl against Arizona State. (Courtesy Grant Halverson/Rutgers Athletic Communications)

James Gandolfini, was present for the ceremonial coin toss before the game. Representing Arizona State was nationally known comedian and talk show host Jimmy Kimmel. A crowd of 43,538 football fans were on hand to watch the game, which was nationally televised. In fact, the 2005 Insight Bowl was the fourth highest rated bowl game on ESPN and ESPN2 that season.

Rutgers drew first blood when Ryan Hart hit tight end Clark Harris with a 1-yard TD pass in the early minutes of the first period. The Arizona State Sun Devils came right back. Quarterback Rudy Carpenter hit Matt Miller with a 43-yard touchdown strike. The Knights' Ryan Hart then rifled a pass to big Brian Leonard, who caught the bullet and raced 31 yards for a second Rutgers touchdown. Jeremy Ito added a 25-yard field goal and Rutgers led 17 to 7 at the end of the first period.

The Sun Devils kicked a field goal in the second quarter to make the score 17 to 10. Brian Leonard's 3-yard touchdown burst gave Rutgers a 24 to 10 bulge over Arizona State. The Sun Devils answered with a touchdown of their own to make it a 24 to 17 game at the half with Rutgers on top.

Arizona State added a touchdown in the third to close the gap. A 23-yard field goal by Rutgers' Jeremy Ito gained back a little ground. Another Sun Devils touchdown combined with a 52-yard Jeremy Ito field goal for Rutgers made the score Arizona State 31 and Rutgers 30 at the end of the third quarter.

Ito got his foot into another kick early in the fourth quarter. His 48-yard field goal attempt was good. It was Jeremy Ito's fourth field goal of the day. Rutgers led 33 to 31. Back came the Arizona Sun Devils. Rudy Carpenter threw a touchdown pass of 42 yards to Matt Miller. Rudy Burgess ran 4 yards for another Sun Devils touchdown. ASU was leading 45 to 33 when Tres Moses caught a 29-yard touchdown pass from Ryan Hart. Jeremy Ito added the extra point. Rutgers ended up on the short side of a 45 to 40 score, but the Knights had played inspired football against a very talented opponent. It was a good day for Rutgers and the state of New Jersey. Scarlet fans knew that even better days were only a season away.

Quarterback Ryan Hart concluded his Rutgers career as the Scarlet's all-time leading passer. In 2005 Hart completed 155 of 255 passes for 2,135 yards and 18 touchdowns. As a Scarlet Knight, Ryan Hart was good on 735 of 1,217 pass attempts for 8,482 yards and 52 touchdowns.

Tres Moses became Rutgers' all-time leading receiver. In 2005 Moses caught 45 passes for 758 yards and 5 touchdowns. Over his career Moses snared a total of 192 passes for 2,522 yards and 16 touchdowns. Tres Moses was named All–Big East. Offensive lineman Jack Glass was selected ECAC All-East and All–Big East Conference.

Ray Rice led the team in rushing with 1,120 yards on 195 carries. He scored 5 touchdowns. Rice was named a Third Team Freshman All-American by the *Sporting News*.

Shawn Tucker made 32 receptions for 484 yards and 1 touchdown. Tucker totaled 109 catches for 1,471 yards and 4 touchdowns over his career.

Tight end Clark Harris caught 38 passes for 584 yards and 4 touchdowns. Clark Harris was voted ECAC All-East and All–Big East Conference.

Willie Foster caught 8 passes for 129 yards in 2005. He returned 30 kickoffs for 736 yards and 1 touchdown. Foster also fielded 15 punts, which he returned for 164 yards and 1 touchdown. Willie Foster was ECAC All-East and All–Big East.

Rutgers tight end Clark Harris scores the first points in the 2005 Insight Bowl on a 1-yard touchdown pass from Ryan Hart. (Courtesy Rutgers Athletic Communications)

Jeremy Ito kicked 20 field goals in 27 attempts in 2005. He was also good on 40 of 40 extra points. Ito's total of 100 points was second best on the team. Joe Radigan punted

BIG EAST
RUTGERS
23

Opposite: The Scarlet Knights' Brian Leonard tallied 2 touchdowns against the Arizona Sun Devils in the 2005 Insight Bowl. (Courtesy Elane Coleman/ Rutgers Athletic Communications)

Above: Coach Greg Schiano talks over defensive strategy with tri-captain Ryan Neill in the 2005 Insight Bowl. (Courtesy Rutgers Athletic Communications)

Left: Rutgers footballers celebrate playing in the 2005 Insight Bowl against Arizona State. (Courtesy Rutgers Athletic Communications)

Right: Tight end Clark Harris caught 6 passes for 85 yards in the Insight Bowl. (Courtesy Rutgers Athletic Communications)

Right: Willie Foster returned a kickoff and a punt for touchdowns in 2005. (Courtesy Grant Halverson/Rutgers Athletic Communications)

Opposite: Val Barnaby had 10 quarterback sacks in 2005. (Courtesy Rutgers Athletic Communications)

60 times for 2,361 yards that same season. Fullback Brian Leonard led Rutgers in scoring in 2005 with 102 points. Leonard tallied 11 rushing touchdowns. He ran for 740 yards on 173 carries. He also caught 55 passes for 568 yards and 6 touchdowns. Brian Leonard was named a First Team All-American by *Pro Football Weekly*. He was also All–Big East.

On defense, end Val Barnaby had 41 tackles and 10 sacks in 2005. Ramel Meekins totaled 63 tackles and 9 sacks. Courtney Greene led the Scarlet Knights with a total of 116 tackles. Greene was a First Team Freshman All-American choice by *College Football News* and the Football Writers' Association of America. He was a Second Team All-American on Rivals.com and a Third Team choice on the *Sporting News* freshman squad.

Defensive end Ryan Neill registered 10 quarterback sacks and 71 tackles in 2005. He had a total of 19 sacks over his career. Neill was an honorable mention All-American on SportsIllustrated.com. In addition, he was ECAC All-East and All–Big East.

Moving on to pro football careers at the conclusion of their college careers were a number of Scarlet Knights. Ryan Neill signed an NFL contract with the Buffalo Bills. Val Barnaby inked a pro deal with the Detroit Lions. Offensive lineman Sameeh McDonald also signed with the Detroit Lions. Wide receiver Chris Baker traveled west to try out with the San Francisco 49ers. Tres Moses went to the Baltimore Ravens. Defensive back Jason Nugent headed north to Canada, where he signed with the Edmonton Eskimos of the Canadian Football League. Wherever they traveled and whatever league they played in after college, Rutgers players would always remember Coach Greg Schiano's advice uttered after the 2005 Illinois game. If things look bleak and the odds seem to be against you, don't give up, just keep chopping!

RUTGERS
94

RUTGERS
91
10
10

Opposite: Defensive end Ryan Neill was Honorable Mention All-America. (Courtesy Rutgers Athletic Communications)

Left: Greg Schiano walks softly but carries a sharp axiom. (Courtesy Patti Banks/Rutgers Athletic Communications)

CHAPTER 15
CHOP . . . CHOP . . . TIMBER! 2006

Would he be back to play another college season or would he turn pro? That was the big question Rutgers fans asked when football talk turned to the topic of Brian Leonard. The Scarlet Knights' star running back was already highly regarded as a pro prospect. It was Brian Leonard's decision to make. Leonard chose to play his senior year at Rutgers. Scarlet football fans across the nation were delighted by his decision.

Coach Greg Schiano and his assistants were also thrilled by Leonard's choice. They quickly began to make plans for the 2006 season. Schiano's support staff was a skilled and experienced group.

Jay Butler played college football at Bucknell. Robert Fraser coached at Holy Cross and Colgate. Chris Demarest coached at North Carolina State. Phil Galiano coached at New Haven and Villanova. Cary Godette coached in the NFL for the Miami Dolphins, the Carolina Panthers, and the Arizona Cardinals. Kyle Flood coached at Hofstra and Delaware. Chris Hewitt played for the New Orleans Saints and coached with the Cleveland Browns. Robert Jackson coached at Oregon State. Joe Susan coached at Bucknell, Princeton, and Davidson. Darren Rizzi coached at Colgate and Northeastern.

Coach Greg Schiano's Scarlet Knights were eager to do some chopping in 2006. (Courtesy Jim O'Connor/Rutgers Athletic Communications)

John McNulty coached at Connecticut and in the NFL with the Jacksonville Jaguars and the Dallas Cowboys. Craig Ver Steeg coached at Cincinnati, Harvard, Utah, and Illinois. In the NFL Ver Steeg worked with the Chicago Bears.

Head Coach Greg Schiano and his staff readied their team for what they hoped would be a banner season in 2006. Record-setting quarterback Ryan Hart was gone, but his replacement was young top gun Mike Teel. Sure-handed receiver Tres Moses had moved on. That receiving vacancy would be filled by Tiquan Underwood, Marcus Daniels, and Kenny Britt. The offensive line was well schooled and stone-wall solid.

Brian Leonard and Ray Rice were soundly backed up by Jean Beljour and Kordell Young. The Knights were well stocked at tight end with All-American candidate Clark Harris, Sam Johnson, and Anthony Cali.

Above: Rutgers was strong on both sides of the ball in 2006. (Courtesy Grant Halverson/Rutgers Athletic Communications)

Below: Rutgers' Ramel Meekins was on the preseason Outland Trophy watch list. (Courtesy Joe Camporeale/Rutgers Athletic Communications)

Opposite: The Scarlet Knights' Courtney Greene was on the Bronko Nagurski Trophy preseason watch list in 2006. (Courtesy Rutgers Athletic Communications)

Defensively the Scarlet Knights had Ramel Meekins, William Beckford, Eric Foster, and Jamaal Westerman to wreak havoc on both passing and rushing downs.

Linebackers Quintero Frierson, Devraun Thompson, Brandon Renkart, and Kevin Malast would anchor an active, swarming defense. In the defensive secondary was Courtney Greene, Joe Porter, Derrick Roberson, Ron Girault, Manny Collins, Jason McCourty, and Glen Lee.

In addition, the Knights were blessed with a group of superb specialists. Joe Radigan was a top-rated punter. Place kicker Jeremy Ito was on his way to rewriting many Rutgers kicking records. Return man Willie Foster had been named the Big East Special Teams Player of the Year.

Preseason pollsters touted the talent of Rutgers running back Brian Leonard. Leonard was rated the top fullback in the country by several experts and publications, including the *Sporting News*. In addition, Brian Leonard became Rutgers' first Heisman Trophy candidate since Bill Austin in 1958.

The Scarlet Knights opened their 2006 season at Chapel Hill, North Carolina. The North Carolina Tar Heels football squad, coached by John Bunting, had posted a record of 5 wins and 6 losses the year before. The Tar Heels returned thirty-seven lettermen in 2006 and had high hopes of going to a bowl at season's end. North Carolina was led by quarterback Joe Dailey, running back Ronnie McGill, and wide receiver Brooks Foster.

After a scoreless defensive tussle for most of the first period, Rutgers broke open the goose egg when Scarlet field general Mike Teel

RUTGERS

R

marched his troops 93 yards in 12 plays. Ray Rice rambled into the end zone from 2 yards out to give Rutgers a 6 to 0 edge. Jeremy Ito added the extra point in automatic fashion.

In the second quarter, the Tar Heels traded punch for punch with the Knights. North Carolina QB Joe Dailey engineered a drive that ended with Dailey's 4-yard dash to pay dirt. The score remained knotted until late in the second when Ray Rice once again broke free from the sticky-fingered Tar Heel tacklers. Rice raced 7 yards to give Rutgers the lead once again. The Scarlet Knights were leading 14 to 7 when North Carolina came calling into Rutgers territory. Tar Heels kicker Connor Barth booted a 47-yard field goal to cut the Scarlet lead. Rutgers had a 14 to 10 advantage at the half.

After the break, Ray Rice churned up big chunks of yardage behind bone-crushing blocking from Pedro Sosa, Jeremy Zuttah, Cam Stephenson, and Darnell Stapleton. Rice notched his third touchdown of the day on a 10-yard sprint. Rutgers raised its lead to 21 to 10.

Late in the fourth, the Tar Heels mustered a rally. Joe Dailey hit North Carolina receiver Hakeem Nicks with a 2-yard touchdown pass. Tar Heels QB Dailey, a New Jersey native from Jersey City, had a hot hand in the air all day. Dailey completed 24 of 36 passes for 234 yards against a veteran Scarlet secondary. However, at a key moment Rutgers' ball hawks came up big. On the important 2-point try, Manny Collins picked off Joe Dailey's pass to make Rutgers' lead 21 to 16 with less than two minutes to play in the game. The Scarlet Knights iced win number one. Ray Rice carried the ball 31 times for a total of 201 yards. He also racked up 3 touchdowns. Rutgers was on the move and football fans across the land were suddenly infected with Scarlet fever.

The Fighting Illini of Illinois squared off against the Knights in Piscataway, New Jersey, for game two. The defense turned up the Scarlet heat early in the contest. Rutgers blocked

Opposite: Ray Rice ran for 201 yards and tallied 3 touchdowns in the Scarlet Knights' opening day win over North Carolina in 2006. (Courtesy Jim O'Connor/Rutgers Athletic Communications)

Below: Devraun Thompson (#55) led a tough Rutgers defense against North Carolina. (Courtesy Grant Halverson/Rutgers Athletic Communications)

Quarterback Mike Teel (#14) guided the Rutgers offense during the 2006 season. (Courtesy Chuck LeClaire/Rutgers Athletic Communications)

an Illinois punt, which was scooped up by senior defensive back Derrick Roberson. Roberson scrambled into the end zone to tally the first points of the contest. The Scarlet Knights were up 7 to 0 when Illinois QB Tim Brasic had a pass pilfered by Rutgers' Devin McCourty. McCourty raced 38 yards with the pigskin for a touchdown. The home team had a comfortable 14 to zip edge when the offense got into gear.

Quarterback Mike Teel capped a fine drive by throwing a 1-yard touchdown toss to tight end Clark Harris. A muffed extra point try made the score Rutgers 20 and Illinois 0. Ray Rice kept the ground game going. Rice ran for 108 total yards and added a touchdown on a 1-yard scoot into the end zone. Jeremy Ito contributed a 37-yard field goal to give Rutgers a 30 to nil lead at the half.

The Rutgers defense sustained their shutout caliber of play in the second half. The Illinois offense never crossed the midfield stripe. Scarlet kicker Jeremy Ito booted a 39-yard field goal in the third quarter to close out the scoring for the day. Rutgers won a big 33 to 0 decision over Illinois. It was win number two.

A strange and interesting story was beginning to unfold. It involved the offense. Heisman Trophy candidate Brian Leonard was now sharing the spotlight with Ray Rice. Rice had gained 309 yards in two games and scored 4 touchdowns. Some sports fans thought tension might develop between the two stars. They were wrong! The two friends didn't care who gained the most yards or who scored the most touchdowns. Leonard and Rice were not concerned about personal glory or individual accolades. The two talented Scarlet Knights backs just wanted to win. When one carried the ball, the other blocked with gusto, and vice versa. The unselfish attitude they shared proved to be a winning one—and win they did.

Coach Frank Solich's Ohio University Bobcats were the Knights' next opponents. Rutgers and Ohio were meeting on the gridiron for the first time since 1937. In that first contest, Ohio had emerged from the fray victorious by the score of 13 to 0. Rutgers was about to pay back the Bobcats for the defeat.

Quarterback Austen Everson made the Ohio offense go. In fact, the Bobcats scored first in the 2006 meeting between the two schools. Everson hit Tom Christy with a 1-yard toss and Ohio jumped out to an early 7 to 0 lead. Rutgers roared back with its defense leading the way. Ron Girault picked off an Ohio pass and returned it 39 yards. Out came the Scarlet offense. Rice broke across the goal line from 4 yards out and the score was tied at 7-all. The game stayed knotted at 7 apiece until the beginning of the second quarter, when Scarlet kicker Jeremy Ito nailed a 29-yard field goal. The kick made the score 10 to 7 Rutgers.

Rutgers' defense continued to pen up the Bobcats offense throughout the first half. The Scarlet aerial attack sputtered and Rutgers stayed on the ground, putting the ball in the hands of Ray Rice 29 times. He responded with a total of 190 rushing yards. Rice tallied a second touchdown by plowing into the end zone from 4 yards out. Before the first half ended, the defense again came up big. Linebacker Brandon Renkart pounced on a Bobcat fumble in the end zone for another Rutgers touchdown. The score was 24 to 7 at the break, and that's where it remained until the end of the game. Rutgers had win number three under its belt. Scarlet running back Ray Rice was off to a phenomenal start. In three games Rice had gained 498 yards and scored 6 touchdowns. Football experts and fans across the nation were starting to notice Ray Rice and Rutgers.

Rutgers defense kept chopping.
(Courtesy Rutgers Athletic Communications)

Linebacker Brandon Renkart recovered a fumble for a touchdown against Ohio. (Courtesy Jim O'Connor/Rutgers Athletic Communications)

Rice was the nation's fourth leading rusher when Rutgers took on Howard in Piscataway, New Jersey, the next week. The contest between the Scarlet Knights and the Division 1-AA Howard Bison was expected to be a mismatch, and that's exactly how it turned out. The Rutgers offense scored touchdowns on 4 of its 8 first-half possessions.

The first Knight to find the end zone was tight end Clark Harris, who pulled in a 45-yard scoring pass from quarterback Mike Teel. Fullback Brian Leonard broke into the scoring column for the first time in 2006 with 2 rushing touchdowns in the first half.

Before the first half ended, Ray Rice tallied his first touchdown of the afternoon with a 3-yard burst into the end zone.

In the third period Rutgers fans were treated to a second helping of Rice as the human dynamo dressed in Scarlet powered the pigskin to pay dirt from the 1-yard line. A short time later defensive back Courtney Greene pilfered a Howard pass. The interception set up a third Ray Rice touchdown.

The game was under Rutgers' control and most of the Scarlet starters gave way to a talented group of backups. On the day Brian Leonard rushed for 63 yards and had 2 touchdowns. Leonard had already rushed for more than 2,450 yards in his career and there were still eight games left on the regular season schedule. Ray Rice ran for 105 yards on the day and tallied 3 touchdowns. He now had six straight games where he'd rushed for more than 100 yards.

The 56 to 7 victory made Rutgers 4–0 on the season. It was the best start for a Scarlet Knights squad since 1980. College football pollsters noticed and rewarded the efforts of Coach Greg Schiano's undefeated Knights. Rutgers was voted number 23 in the national poll of college teams. It was the first time a football squad from the State University of New Jersey had been ranked in the Top 25 in thirty years. The University of South Florida was next on the chopping block.

The Big East gridiron clash between South Florida and Rutgers was nationally televised on ESPN.

South Florida quarterback Matt Grothe was a double threat on offense. He could run as well as he could throw. Defending against Grothe would be no easy chore. The best way to combat Grothe's skills was to keep the Bulls' offensive on the sidelines.

Rutgers controlled the game's tempo in the early going. QB Mike Teel engineered a 12-play, 29-yard drive march that ended with Ray Rice bounding into the end zone from the 3. Rutgers took an early 7 to zip lead. South Florida mustered a march of its own, but a Mike Benzer field goal attempt fizzled.

Rutgers' superb place kicker Jeremy Ito got the chance to show off his leg strength and boomed a 32-yard bullet through the uprights. Rutgers increased its lead to 10 to nothing.

Left: Heisman Trophy candidate Ray Rice was a fan favorite. Rice ran for 202 yards in the Scarlet Knights' win over South Florida. (Courtesy Tom Ciszek/Rutgers Athletic Communications)

Below: Courtney Greene had a big game on defense against the Howard Bison. (Courtesy Patti Banks/Rutgers Athletic Communications)

23
81
GERMANY
99

Brian Leonard (with football) tallied a pair of touchdowns in Rutgers' 56 to 7 victory over Howard in 2006. (Courtesy Elane Coleman/Rutgers Athletic Communications)

The Rutgers–South Florida football clash was on national television. (Courtesy Joe Camporeale/Rutgers Athletic Communications)

However, the Scarlet lead didn't hold, as quarterback Matt Grothe ran for 2 South Florida scores before the half ended. South Florida was on top 14 to 10 over Rutgers at the break.

In the second half, Rutgers' Jeremy Ito made it a 1-point contest as he kicked a successful 40-yard field goal. It was South Florida 14 and Rutgers 13 early in the third. Ray Rice got back into overdrive in the fourth quarter and scored the go-ahead points on a 7-yard touchdown scamper. Rutgers went for 2 points and the attempt fell short. It was Rutgers 19 and South Florida 14.

Rutgers' defense stiffened and the South Florida offense went three and out on the next series. Rutgers' offense suffered a slight stall and Jeremy Ito was pressed into service to try a 53-yard field goal. Ito was good on the longest kick of his young career and the Rutgers advantage over South Florida was increased to 22 to 14.

There were less than three minutes to play in the game when Jeremy Ito was again called on to try a long field goal. This time the kick attempt was blocked by the Bulls. South Florida pounced on the pigskin at the Rutgers 36-yard line. A touchdown and a 2-point play would tie the game.

South Florida signal caller Matt Grothe went to work. A pass completion and a penalty for roughing the passer gave South Florida a first down at the Rutgers 19-yard line. After a questionable pass interference call against Rutgers gave the Bulls the ball at the 6-yard stripe, an illegal block call against South Florida wiped out a Bulls touchdown pass. With time ticking down, Matt Grothe fired a completion to Ean Randolph in the back of the end zone. The score was Rutgers 22 and South Florida 20 with fifteen seconds left to play. South Florida lined up for the 2-point attempt to tie the contest. Scarlet defensive back Jason McCourty then made the play that saved the day. McCourty knocked down Matt Grothe's pass on the 2-point play to preserve the Rutgers win. The Knights emerged victorious with a 22 to 20 hard-fought victory.

Jeremy Zuttah and the Rutgers offensive line provided the blocking that helped Ray Rice rush for 202 yards and 2 touchdowns against South Florida. (Courtesy Patti Banks/Rutgers Athletic Communications)

Tiquan Underwood caught 2 touchdown passes against Navy in 2006. (Courtesy Chuck LeClaire/Rutgers Athletic Communications)

On the day, Rutgers' Ray Rice rushed for 202 yards and 2 touchdowns before a national TV audience. Whispers began to be uttered about Rice's accomplishments. His name was mentioned as a potential Heisman Trophy candidate. Rutgers was also a football buzzword. Everyone was talking about the surprising Cinderella team of the East. The 5–0 Scarlet Knights were a force to be reckoned with.

Navy hoped to turn the tide on the sudden wave of Rutgers hype flooding media outlets. Coach Paul Johnson's Midshipmen were a very sound football squad. Navy had a record of 5 wins and 2 losses and averaged more than 350 rushing yards per game. For the second week in a row the Rutgers defense would be sorely tested.

The Navy offense was spearheaded by star quarterback Brian Hampton. Hampton was a better runner than Matt Grothe of South Florida, who'd been a terror for Rutgers to defend against. Rutgers' defense, which was personally coached by Greg Schiano, played inspired football that day. Navy's feared option offense sputtered and the game was scoreless for the first half. The Navy team suffered a serious setback when their leading rusher, Brian Hampton, injured his knee and could not finish the game. The Navy offense never fully recovered from the loss of its star quarterback.

Rutgers' offense got its act together in the second period. Jeremy Ito blasted a 30-yard field goal to put up the first points of the day. On their next offensive possession, Scarlet QB Mike Teel was on target with a 25-yard touchdown pass to Tiquan Underwood. Rutgers went up 10 to 0 over Navy.

Navy's first offensive possession of the third period proved disastrous. The Midshipmen were quickly forced to punt, and Rutgers' Tim Brown rushed in to block the kick. The Scarlet Knights offense took over and scuttled the Navy defense. Field general Mike Teel fired a 9-yard touchdown pass to Tiquan Underwood to cap the drive. Underwood's second TD catch of the day made the score 17 to 0 in favor of Rutgers.

When another Navy offensive drive fizzled, the Midshipmen were forced to punt again. This time defensive back Glen Lee was Johnny-on-the-spot for Rutgers. Lee bolted in to smother the kick. Rutgers recovered the ball and the offense took over. The block resulted in a 24-yard field goal by Jeremy Ito. The Rutgers advantage jumped to 20 to zip.

Rutgers continued to dominate on defense and offense. Scarlet quarterback Mike Teel connected with receiver James Townsend on a 30-yard scoring play. It was Teel's third touchdown pass of the day. He completed 15 of 26 passes for 215 yards in the contest.

Running back Kordell Young added a short touchdown run late in the fourth period to close out the scoring for Rutgers. The final was Rutgers 34 and Navy 0. Ray Rice, Rutgers' star running back, ran for 93 yards on the day, ending his streak of consecutive games in which he rushed for 100 yards or more. Rice gave little if any thought to the end of the streak. He was happy about the victory, which made Rutgers bowl eligible for the second straight year. The Scarlet Knights owned a 6–0 record and were hungry for more victories.

Rutgers moved up in the national polls and was ranked 19th in the nation before its game against the Pittsburgh Panthers. The game was touted as a key Big East matchup. Pittsburgh, coached by ex-NFL gridiron mentor Dave Wannstadt, was led by its outstanding quarterback, Tyler Palko. When the game began, the high-powered Panther offense

was successfully stymied by the Scarlet defense. Rutgers held the Panthers scoreless in the first half and allowed Pittsburgh just 58 yards in offense. Rutgers' big offensive machine misfired slightly and could manage only 2 field goals by the Scarlet's star kicker, Jeremy Ito.

The Panthers, who had won four games in a row coming into the Rutgers contest, trailed the Knights 6 to 0 at the half. Pittsburgh stormed back in the third period. After a Panthers drive stalled, Pittsburgh's Conor Lee kicked a 46-yard field goal. The score was 6 to 3 and Rutgers needed to generate some offense if it hoped to remain unbeaten.

The Scarlet Knights regrouped on offense and responded with a 72-yard drive on 9 plays, which concluded with a Mike Teel to Tiquan Underwood touchdown. The big play on the drive was a spectacular 21-yard scamper by fullback Brian Leonard. Rutgers was up 13 to 3, but the game was far from over.

Tyler Palko sparked the Pittsburgh offense by completing long passes to Oderick Turner and Darrell Strong. Palko connected with Turner on an 8-yard touchdown strike in the fourth period. The Panthers closed the scoring gap, making it Rutgers 13 and Pittsburgh 10. Rutgers' undefeated season suddenly seemed to be in jeopardy. Momentum was swinging to the Panthers' sideline.

Rutgers offense was experiencing a short hiccup when Ray Rice turned the tide for the Scarlet. Rice took a handoff from Mike Teel and looked for daylight. The offensive line parted the Panthers defenders like Moses facing the Red Sea. Rice burst through the line and blazed down the field for a 63-yard gain that broke the back of the Panther defenders.

Opposite, top: Rutgers celebrated its sixth straight victory of the 2006 season with a win over Navy. (Courtesy Rutgers Athletic Communications)

Opposite, bottom: Cam Stephenson and the offensive line made some big blocks in Rutgers' game against Pittsburgh in 2006. (Courtesy Patti Banks/Rutgers Athletic Communications)

Above: Ray Rice rushed for 225 yards against Pittsburgh in 2006. (Courtesy Tom Ciszek/Rutgers Athletic Communications)

After a short run by Brian Leonard and a penalty against Pittsburgh, Rice rammed into the end zone to give Rutgers a 20 to 10 lead.

Pittsburgh's Tyler Palko tried to regroup, but was pressured and pressured by the relentless Rutgers defense. The Knights' Jamaal Westerman dropped Palko for an important sack. Palko was further pressured into throwing three incompletions. Rutgers took over and successfully killed the clock. Ray Rice had had another big day. He carried the ball 39 times for 225 yards. Rice was looking more and more like a Heisman Trophy contender and Rutgers was looking more and more like a Top 10 team.

Rutgers jumped up in the polls. The Scarlet Knights were ranked number 15 in the country prior to their meeting with the Connecticut Huskies. Only two other Rutgers teams in history had been ranked so high. They were the undefeated teams of 1961 and 1976. Rutgers was bowl eligible and undefeated after seven regular-season games. The Scarlet Knights were the talk of college football and the surprise team of the 2006 season. They were the number 12 team in the Bowl Championship Series rankings, which determined the eventual National Champion. However, Rutgers wasn't thinking about BCS bowls when it played the University of Connecticut in Piscataway. The Scarlet Knights had but one thought. That thought was to win.

The Rutgers-Connecticut gridiron clash was played on Thursday night and televised. Rutgers first scored when Ray Rice rumbled into the end zone from the 5-yard mark.

Quarterback Mike Teel guided Rutgers to a victory over Connecticut. (Courtesy Chuck LeClaire/Rutgers Athletic Communications)

The Scarlet touchdown was set up by a 22-yard pass completion from Mike Teel to Brian Leonard.

After Rutgers' opening offensive march, the Scarlet defense took over. Defensive end Jamaal Westerman from Brampton, Ontario, smashed into Connecticut's D. J. Hernandez as he attempted to pass. Westerman's hit forced a fumble. Rutgers' Manny Collins vacuumed up the bouncing ball and was escorted into the end zone by defensive tackle Ramel Meekins. The Knights jumped out in front of the Huskies 14 to 0 before the half ended. Jeremy Ito blasted an impressive 51-yard field goal to increase the Scarlet lead to 17 to zip.

Rutgers' Jamaal Westerman makes the big play of the day on defense against the Connecticut Huskies in 2006. (Courtesy Tom Ciszek/Rutgers Athletic Communications)

In the second half, the Rutgers defense ran roughshod over the Huskies offense. The defensive unit led by Westerman, Ramel Meekins, and Quintero Frierson recorded a total of 6 sacks in the contest. Jamaal Westerman personally accounted for 2.5 quarterback sacks.

Connecticut finally battled back in the third and fourth. The Huskies scored 2 touchdowns on runs of 65 and 7 yards by Donald Brown. A muffed PAT made the score Rutgers 17 and Connecticut 13.

Rutgers' offense sputtered for much of the evening. Ray Rice was saddled with a slight ankle injury suffered early in the game. Rice played through the pain, but managed to gain only 29 yards in the contest. Brian Leonard was also unable to break off any big plays.

The score stayed stuck at 17 to 13 until Jamaal Westerman made his highlight-reel move. Westerman bulled his way through Connecticut blockers to block a Chris Pavasaris punt. The ball bounced into the end zone, where it was covered by Rutgers' Quintero Frierson for a Scarlet touchdown. Rutgers held a 24 to 13 advantage until time ran out. The Scarlet Knights were 8–0 going into their last four gridiron contests. They were 3–0 in Big East Conference play. Rutgers had chopped its way into the national spotlight. However, the Scarlet Knights were still in the woods. The biggest game in the history of Rutgers football lay just ahead.

At the time, Rutgers was one of three undefeated Big East teams. West Virginia and Louisville had not lost a single contest. Both schools were Top 10 teams. West Virginia was

Ticket demand for the gridiron matchup between unbeaten Rutgers and undefeated Louisville was unbelievable. (Courtesy Rutgers Athletic Communications)

the number 3–ranked team in the nation. Louisville was ranked number 5 in the country. Number 15–ranked Rutgers still had to play both West Virginia and Louisville. Louisville and West Virginia were scheduled to play each other before either club took on Rutgers. Something had to give.

Rutgers' Ray Rice rested his sore ankle. Rice, Brian Leonard, and their teammates sat back and watched West Virginia and Louisville battle it out on national TV the week before the Louisville Cardinals were scheduled to come to New Jersey. West Virginia, coached by Rich Rodriguez, had a two-star offense that featured the running talents of quarterback Pat White and running back Steve Slaton.

Coach Bobby Petrino's Louisville squad had a high-powered offense fueled by the pass-catching skills of speedster Harry Douglas and dart-throwing quarterback Brian Brohm, a potential first-round NFL draft pick.

Rutgers quietly watched and waited as the two old heavyweights of the Big East Conference slugged it out. Rutgers, the great Scarlet hope from New Jersey, was the top contender standing in the wings. The Mountaineers of West Virginia were gunned down by the Louisville Cardinals 44 to 34 in the historic shootout in Kentucky. In an instant, West Virginia's hopes of winning a National Championship vanished. Louisville was suddenly the team with championship aspirations. Only one thing stood in the way of the Cardinals. That stumbling block was a team named Rutgers and Rutgers was eager and ready to do some chopping.

The publicity and sports hype that preceded the Rutgers-Louisville game was nothing less than astounding. Football talk across the country centered on the nationally televised game between two Big East unbeatens on Thursday night in Piscataway, New Jersey. Billboards up and down the New Jersey Turnpike urged on the Scarlet Knights. Reporters and TV crews from everywhere poured into Piscataway. On the Rutgers campus, students camped out near the stadium in the hope of securing tickets to the big game. When Rutgers head coach Greg Schiano saw the long line of student fans braving the elements, he personally paid for enough pizzas to feed the faithful Scarlet multitude. In New York City, the Empire State Building was draped in a Scarlet glow to show support of Rutgers against Louisville. New Jersey college football fans never witnessed anything quite like the hoopla created by the Rutgers-Louisville gridiron clash. A crowd of fifty thousand was expected to be on hand to witness the Thursday night rumble near the old Raritan River.

The game was one of the biggest amateur sporting events ever held in New Jersey, if not the biggest. Louisville came into New Brunswick as the number 3 team in the country. Rutgers was number 15 in the AP poll. The contest matched two of the country's five remaining undefeated teams (Ohio State, Boise State, and Michigan were the other three).

On hand at the contest were scouts from the Sugar Bowl, the Fiesta Bowl, the Gator Bowl, the Sun Bowl, the Texas Bowl, and the Orange Bowl. One of the Orange Bowl scouts was a former circuit court judge who graduated from Rutgers in 1971. Orange Bowl scout Mike Chavies played quarterback on the Rutgers freshman football team and was a pitcher on the Rutgers baseball team during his days on the banks of the old Raritan.

Finally! Game time arrived. Coach Greg Schiano's defense, which was ranked number 1 in the Big East Conference in three categories (scoring defense, total defense, and pass defense), would match up against Coach Bobby Petrino's heralded offense, which was ranked number 1 in the conference in two categories (total offense and pass offense). The clash of wills spilled out onto the field before a throng of screaming fans and countless TV viewers.

The Louisville Cardinals offense had its way early in the contest. The Cardinals, under the guidance of playmaster Bobby Petrino and QB Brian Brohm, methodically moved into Rutgers territory. Running back Anthony Allen capped off the Cardinals' march with a 2-yard run into the end zone. Arthur Carmody added the extra point and Louisville led 7 to 0.

Rutgers didn't falter and came roaring back after a timely interception by Devraun Thompson. Scarlet signal caller Mike Teel dropped a perfect pass into the hands of Tiquan Underwood as the wideout broke down the middle of the field. Underwood pulled in the pigskin and raced 26 yards into the end zone for the score. Jeremy Ito came on to chalk up the extra point and it was 7-all. On the following kickoff Louisville's JaJuan Spillman made the Rutgers faithful gasp in horror as he collected the ball and outraced every Scarlet player on the field, streaking 100 yards for a touchdown. Anthony Allen ran the ball in on the 2-point try, and in the blink of an eye Louisville led 15 to 7.

In the second quarter Brian Brohm led his team to pay dirt after a successful fake punt play. Brohm hit Jimmy Riley with a 5-yard touchdown toss. Arthur Carmody kicked the PAT.

Just when things looked bad for the Scarlet Knights, Ray Rice demonstrated why he was one of the top backs in the country. After a screen pass to Kordell Young netted a 36-yard gain, Rice went to work. He took a pitch-out and scrambled 18 yards for a touchdown.

RUTGERS
55
56

Ito kicked the extra point. The teams went to the lockers with Louisville out in front 25 to 14. It looked like Rutgers' unbeaten run might come to a screeching halt.

No one in the Rutgers locker room was worried about the score. There was no panic or alarm. The Scarlet Knights were ready to chop. Early in the second half, quarterback Mike Teel hooked up with receiver Kenny Britt for a 67-yard pass completion. Britt had the ball stripped away by Louisville's William Gay, but covered his own fumble at the 4-yard stripe. Ray Rice then boiled over the goal line behind his blockers to tally the touchdown. Teel then threw to Dennis Campbell to complete a successful 2-point play. The scoreboard told the tale. Rutgers was back in the game. The score was Rutgers 22 and Louisville 25.

Rutgers' defense then dialed it up a notch and unleashed a fearsome pass rush, which continually shredded the Cardinals' offensive line. Brian Brohm had to run for his life. Ramel Meekins sacked Brohm twice. Devraun Thompson dropped the opposing quarterback two times. In all, Brian Brohm was sacked 5 times in the game. The Cardinals' high-flying offense did not make a first down for the first twenty-six minutes of the second half.

Rutgers managed enough offense on each possession to get into field goal range for Jeremy Ito. In the beginning of the fourth, Ito kicked a 46-yarder to knot the score at 25-all.

Brian Brohm continued to get pounded as time ticked away in the contest.

Opposite: Devraun Thompson and the Rutgers defense held Louisville scoreless in the second half of their nationally televised gridiron clash. (Courtesy Jim O'Connor/Rutgers Athletic Communications)

Below: Jeremy Ito prepares to kick the game-winning field goal in Rutgers' amazing upset win over Louisville in 2006. (Courtesy Tom Ciszek/Rutgers Athletic Communications)

Rutgers got the ball back and was in Louisville territory with less than a minute to go. Jeremy Ito was called on to try a last-ditch 33-yard game-winning field goal before overtime. Rutgers fans held their breath. The snap was good. Ito got his foot onto the ball. The pigskin flew toward the goal posts, but hooked to the side. It was no good.

Before Rutgers fans could exhale in despair, flags appeared on the field. Louisville's William Gay was offsides on the play. Jeremy Ito would get a second shot at instant immortality. If his kick was good, the moment would live forever in the minds of Rutgers football fans. There were thirteen seconds left in the game as Ito waited for the snap. The ball was placed. Jeremy Ito gave it the boot. The 28-yard kick sailed through the uprights. It was good! Rutgers won 28 to 25! The Scarlet Knights and their fans celebrated as time expired. Rutgers had come back to beat the number-3 team in the country and in doing so had shattered Louisville's dream of winning a National Championship. A new team now had that very dream thrust upon them. Rutgers was 9 and 0. If the Scarlet Knights could win their last three games, a National Championship was a real possibility. Winning

Kenny Britt (#88) celebrates a Scarlet victory with a Rutgers teammate. Britt made 2 pass receptions for 82 yards against Louisville. (Courtesy Rutgers Athletic Communications)

the Big East Conference was also possible. The win over Louisville on national television would go down in history as one of Rutgers' greatest victories.

"This," said Rutgers coach Greg Schiano after the contest, "is the way college football is supposed to be."

The following week Rutgers vaulted up the rankings. The Scarlet Knights were voted the number-7 team in the country by the Associated Press. No Rutgers team had ever climbed to such a lofty position in the poll. Rutgers was also rated number 6 in the Bowl Championship Series behind Ohio State, Michigan, USC, Florida, and Notre Dame. The Scarlet Knights basked in the limelight, but only for a moment. The glory of victory was a treat to be enjoyed at the end of the season. There was more chopping to do. Games against Cincinnati, Syracuse, and old nemesis West Virginia remained.

Rutgers' contest against Cincinnati was televised. A win over the Bearcats would solidify Rutgers' chances for a BCS berth and increase the Knights' chances of capturing the Big East Conference crown. The Cincinnati contest was also a trap game. A trap game is a

Rutgers fans across the country celebrated the Scarlet's win over Louisville for the Knights' ninth consecutive victory of the season. (Courtesy Rutgers Athletic Communications)

BIG EAST
UTGERS
81
81

contest of seemingly less significance that comes after or before a so-called "big game." Football coaches, players, and real fans know all gridiron contests are important. Football is a funny game as far as fate is concerned. Any team can beat a higher ranked team given the right circumstances and a little bit of luck. Rutgers was 9–0 and Cincinnati was 5–5. The Bearcats needed a win to become bowl eligible. Coach Mark Dantonio's Bearcats were a sound squad. They saw Rutgers' upset of Louisville on television. Cincinnati believed they could do the same to Rutgers even though their regular starting quarterback, sophomore Dustin Grutza, might be unavailable for action due to an injury. Senior QB Nick Davila, who had never started a college game, might be behind center for the Bearcats in their game against the Knights.

The trap was set. Even though Rutgers was mentally and physically prepared to play, the Knights were tripped up. It could be called a letdown. It could be called falling into a trap. However, it's best to call the contest what it really was. Guided by a surprise substitute quarterback, the Cincinnati Bearcats played a great game. On that day they were better than Rutgers. It happens in sports. That's why the word *upset* is in the dictionary.

Cincinnati scored first on a 32-yard field goal by Kevin Lovell. The Bearcats increased their lead when Cincinnati quarterback Nick Davila engineered a drive that ended with Davila scoring a touchdown on a 1-yard run. In the second period, Cincinnati boosted its advantage to 17 to 0 when cornerback DeAngelo Smith picked off a Mike Teel pass and returned it 70-plus yards for a Bearcat TD.

Jeremy Ito's 33-yard field goal late in the second quarter made the score Rutgers 3 and Cincinnati 17. Rutgers' great running game was outmanned at the line, forcing the Scarlet Knights to utilize the pass more than usual. The absence of veteran Scarlet receiver Shawn Tucker, who'd been out of action since early in the season due to an ankle

Opposite: Tight end Clark Harris made 5 pass receptions for 102 yards against Cincinnati. (Courtesy Tom Ciszek/Rutgers Athletic Communications)

Below: Rutgers celebrates Senior Day against Syracuse in 2006. (Courtesy Rutgers Athletic Communications)

injury, proved costly. Rutgers just couldn't jump-start its offense, even though freshman receiver Kenny Britt caught 9 passes for 91 yards on the day. Tight end Clark Harris pulled in 5 passes for 102 yards. Rutgers' rushing star, Ray Rice, tallied the Knights' only touchdown on a 1-yard plunge. Rice was held to a season-low total of just 54 yards on 18 carries.

The day belonged to Cincinnati and Bearcat quarterback Nick Davila, who threw an 83-yard touchdown pass to tight end Brent Celek in the third. Cincinnati added Kevin Lovell field goals in the third and fourth periods to upset the Rutgers Scarlet Knights 30 to 11. Rutgers' bid for an undefeated season ended. The chance to play for a possible National Championship was a dream shifted to the back burner. However, Rutgers was 9–1 with other goals still within reach.

Rutgers came home to play Syracuse on Senior Day.

Rutgers rebounded against Syracuse with a vengeance. The Scarlet Knights steamrolled 88 yards in 8 plays for a touchdown on their opening drive of the contest. Ray Rice crossed the goal line at the end of a 10-yard run to give Rutgers an early 7 to 0 lead. Freshman receiver Kenny Britt sparkled as he pulled in a pass from QB Mike Teel and scampered 38 yards to pay dirt in the first. Jeremy Ito's 2 extra-point kicks gave the Knights a fast 14 to nil advantage.

In the second quarter the Mike Teel to Kenny Britt passing combo clicked again. Teel hit Britt with a 28-yard scoring strike.

From that moment on, it was the Brian Leonard and Ray Rice run-and-stun show. Leonard tallied 2 touchdowns, each on a run of 2 yards. He carried the ball 19 times for a total of 106 yards. Leonard also caught 4 passes for 27 yards. Ray Rice rambled for 107 yards on 23 carries and scored 1 touchdown. Jeremy Ito added a 32-yard field goal for Rutgers in the fourth quarter. J. J. Nesheiwat pulled in a 14-yard touchdown pass from Perry Patterson for Syracuse's only points of the day. The final score was Rutgers 38 and Syracuse 7, as the Scarlet Knights notched their tenth victory of the season. In the contest, Brian Leonard scored the 266th point of his career to become Rutgers' all-time leading scorer. Leonard passed kicker Kennan Startzell, who totaled 261 points over his career (1976 to 1979).

On the same day that Rutgers walloped Syracuse, West Virginia was upset by South Florida 24 to 19. If Rutgers could top the Mountaineers in the final game of the regular season for both schools, Rutgers would claim the Big East Championship.

The Rutgers–West Virginia game was televised nationally on ESPN. The contest pitted two of the nation's best rushers against each other. Rutgers' Ray Rice and West Virginia's Steve Slaton were two of the finest backs in America. The Mountaineers' shifty quarterback, Pat White, was also better known as a runner than as a passer. Going into the contest, Rutgers' Ray Rice had rushed for 1,495 yards and 17 touchdowns. West Virginia's Steve Slaton had rushed for 1,621 yards and 14 TDs. Slaton's backfield mate Pat White had rushed for 1,074 yards and 17 touchdowns.

Rutgers was now ranked number 13 in the country. West Virginia was ranked number 15. If Rutgers won, it would capture the Big East title and earn a berth to a BCS bowl, which might be the Orange Bowl. If Rutgers lost, it would still go to a high-profile bowl game. If West Virginia (9–2) won, Louisville (which beat Connecticut in its final game) would claim the Big East crown and the BCS bowl bid. West Virginia would also go to a top bowl. The stakes were high in Morgantown, West Virginia, when the two teams took the field.

Fullback Brian Leonard became Rutgers' all-time leading scorer in 2006. (Courtesy Elane Coleman/Rutgers Athletic Communications)

For the second time in three games, Rutgers was surprised to learn that its opponent's starting quarterback would not play. An injured Pat White would stand on the sidelines while Jarrett Brown would handle the signal calling for the Mountaineers. Brown would make his first career start for West Virginia against Rutgers.

The contest proved to be the nip and tuck battle everyone expected it to be. Rutgers scored first. The Scarlet Knights' super sophomore and Heisman Trophy candidate Ray Rice dashed to pay dirt from 16 yards out. Jeremy Ito's kick gave the Knights an early 7-point advantage.

West Virginia, led by young quarterback Jarrett Brown, generated enough offense to answer Rutgers' first score with a 38-yard field goal by Pat McAfee. Jeremy Ito traded McAfee point for point and booted a 36-yard field goal to close out the scoring in the first period. Rutgers led 10 to 3. In the second quarter, both defenses held their foes away from the goal line. Neither offense got a sniff of the other's end zone. The only points scored

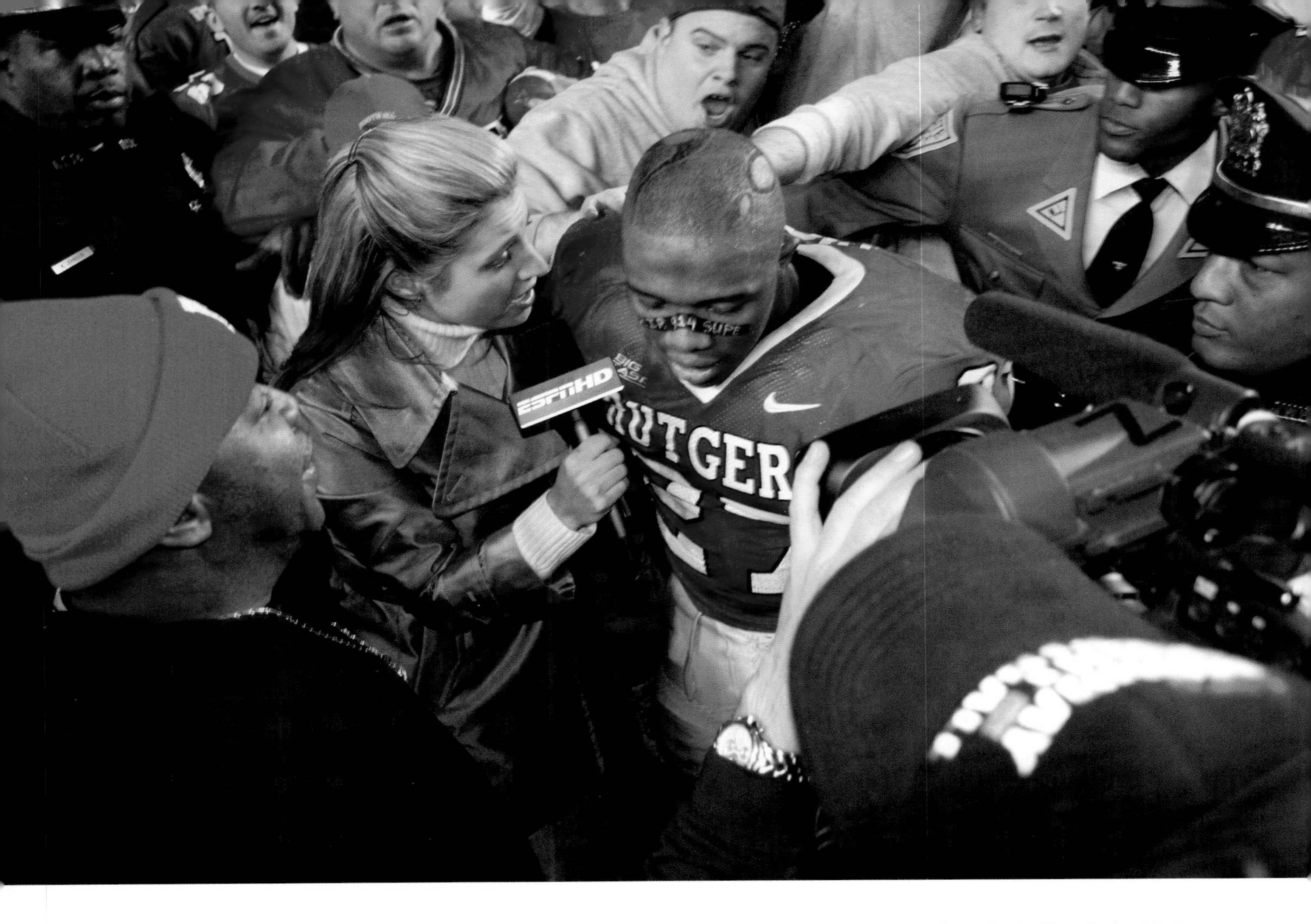

Rutgers football fans, coaches, and players had plenty of reasons to celebrate in 2006. The Scarlet Knights posted a season record of 10 wins and 2 losses and were invited to play in the Texas Bowl. (Courtesy Rutgers Athletic Communications)

came in a 32-yard field goal by the Mountaineers' Pat McAfee. The half ended with Rutgers out in front 10 to 6.

In the third quarter both offenses got busy. Steve Slaton capped a drive with a 1-yard plunge for his 15th touchdown of the season. Jarrett Brown then wove through Rutgers defenders to score a touchdown on a 40-yard ramble. Pat McAfee provided the PATs. Rutgers freshman receiver Tim Brown then hooked up with QB Mike Teel for a 72-yard pass completion, which was good for a touchdown. Jeremy Ito added the kick, and the score at the conclusion of the third quarter was West Virginia 20 and Rutgers 17.

In the fourth and final quarter, Jeremy Ito accounted for all of Rutgers' point production. Ito made field goals of 21 yards and 31 yards. The Scarlet Knights held a slim 23 to 20 lead over the Mountaineers late in the contest. West Virginia rallied its offense and managed to move into field goal range with less than a minute to go. Pat McAfee nailed a 30-yard field goal with fifty-three seconds remaining to tie the game at 23-all, sending the contest into overtime.

In the first overtime period, the two gridiron combatants traded field goals. West Virginia's McAfee booted a successful 43-yarder. Rutgers' Ito duplicated the feat. The score was knotted at 26 apiece.

On went the contest. The two pigskin pugilists traded punch for punch. Rutgers' Brian Leonard tallied a touchdown on a 1-yard run to begin the second overtime. Ito added the kick. West Virginia's Steve Slaton countered with a 1-yard touchdown run. McAfee provided the PAT. At the end of the second overtime, Rutgers and West Virginia were locked at 33-all.

The NCAA has a rule about overtimes. Starting with the third overtime, teams must go for a 2-point conversion after a touchdown. Mountaineers signal caller Jarrett Brown hit receiver Brandon Myles with a 22-yard touchdown pass to start the third overtime. On the 2-point try, Brown fired a bullet to Dorrell Jalloh, who caught the rocket to complete the play. West Virginia led 41 to 33.

Rutgers roared back. Ray Rice capped a drive with a 1-yard plunge into the end zone. Rutgers needed the 2-point play to stay in the game. Scarlet quarterback Mike Teel looked to pass. He fired toward Ray Rice in the end zone. West Virginia's Vaughn Rivers raced over to knock down the pass. The hometown West Virginia fans went wild as the Mountaineers defeated the valiant Scarlet Knights 41 to 39 in three overtimes.

In the contest, West Virginia's Steve Slaton carried the ball 23 times for 112 yards and scored 2 touchdowns. Rutgers' Ray Rice lugged the pigskin 25 times for a total of 129 yards. Rice also scored 2 touchdowns.

Rutgers finished the year with a record of 10 wins and 2 losses. The Knights were denied the Big East Championship and a BCS berth, but the team had come close to achieving the impossible dream. The 2006 season would live forever as one of Rutgers' finest football accomplishments.

Prior to the West Virginia–Rutgers football clash, rumors began to circulate that the University of Miami was interested in Greg Schiano. Miami was in need of a new head coach and Rutgers coach Schiano was the frontrunner for the position. Rutgers fans wondered if Schiano would stay or go. Coach Greg Schiano made his position very clear and Rutgers fans rejoiced when they learned of it.

"I'm very happy here," Schiano told reporters. "I have no plans of going anywhere else." The Jersey guy was staying home. His ultimate goal was to bring a National Championship to the banks of the Raritan.

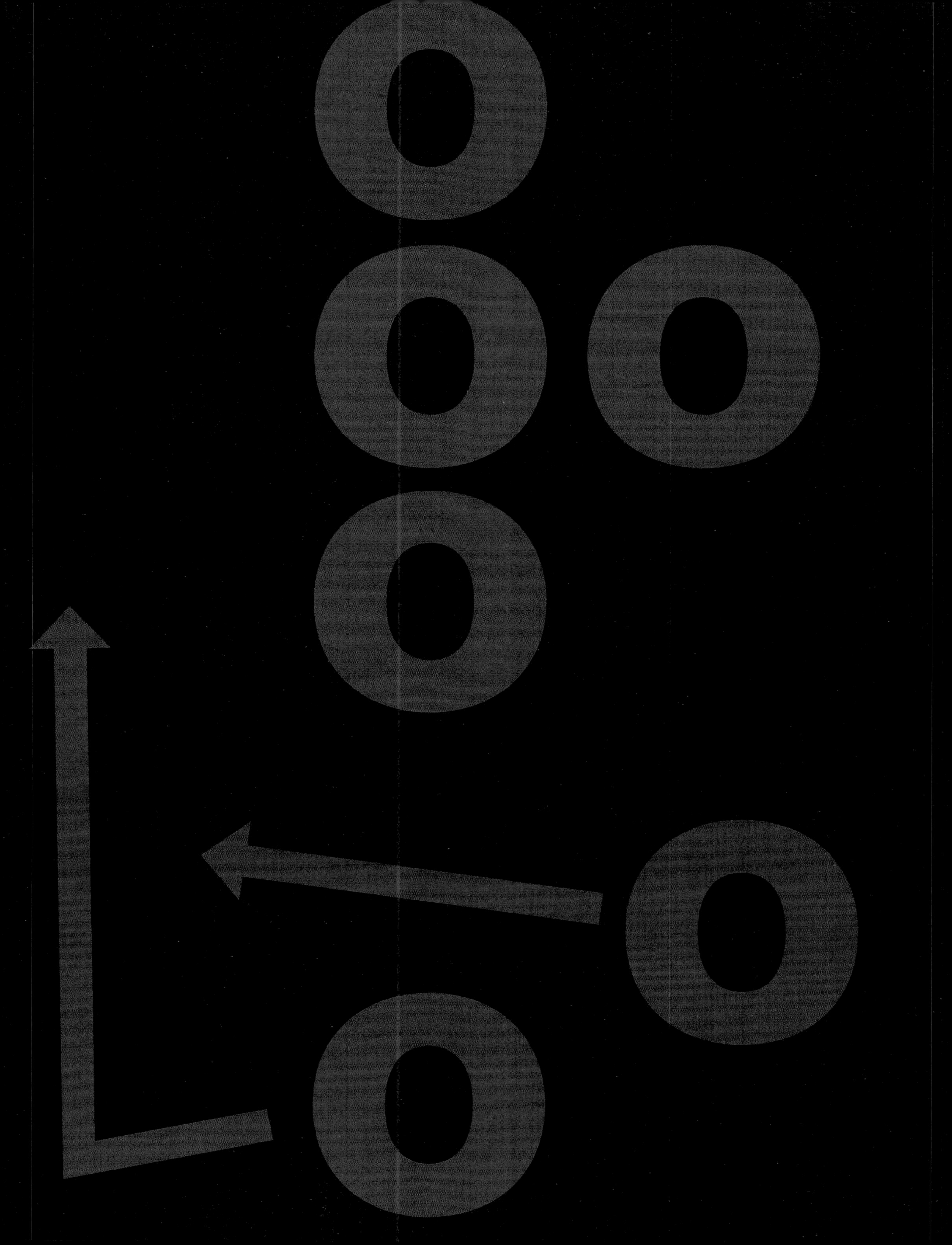

CHAPTER 16
STARS, BOWLS, AND BEYOND

The Scarlet Knights were invited to play in the Texas Bowl in Houston. Rutgers' opponent was Kansas State, which had a season record of 7 wins and 5 losses.

Prior to the team's second straight bowl appearance, Rutgers coaches and players garnered a bonanza of individual honors and awards.

Coach Greg Schiano was named the Home Depot National Coach of the Year. The announcement of Schiano's selection was made live on a national ESPN broadcast.

Coach Schiano was also awarded the inaugural Liberty Mutual Coach of the Year Award in 2006. The award honors the nation's top college football coach who best exemplifies responsibility and excellence on and off the field.

The Scarlet gridiron mentor was honored as the National Coach of the Year by the Walter Camp Football Foundation. In addition, Greg Schiano was selected the Big East Coach of the Year. Schiano was the first coach in Rutgers history to guide the Scarlet Knights to a Top 10 national ranking.

Greg Schiano of Rutgers won several National College Football Coach of the Year honors in 2006. (Courtesy Jim O'Connor/Rutgers Athletic Communications)

Rutgers fullback Brian Leonard was awarded the Draddy Trophy. The Draddy Trophy is awarded to the college football player who best combines academic, football, and leadership excellence. Leonard was not only a remarkable athlete at Rutgers, he was also an outstanding student. In fact, most Rutgers football players excel both on the playing field and in the classroom. In 2006, Rutgers rated 9th out of 64 bowl-eligible teams in terms of NCAA academic performance. Leonard was also a National Scholar-Athlete. Brian Leonard was later selected by the St. Louis Rams in the second round of the 2007 NFL draft.

Tight end Clark Harris was All–Big East and was picked to play in the Senior Bowl. Harris was later a seventh-round NFL draft pick of the Green Bay Packers. Offensive lineman Cameron Stephenson was All–Big East and a fifth-round draft pick of the Pittsburgh Steelers in the 2007 NFL draft.

Defensive tackle Eric Foster was named a First Team All-American by the Football Writers' Association of America. He was a Third Team

Scarlet tight end Clark Harris was selected to play in the Senior Bowl game. (Courtesy Tom Ciszek/Rutgers Athletic Communications)

All-American pick by the Associated Press. Punter Joe Radigan and offensive lineman Jeremy Zuttah were All–Big East.

Rutgers kicker Jeremy Ito was an Honorable Mention All-American and Second Team All–Big East. Other Rutgers stars selected to the All–Big East Second Team were safety Ron Girault, safety Courtney Greene, defensive tackle Ramel Meekins, defensive end Jamaal Westerman, linebacker Devraun Thompson, and offensive lineman Pedro Sosa.

Running back Ray Rice was the first Rutgers player in history to be named a finalist for the Maxwell Trophy. Rice was also a Doak Walker Award semifinalist. Ray Rice finished seventh in the balloting for the Heisman Trophy, which was won by Ohio State quarterback Troy Smith. In addition, Rice was selected a Second Team All-American by the Associated Press, the *Sporting News,* the Walter Camp Foundation, and Rivals.com.

In December 2006, Rutgers coaches and players tucked away their awards and trophies and prepared to play in a bowl game for only the third time in the history of the Scarlet Knights program.

Left: Defensive tackle Eric Foster won All-America honors in 2006. (Courtesy Tom Ciszek/Rutgers Athletic Communications)

Page 242, top: Fullback Brian Leonard (left) won the Draddy Trophy in 2006. That same season, halfback Ray Rice became the first player in Rutgers history to be named a finalist for the Maxwell Trophy. (Courtesy Joe Covino/Rutgers Athletic Communications)

Page 242, bottom: Rutgers played Kansas State in the 2006 Texas Bowl. (Courtesy Heather Morrison/Rutgers Athletic Communications)

Page 243: The Texas Bowl was held in Houston on December 28, 2006. (Courtesy Heather Morrison/Rutgers Athletic Communications)

2006
TEXAS
RUTGERS
RUTGERS
27
2006
TEXAS
BOWL

Reliant Stadium
TEXANS
Reliant Stadium
R
R

Rutgers fans from around the nation flocked to the Texas Bowl to support their Scarlet Knights. (Courtesy Heather Morrison/Rutgers Athletic Communications)

The Texas Bowl was played at Reliant Stadium in Houston, Texas. Rutgers, with a record of 10–2, was ranked number 16 going into the contest.

Coach Ron Prince's Kansas State Wildcats were led by their freshman phenom quarterback, Josh Freeman. Freeman passed for more than 1,650 yards in his first season. He engineered impressive wins over Texas and Colorado during the regular season.

The Rutgers Scarlet Knights wasted no time in taming the Kansas State Wildcats on offense and defense. The first period belonged to the Knights. Rutgers marched 35 yards with the help of a personal-foul penalty against the Wildcats to score the first points of the bowl clash. Scarlet quarterback Mike Teel hit wide receiver Tim Brown with a 14-yard scoring strike. Jeremy Ito was good on the kick and Rutgers led 7 to zip. After the Rutgers defense shut down the Kansas State offense, Teel went back to work. He fired a 49-yard touchdown toss to Tim Brown. Brown's second TD reception resulted in a 14 to 0 advantage after the Jeremy Ito PAT.

In the second quarter, Kansas State kicker Jeff Snodgrass got the Wildcats on the board with a 44-yard field goal. After a Rutgers offensive series misfired, Kansas State return man Yamon Figurs electrified the crowd by returning a Joe Radigan punt 76 yards for a Wildcats touchdown. Figurs's run made the score Rutgers 14 and Kansas State 10. Before the half ended, the Scarlet Knights' Jeremy Ito came on to boot a 37-yard field goal to boost Rutgers' edge to 17 to 10. Ito's field goal was set up by Mike Teel pass completions to Kenny Britt for 22 yards and to Clark Harris for 26 yards.

From the moment the Scarlet Knights exited the lockers after the halftime break, the rest of the game belonged to Rutgers. The Scarlet defense limited the Kansas State offense to a total of 162 yards in the game. The Wildcats made only 6 first downs in the contest. Rutgers senior linebacker Quintero Frierson, from Coral Gables High School in Florida, made the big defensive play of the game. Frierson picked off the first pass thrown by Wildcats quarterback Josh Freeman in the second half. The Rutgers linebacker tucked away the pigskin and raced 27 yards for a Rutgers touchdown.

The Scarlet offense continued to roll. Ray Rice, who had gained 77 yards on 13 carries in the first half, squirted through the middle of the line and raced 46 yards for a touchdown. Rutgers was ahead of Kansas State 31 to 10 by the end of the third quarter. In the last period, the Scarlet's Jeremy Ito hit on field goals of 23 yards and 21 yards to make the final score 37 to 10 in favor of Rutgers.

The first-ever meeting between Kansas State and Rutgers resulted in Rutgers' first bowl victory in history. Ray Rice gained 170 yards on 24 carries and tallied 1 touchdown. Rice was named the Most Valuable Player of the Texas Bowl.

Ray Rice shattered Jim "J. J." Jennings's single-season rushing mark at Rutgers by running for 1,794 yards in 2006. Rice also scored 20 touchdowns, which was 1 shy of Jennings's single-season mark of 21 TDs set in 1973. Scarlet quarterback Mike Teel had an outstanding game against Kansas State in the Texas Bowl. Teel completed 16 of 28 passes for 268 yards and 2 touchdowns.

Rutgers' first bowl victory was celebrated all over the state of New Jersey and all over the country by Scarlet alums and fans. Rutgers football, with its long tradition, had returned to the national sports spotlight. The Scarlet Knights were ranked number 12 in the nation in the final AP poll of 2006.

Left: Quarterback Mike Teel takes a snap from center Darnell Stapleton. Teel tossed 2 touchdown passes in the 2006 Texas Bowl. (Courtesy Chuck LeClaire/Rutgers Athletic Communications)

Right: Ray Rice of Rutgers was named the Most Valuable Player of the 2006 Texas Bowl. (Courtesy Joe Covino/Rutgers Athletic Communications)

Left: Greg Schiano coached Rutgers to an 11–2 record in 2006, including a 37 to 10 win over Kansas State in the Texas Bowl. (Courtesy Joe Covino/Rutgers Athletic Communications)

Right: Rutgers University president Richard L. McCormick holds the Texas Bowl Trophy. (Courtesy Joe Covino/Rutgers Athletic Communications)

Pages 248–249: In 2006 the Rutgers Scarlet Knights recorded their first bowl victory in school history. (Courtesy Joe Camporeale/Rutgers Athletic Communications)

When Coach Greg Schiano and his Scarlet Knights returned home to New Jersey after their initial bowl victory, they were welcomed back by officials of the state government. The Rutgers team was applauded in the Senate and on the floor of the State Assembly. The Scarlet Knights were presented with ceremonial resolutions. Governor Jon Corzine also added his congratulations at a ceremony held at the Louis Brown Athletic Center on the Rutgers campus. A Cinderella season came to a close, but it was not the end of the story. There is more sports history to be made at Rutgers.

"The Rutgers football team became a source of pride for the people of New Jersey," wrote Rutgers University president Richard L. McCormick. He continued, "Rutgers' football success [also] has brought greater national visibility to our university and our state."

College football was born in New Jersey. Rutgers was a gridiron pioneer and trailblazer. The Scarlet Knights now have their sights trained on new goals, like winning the Big East Conference crown and perhaps even a National Championship. It will take some intense chopping, but anything is possible if the ax is sharp enough. Whatever the future holds, let this fact be known: The Rutgers football tradition sparked back in 1869 was rekindled in 2006. The Scarlet gridiron tradition is a blazing flame that will burn on as long as the sport of college football is played.

AFTERWORD

The noted sportswriter Grantland Rice once wrote, "When the One great Scorer comes to write against your name— / He marks—not that you won or lost—but how you played the game." In truth, life is the only game in which how you perform is really important . . . because God is the referee.

RUTGERS FOOTBALL LETTERWINNERS

The names you see here have created a tradition that has endured for more than 135 years. These student-athletes' dedication, determination, and self-sacrifices should never be forgotten.

-A-

Abbott, R. J. (Mgr.)
Acanfora, Gerry
Ackroyd, Samuel
Adams, Gene
Adams, J.
Adkins, Doug
Ahern, John
Ahmed, Haney (Mgr.)
Alexander, John (1)
Alexander, John (2)
Alken, Frederick
Allen, Frederick
Allen, John
Allen, Raymond
Allen, Ron
Allen, Scott
Allen, Steve
Allgair, John
Allison, Matt
Allmer, Chris (Mgr.)
Altomare, Joe
Alverson, James
Alvord, Greg
Ambrose, Joseph
Amling, Harry (Mgr.)
Anderson, Claremont
Anderson, H.
Anderson, Howard
Anderson, John (Mgr.)
Anderson, Karl
Anderson, Mark
Anderson, Milton
Anderson, Ravon
Anderson, William (1)
Anderson, William (2)
Andiorio, Ken
Andre, Jerry
Andrews, Alan
Angelillo, John
Angstadt, Tom
Angus, Harry
Angyal, Joseph
Anstatt, Joseph
Anthony, Brian
Anzidei, Chris
Archambault, Victor
Archibald, Lauren
Arnold, Burt
Arthur, John
Arthur, Walter
Arway, William
Asberry, Dondre
Ashby, Kenneth
Ashton, George
Astridge, Ronald
Atkinson, Asher
Atwood, Donner
Aubry, Robert
Augustine, Harold
Austin, Jean
Austin, Raymond
Austin, William
Aydelott, John
Ayres, Louis (Mgr.)
Azzarita, Frank

-B-

Babcock, James
Bachman, Matt
Baer, William
Bailey, Bill
Bain, Alan
Baker, Andrew (1)
Baker, Andrew (2)
Baker, Chris
Baker, Clifford
Baker, Derek
Baker, James
Baker, Jerome
Baker, John
Baker, Timothy
Bakst, Murray
Baldwin, George
Baldwin, Richard
Ball, Madison
Balogh, W. Arpad
Bankos, George

Banks, Gordon
Banks, Roland
Barnaby, Val
Barnes, Corey
Barnes, Darian
Barone, Joe
Barone, Steve
Barr, Michael
Barr, Robert
Barr, Thomas T. (Mgr.)
Batchelder, Walter
Battaglia, Marco
Battle, Bernarr
Bauer, John
Bauman, Richard
Beachem, T. (Mgr.)
Bear, Robert
Beckett, Andrew
Beckford, William
Beckwith, Arthur
Beddoe, Gary
Bednard, Paul
Beekman, Myron
Beekman, Theodore
Behnke, Craig
Behrend, John
Beierle, Brill
Belh, Mike
Beljour, Jean
Bell, Arthur
Bell, Gary
Bellamy, Jay
Bellezza, Len
Benante, Marty
Bender, Brian
Bender, Cuno
Bender, David
Bender, Peter
Benedict, James
Benestad, John
Benke, Gary
Benke, Paul
Benkert, Henry
Bercier, Ken
Berdine, George
Bergamini, Herbert
Berkowitz, Joseph
Berkowitz, Simpson
Bernath, Fred
Bernstein, Howard
Berry, Tony
Berson, Steven
Beschne, Bill
Bethea, Andrew (Mgr.)
Bethune, T. R.
Beugless, Francis
Bido, Luis
Bierman, Moses
Biernacki, Dan
Bilderback, Willis
Billock, Fred
Bing, Richard
Bishop, Ellis (Mgr.)
Bishop, James, Jr.
Bishop, John
Black, Cunningston
Black, John
Black, Shin
Blackwell, J. G. (Mgr.)
Blackwell, Julius
Blackwell, Ted
Blackwood, Howard
Blanchard, Jeff
Blanchard, Tim
Blanche, Scott
Blanchfield, Robert
Blanton, John
Blauvelt, Louis
Bleich, John
Bliss, William
Block, Norton
Bloom, Jack
Blum, John
Blumberg, Edward
Blumenstock, Marvin
Bobrowski, C.
Boehrer, Bryan
Bohnel, Jay
Bokesch, Randy
Bolash, Bill
Bonosoro, John (Mgr.)
Bonsall, Richard
Boocock, Philip
Boone, Len
Booz, Louis
Bosch, Chad
Bossow, Kenneth
Boswick, Keith (Mgr.)
Botti, Michael
Bouchard, Mike
Bouchard, Phil (Mgr.)
Bounty, Charles
Bowen, Edward
Bowen, Paul (Mgr.)
Bowers, Charles
Bowlby, Robert
Bracher, Elmer
Brackett, Gary
Bradley, Addison
Bradley, William
Brady, Aaron
Brandes, Raymond
Brantley, Chris
Breckley, Joseph
Brendel, Robert
Brennan, E. Gaynor
Brenner, Michael
Brestle, Mike
Brett, Philip
Bridges, Wes
Brinckerhoff, James
Britt, Kenny
Brittingham, Darryl
Broadbent, Travis
Brody, David
Brogger, Adolph
Brooks, David
Brown, Albert
Brown, Alfred
Brown, Cedric
Brown, Conger (Mgr.)
Brown, Elisha
Brown, Fred
Brown, Gene
Brown, George
Brown, Larry
Brown, Matt
Brown, Melvin
Brown, Sampson
Brown, Tim
Browning, Howard
Brundage, Warren
Bruni, Arthur
Brush, Robert
Bruyere, Holmes
Bruyere, Walter, III
Bryan, Dusty
Bryant, Keif
Bryant, Taman
Bucci, John
Buchowski, Barry
Budd, DeWitt
Buffington, Darrell
Bugg, Ron
Bullard, Maurice
Burd, Bill (Mgr.)
Burke, Joe
Burkhardt, Arthur
Burkowski, Edward
Burnett, Albert
Burnett, Daniel
Burnett, William
Burns, Frank
Burns, Joseph
Burns, Kevin
Bursch, Robert
Butkus, Peter
Butler, Rickey
Byers, Andy
Bynes, Terry
Byrd, Arnold
Byrne, Albert

-C-

Cairns, David (Mgr.)
Calbi, Jill (Mgr.)
Calhoun, Vaughn
Cali, Anthony
Callaghan, John

Callahan, Neil
Campanile, Anthony
Campassi, Joseph
Campbell, Bruce
Campbell, Dennis
Campbell, Jeremy
Campion, Albert
Canal, John
Canavan, John
Cann, James
Cantine, Charles
Capestro, Stephen
Cappelletti, Thomas
Capraro, Frank
Capraro, Patty (Mgr.)
Capria, Richard
Card, Clellan
Carino, Andy
Carlucci, John
Carollo, Andrew, Jr.
Carney, Bob
Carney, John
Carpender, John
Carpender, William
Carroll, Charles
Carswell, Trohn
Carter, George
Carty, Sean
Carujo, Robert (Mgr.)
Caruso, Andrew
Case, Clifford
Casey, John
Catanho, Alcides
Cauthen, Anthony
Cebula, Chris
Celigoi, Rudolph
Cella, Tony
Cerone, Frank
Chadwick, Cameron
Chadwick, John
Challen, Paul
Chamberlain, Jacob
Chamberlain, Lewis
Chamberlain, William
Chandler, W.
Chando, Leon
Chapman, Sam
Chergey, Tom
Cherrie, Stanley
Cherry, Deron
Cherry, Duane
Chesna, Bill
Chizmadia, Albert
Christ, Bob
Christ, Tim
Christiansen, Woodrow
Christoff, Larry
Ciaffoni, Joe
Ciampaglio, Bob
Cinquergrana, Denton
Cintolo, William
Cipriano, Lou
Cirone, Joseph
Ciurciu, John
Clancy, Mike
Clark, Dave
Clark, Davon
Clark, Heath
Clark, Otis
Clark, Pete
Clark, Robert
Clarke, Bill
Clarke, Peter
Clary, Bob (Mgr.)
Clemens, Thomas
Clements, Jim
Cloke, Allen
Clymer, Bruce
Clymer, Larry
Coan, Wilson
Cobb, Brian
Cobb, Robert
Cobbs, Melvin
Codington, Horace
Coen, Thomas
Cohen, Bernard
Coker, Jennifer (Mgr.)
Cole, Hugh
Coleman, J. M. (Mgr.)
Coley, Omar
Collareno, Nunzio
Collier, Arthur
Collier, William
Collins, Leslie
Colon, Nate
Colville, A. R. (Mgr.)
Combiths, Thomas
Comeau, Ryan
Comiskey, John
Conger, Frederick
Conklin, Marion
Conlan, Mike
Conley, Craig (Mgr.)
Conlin, Kevin
Connelly, Tom
Connors, Harold
Conover, David
Cook, George
Cook, Robert
Cook, William
Cooke, Leonard
Cooper, Henry
Cooper, Jarrett
Coppalo, Bob
Coppin, Samuel
Corbin, Charles
Corbin, Joe
Corcoran, Jack
Corda, Michael
Corizzi, Harold
Corle, M. M.
Corrigan, Paul
Cortese, Mike
Cory, Donald
Cos, Harry
Costin, Del
Coursen, Donald
Courtney, Robert
Cox, Andre
Coyle, Chris
Craft, William
Craig, Charles
Craig, Edmond (Mgr.)
Cramer, Richard
Cramer, William
Crawford, Norris
Crawford, Raishard
Crawford, Sydney
Crenshaw, Robert
Crockett, Brian
Cronin, George
Cronin, Jerry
Crooks, Jacki
Crosby, Charles
Crowder, Aaron
Crowl, Richard
Cubit, Ryan
Cuddeback, Samuel
Cummins, John
Cunningham, Brad
Cuozzo, Frank
Curley, Lee
Curry, Jason
Curry, Joe
Cutler, Willard
Czellecz, Darrin

-D-

Daddario, Joseph
Daisley, Brook
Dalton, Willim
D'Amato, Robert
Dammann, Ken
D'Andrea, Henry
Daniels, Marcus
Danner, Julius
D'Antonio, Jim
Dargin, John
Darkes, Leroy
Darlington, George
Darwent, Alvin
Dato, Clint
Daverport, Kerry
Davis, Alan
Davis, Doug
Davis, Edwin
Davis, George
Davis, James
Davis, Len

Davis, Luther
Davis, Mitchell
Davis, Robert
Davis, Sam
Davis, Titus
Day, Robert
Dazer, Charles
Debes, Mark
Decker, Fred
Deering, Eric
Delamater, Ezra
Dell Angela, Silvio
Del Tufo, A. (Mgr.)
DeLucia, Mike
Demarest, Nathan
Demarest, Samuel
Demarest, William
DeMarrais, Douglass
Demier, Dan
Demyen, Marc
Denardo, Jack
Denardo, Mike
Denise, Charles
Dennis, Nicholas
Dennison, Jerry
DeRensis, Henry
DeRosa, Jack
DeSantis, Anthony
Deshler, Frederick
Devera, Voltaire (Mgr.)
Devido, Joseph (Mgr.)
Devlin, Shawn
DeWitt, John (1)
DeWitt, John (2)
DeWitt, Theodore
Diaz, Donny
Dickerson, Edgar
Dickerson, Rawson
Dickinson, Edward
Diederich, David
Diehl, Gerard
DiGiacinto, James
Diggs, Joe
DiGilio, Joe
Digney, James
DiLemma, Patrick
DiLiberti, Charles
Dillard, Bob
Dillon, Mike
D'Imperio, Joseph
D'Imperio, Ryan
Dinsmore, Rob
DiPonziano, Charles
Dixon, George
Dixon, Romeo
Dodson, Gordon (Mgr.)
Doliber, William
Donaldson, Bill
Donato, Joseph
Donnelly, Pete
Donofrio, Mike (Mgr.)
Donovan, Keith
Dorn, David
Dorn, Wilfred
Dornlas, Todd
Dorsey, Tekay
Douglas, Phillip
Dowd, Pat
Drake, Edward
Drake, Scott
Dreher, Art
Dreier, Donald
Drury, Francis
Drury, Michael Pace (Mgr.)
Dubiel, William
DuBois, Clarence
DuBois, Roelif
Duborg, Eddie
Duda, Edward
Duffy, Brian
Duffy, James
Duffy, Paul
Duffy, Thomas
Dulin, Loren (Jim)
Dumont, Jim
Dumont, Robert
Duncan, Donald
Dunham, Richard
Dunlop, Archie
Dunn, Nasario
Dunn, William
Dunne, David
Dunster, Will
Durango, Bryan
Dutch, Dennis
Dyevich, Kevin
Dyke, Chalmers

-E-

Echerson, Frank
Eckels, Dennis
Eckert, Fred
Eckhardt, Joseph
Edgar, Blanchard
Edgar, David
Edmonds, Brendan
Edmons, R.
Edwards, Curt
Edwards, Ernest
Edwards, Job
Egan, Ron
Eli, Henry
Elias, George
Elliott, John
Elliott, Robert
Ellis, Milton
Elmendorf, John
Elmendorf, Nicoll
Elting, Howard
Ely, Richard (Mgr.)
Emanuel, Nick
Emery, John
Emmer, Jack
Enander, Ellis
Enberg, Edward
Endick, Joel (Mgr.)
Engle, Marvin
Engle, Maurice
English, Rae Ann (Mgr.)
Epps, Joe
Erickson, Jeffrey
Erney, Scott
Errico, Dan
Esposito, Michael
Esselstyn, Charles
Evans, Chris
Evans, Edward
Evarts, Chris
Evina, Lance

-F-

Facyson, Markis
Faherty, William
Fairchild, Ralph
Falcinelli, Alex
Fallon, Jim
Falussy, Aloysius
Farkas, Andy
Farley, John
Farnham, John
Farrell, Edward
Farrell, Wayne
Fauntleroy, Gary
Fedorchak, John
Fego, Paul
Feitner, William
Felber, Donald
Feller, Daniel
Fenn, Bill
Fennell, James
Fennell, John
Fenstemacher, Albert
Ferrara, Anthony
Ferrughelli, Steve
Fiedler, George
Field, Peter
Figueora, Dave
Fine, Glenn
Finelli, Peter (Mgr.)
Finetti, Mike
Firkser, Boaz
Fischer, Elias
Fischer, Robert
Fisher, Douglas
Fisher, Gary
Fisher, Michael (1)
Fisher, Michael (2)
Fisher, W. A. (Mgr.)

Fisher, Walter
Fithian, Erkuries
Fitz-Randolph, Thomas
Fitzsimmons, Bob (Mgr.)
Flachbarth, Louis
Fladell, Mike
Fleming, Matt
Fleming, Mike
Fletcher, Delrico
Flower, Robert
Flynn, Michael
Foertner, Frederic
Follensbee, Brandley
Forbes, Alex
Forbes, Donald
Forbes, William
Ford, Allen
Forgash, Andrew
Forman, Brian (Mgr.)
Fortay, Bryan
Foster, Eric
Foster, Raymond
Foster, Samuel
Foster, Willie
Fox, Adin
Fox, Edward
Francisco, Kenneth
Francke, Valentine
Francke, William
Frank, Leonard
Frankiewicz, Martin
Fraser, George
Frauenheim, Pierce
Frazier, Anthony
Frederickson, Charles
Freed, Joe
Freedman, Bernard
Freeman, Mark
Freeney, Tarell
Frelinghuysen, John
French, Benjamin
French, Walter
Frentrop, Werner
Freystadt, Everett
Friday, Jerred
Frierson, Quintero
Frothingham, Richard
Fuchs, Carl
Fuller, Howard
Fuller, Perry
Fullman, Michael
Funderburk, Bob
Funderburk, Reggie
Furnari, Joseph

-G-

Gaebele, Andrew
Gagas, Melanie (Film Mgr.)
Gagliardi, Joe
Gallagher, Eugene
Gallin, Lawrence
Gallo, John
Gannon, Robert
Gano, Stephen
Gant, Charles (Mgr.)
Gardner, Ernest
Gardner, Hector
Gardner, Robert
Gardner, William
Garea, Ivan
Garea, Paul
Garefino, Joe
Gargan, Thomas
Garlock, Steve
Garrabrant, John
Garreston, Richard
Garrett, Alfred
Gasienica, Leo
Gates, Charles
Gatt, Charles
Gatyas, William
Gay, William
Geckeler, Tim
Gelman, George
Genkinger, David
Gennarelli, Francis
George, Jeff
George-Shields, Ansel
Gesbocker, Bradford
Getty, George
Getz, Lee
Getzendanner, Jay
Giacobbe, Joe
Giangeruso, Jill (Film Mgr.)
Gibbs, John
Gibbs, Jonathan
Gibson, Aaron
Gibson, Benjamin
Gibson, Gary
Giddings, Rahsaan
Giebelhaus, August
Gies, William
Giesler, Doug
Gilbert, Frank
Giles, Carter
Giles, Dwight
Gilkison, Will
Gillam, Edward (Mgr.)
Gillam, L. G. (Mgr.)
Gilmartin, Mike
Gilmore, Edward
Gimbl, R. J. (Mgr.)
Girault, Ron
Glander, Frederic
Glasier, George
Glass, John
Glassman, Armand
Glatzer, Joseph
Goldberg, Alan
Goldberger, Robert
Goldschmidt, Edward
Goode, E. Trescott
Goodkind, Carol (Mgr.)
Gordon, Allen
Gordon, G. M. (Mgr.)
Gorman, Pat
Gottlieb, Arthur
Gould, Louis
Gould, Scott
Gowen, Isaac
Graham, Ian
Grant, Jason
Grasso, Louis
Gray, Dan
Gray, William
Greaves, A. Michael
Greczyn, Jeff
Green, C. W. (Mgr.)
Green, Harold
Green, Lamont
Green, Ron
Green, Toni (Mgr.)
Green, William
Greenberg, Alan
Greenberg, Benjamin
Greenberg, Gilbert
Greene, Courtney
Greif, Herman
Greif, J. Leonard (Mgr.)
Griffin, David
Griffin, John
Grimes, Eddie
Grimsley, Harvey
Griswold, Elmer
Grogan, Tim
Grossman, Jack
Grossman, Morris
Grote, Jeff
Grower, Louis
Guarantano, James
Guarnera, Jim
Guglielmo, Jerry
Gustin, Paul
Guthrie, John

-H-

Hackett, Jim
Haddow, Hugh, Jr.
Hadrava, Jim
Haegley, Marshall
Hairston, Justise
Halada, Paul
Hall, Ken
Hall, Newton
Hall, Vince
Hambrecht, William
Hampton, Wayne
Hand, Kenneth

Hanf, Lester
Hannis, Randy
Hannoch, F., Jr. (Mgr.)
Hansen, Jeff
Hansen, Leonard
Hanson, Thomas
Haring, Cornelius
Harker, Mahlon
Harley, David
Harmon, Mark
Harper, Steven
Harris, Bertram
Harris, Clark
Harris, Don
Harrison, Robert
Hart, Frederick
Hart, Ryan
Harvey, Paul
Hasbrouck, Albert
Hasbrouck, Gilbert
Hasbrouck, John
Haskins, Jeff
Hatchett, William
Hauser, Percy
Hausner, Frank
Haven, R. C. (Mgr.)
Havran, Steve
Haw, Brandon
Hawxhurst, Daniel
Hazel, Homer
Hazelet, Leilani (Mgr.)
Headley, A. A.
Heath, George E.
Hedgeman, Josh
Hedgeman, Mercer
Heenan, Francis
Heggie, Torrance
Heilman, Don
Heinfelden, Curt
Hemmer, Richard
Henderson, Henry
Hendrickson, Hendrick
Henry, Mario
Herbert, Carl
Herbert, Henry
Herbert, John W.
Hering, Herman
Hering, Robert
Heritage, Harold
Herman, Albert
Hermerda, Louis
Herold, A. J.
Hess, Jeff
Heyd, Edward
Hibbs, Gregg
Hicks, Douglas
Hiecke, George
Higgins, James
Higgins, M. Harold
Higgins, Robert (1)
Higgins, Robert (2)
Highlander, Richard
Hill, Frederick
Hill, Maurice
Hill, Otto
Hill, William (1)
Hill, William (2)
Hilliard, A.
Hines, Maurice
Hinton, Travis
Hipolit, John
Hiros, William
Hirshhorn, Lloyd
Hitchner, Alfred
Hlavach, Steve
Hoare, Thomas
Hobbs, Josh
Hochberg, Eric
Hoeflinger, Anton
Hoffman, Paul (Mgr.)
Hoffman, Steve
Hoffner, Craig
Hogan, Christina (Film Mgr.)
Hohmann, Brian
Hohne, Paul
Hohnstine, Jack
Hoke, Alec
Holland, Andrew
Holmes, Gregory
Holmes, Tom
Holsten, Franklyn
Honeyford, Peter
Hooper, Dwayne
Hoover, Roy
Hopkins, John (Mgr.)
Hopkins, Nelson
Hopper, Thomas
Hopwood, William
Horenle, William
Horn, Stanley
Horner, Jim
Horsford, G. S. (Mgr.)
Horton, Lester
Horvath, Joseph
Hosoda, Toshimasa
Hotaling, Henry
Hotchkiss, Douglass
Hotz, Jack
Hovey, Harold
How, John
Howard, Carl
Howard, Clarence
Howard, Robert
Howell, Darren
Hubbard, Robert
Huber, William (Mgr.)
Hudak, Keith
Hugger, Peter
Hughes, Jim
Hughes, Sarah (Mgr.)
Hults, Willard
Hummel, Charles
Humphreys, Rick
Hunt, Clint
Hunton, Jay
Hurt, John
Hutchinson, Berkeley
Hutton, Chris
Huyler, John
Huyssoon, Peter
Hyman, Corey
Hynes, Joseph
Hynoski, Robert
Hynoski, Walt

-I-

Iannucci, Angelo
Irwin, Joseph
Ito, Jeremy
Ivey, Ralph

-J-

Jackman, Leslie
Jackson, Jamil
Jackson, John
Jackson, Malik
Jackson, Randy
Jahn, Julius
Jefferds, Jerome
Jefferson, Riley
Jeffries, Roger
Jenerette, Ron
Jenkins, George
Jenkins, Henry
Jenkins, James
Jennings, Frank
Jennings, Jim "J. J."
Jeter, Kent (Mgr.)
Johnson, August
Johnson, Bruce
Johnson, C. Stanley
Johnson, Eric
Johnson, Errol
Johnson, Ezra
Johnson, Frederick
Johnson, George
Johnson, Jarvis
Johnson, Joseph (Mgr.)
Johnson, Lester
Johnson, Robert (Mgr.)
Johnson, Sam
Jones, Donald
Jones, Ed
Jones, Joey
Jones, Marcus
Jones, Mark
Jones, Michael
Jones, Nathan

Jordan, Ed
Jovanavic, Paul
Julian, James
Julie, Howard
Julien, Joseph

-**K**-

Kaczorowski, Krzysztof
Kahle, Cornell
Kahle, John
Kahn, Howard (Mgr.)
Kalinger, Roger
Kane, Orlando
Kaplan, Robert
Kaplan, Saul
Karakas, Harry
Karpinski, Jed
Karwacki, Mike
Katchen, Jeffrey (Mgr.)
Kaup, Ken (Mgr.)
Kavulich, Doug
Kearney, Edward
Keating, James
Keating, John
Keating, Tom
Keefe, Stephen
Kehayas, Nicholas
Kehler, Glen
Keller, Henry
Keller, Ron
Kelley, Frank
Kelley, Robert
Kelly, David
Kelly, Thomas
Kemlo, James
Kempson, Norman
Kennedy, Chris
Kennedy, Justin
Kenney, John
Kenney, Ronald
Keough, John
Kieman, James
Kiley, Al
Kinch, Ray
King, Robert
King, Walter
Kingman, William
Kitchen, Zaire
Kizis, Michael
Klein, Leon
Klitchko, Frank
Klosky, Simon
Knabb, George
Knauss, Richard
Knight, Mike
Koar, William
Kocaj, Thomas
Koehler, George (1)
Koehler, George (2)
Kofitsas, Pete
Kokoskie, Doug
Kolstery, Jeff
Koos, Frank
Koprowski, Richard
Kornicki, Peter
Kosup, Bert
Kowalski, Joseph
Kozak, Kory
Kozicky, Myron
Krafchick, Max
Kramer, George
Kramer, Vincent
Krapf, Shirley (Mgr.)
Krasnavage, Paul
Krause, Aaron
Krayer, Keith
Kroll, Alex
Krupka, Dawn (Film Mgr.)
Kubas, Mike
Kuch, Frank
Kucowski, Joe
Kull, Frank
Kurdyla, Jeff
Kurdyla, Kevin
Kushinka, Candy (Mgr.)
Kushinka, Michael
Kutz, John

-**L**-

Labiner, Gerald
Ladley, John
Lamb, George
Lamicella, Pete
Land
Landi, Keith
Lane, Todd
Lang, H. Titus
Langenus, John
Lansing, Howard
Lapkowicz, Vic
LaPrarie, Jacque
LaPrarie, Walter
Large, George
Larkin, Thomas (Mgr.)
Lasher, Winfield
Lassiter, Mark
Latimer, George
Latore, Dan
Laubenheimer, John
Laverty, John
Law, John
Lawes, Ernest
Lawrence, Bruce
Lawrence, Richard
Lee, Glen
Leek, Ralph
Lefferts, D. W. (Mgr.)
Leggett, William
Lentz, August
Leonard, Brian
Leonard, Nate
Leslie, Edwin
Leslie, Jesse
Lester, Tim
Letson, Walt (Mgr.)
Lewendon, J. Scott
Lewis, Chenry
Lewis, Clifford (Mgr.)
Lewis, Paul
Lezdey, John
Libby, William
Liddy, Jack
Liddy, John
Light, Liz (Film Mgr.)
Liguori, Jim
Lilburn, George
Lillis, James
Lincoln, Robert
Linquist, Wallace
Linton, Dimitri
Lipetz, David
Lippman, Robert
Lipscomb, Dwight
Lipsett, Daniel
Liska, Gary
Listori, Brad
Littel, Bloomfield
Loblein, Eldon
Locke, Jason
Lockwood, Henry
Long, Pete (Mgr.)
Loomis, Chris
Lopez, Joseph
Loppacker, Raymond
Lord, John
Lorenz, Herbert
Losee, Harvey
Loud, John
Lovelace, Antoine
Lubin, Rachel (Film Mgr.)
Lucas, Ray
Luderman, Robert
Ludlam, Malcolm
Ludlow, Gabriel
Ludlow, George
Ludlum, Howard
Lufborrow (Mgr.)
Lugossy, Frank
Lukabu, Piana
Lull, Richard
Lummis, William (Mgr.)
Luna, Marcus
Lundwall, Albert
Lusardi, LeRoy
Lusardi, Robert
Luthman, Carol (Mgr.)
Lyall, John
Lydecker, George

Lyman, Robert
Lynn, Gwendolyn
Lyon, Wilson
Lysack, Wesley

-M-

Mabius, Len
MacCauley
MacDonald, Kenneth
MacFarlin, Donald
MacNeil, John
MacNeil, William
Maddalena, Al
Magin, Franklin
Magoo, Quincy
Makarevich, Larry
Maki, Matt (Mgr.)
Malakoski, Jason
Malanga, Gerald
Malast, Kevin
Malekoff, Albert
Malekoff, Andy
Malinak, Roy
Maloney, Francis
Maloney, Jom
Malven, Stephen
Manfred, F.
Mangiero, Dino
Manhoff, Bert
Mann, Arthur
Mann, Oliver
Manning, Sherman
Mannix, Kevin
Mannon, Tom
Mansbach, Howard (Mgr.)
Marcali, Kalman (Mgr.)
Marco, James
Marcus, Paul
Marelli, Henry
Marinkovich, George
Marino, Dave
Mark, Barnard
Marker, Harry
Marks, E. Robert
Marotta, Nick
Marshall, W. B.
Martello, Jim
Martin, Aaron
Martin, Ben
Martin, Bill
Martin, Charles
Martin, Gary
Martin, William
Martinak, Joe
Martine, Abram
Mason, Charles
Mason, D. T. (Mgr.)
Mason, Howard
Mastrolia, Ronald
Mattern, Trent
Matthews, Wayne (Mgr.)
Mattia, Hector
Max, Robert
Maxwell, George
Mayall, Karl
Mayes, Ivan
Mayes, Marty
Maynard, Hiram
Maynard, Oscar
Mayne, Robert
Mazur, Andy
Mazurkiewicz, Agnus (Mgr.)
Mazza, Rich
McAllister, Claude, Jr.
McBroom, Len
McCord, Derek
McCormack, Dennis
McCourty, Devin
McCourty, Jason
McDonald, Marshall "Lee"
McDonald, Sameeh
McDougall, Neil
McGoey, Bill
McGorry, Dennis
McGovern, John
McGuire, Damian
McHarris, Dan
McKanna, A. Gregory
McKee, William
McKelvey, John
McKiernan, Jack
McKnight, William
McKoy, Vaughn
McLaren, George
McLaren, Malcolm
McMahon, Dan
McMahon, Mike
McMahon, William
McManis, Rich
McManus, Eugene
McMichael, Arthur
McMichael, Ed
McNamara, Peter
McQueen, Tyrone
Meddalane, Al
Medley, Ishmael
Meekins, Ramel
Melcon, Jerry
Mele, Joe
Mellor, John
Melly, Kevin
Melrose, John
Melton, Gary
Melusky, Diane (Mgr.)
Mendez, Peter
Mersola, Brett
Meryer, James
Merz, William
Messe, David
Messler, Isaac
Metzger, Roscoe
Metzler, Robert
Michaelson, Stanley
Mike-Mayer, Nick
Milano, William
Milburn, Rich
Milea, Paul
Millard, Jack (Mgr.)
Miller, Alan
Miller, Anthony
Miller, Bruce
Miller, David
Miller, Glenn
Miller, Harold
Miller, John
Miller, Leslie
Miller, Richard
Miller, Scott
Miller, Seaman
Milliken, Peter
Mills, John
Mills, Travis
Mills, William
Miner, D. B. (Mgr.)
Mischwitz, Edmund
Mitchell, Allen
Mitchell, H. Bryant
Mitchell, Jason
Mitchell, Matt
Mitchell, Sheddrick
Mitchell, William (Mgr.)
Mitlehner, Alfred
Mitter, Craig
Moffett, Thomas
Mohn, Otto
Molina, Ulysses (Mgr.)
Monahan, James
Montigney, Bruce
Moody, Mahiri
Moon, Ridgeway
Moore, Antoine
Moore, Bryant
Moore, Jabari
Moore, Ray
Moore, Warner
Morehead, John
Morfoot, G.
Morgan, Walter
Moro, Luis
Morris, Austin
Morris, Frank
Morris, George
Morris, James
Morris, Joseph
Morris, Ralph
Morrison, John
Morrison, Mahlon
Morse, Wayne
Morton, Bob

Moscowitz, David
Moses, Tres
Mosher, Robert
Moultrie, Reggie
Mound, Chuck
Mount, George (Mgr.)
Mount, Wilton
Mozzochi, Donald
Mudie, Charles
Mudie, Sam
Mullen, John
Mullert, Paul
Mullowney, Thomas
Muno, Larry
Murar, Richard
Murphy, J. Harvey
Murphy, John
Murray, Brian
Murray, Norbury
Muschiatti, Lawrence
Myers, William

-**N**-

Naporano, Andrew
Naporano, Anthony
Nash, Robert
Nasholds, William
Naso, Robert
Nathaniel, Thomas
Nave, Glen
Naylor, Frank
Nebb, William
Nedvins, Ernest
Neiley, Nick
Neill, Ryan
Nelson, Milton
Nelson, Oswald
Neumann, William
Neuschafter, Alfred
Nevius, George
Newman, Jeffrey
Nielsen, Craig
Niemyer, John
Nilan, Joseph
Nobel, John
Norris, John
Norton, Robert
Notaro, Gianii
Novak, Richard
Novelli, Leonard
Nugent, Jason
Nutt, Robert

-**O**-

Oake, Roy
Oberlander, Richard
O'Brien, James
Ochs, Robert
O'Connell, Matthew
O'Conner, Kevin
Odell, Tim
Ogden, William
O'Halloran, Jim
O'Hara, Shaun
O'Hearn, John
Ohene, Jason
Oldt, Bob
Oliva, Anthony (Mgr.)
Olsen, Jeff
Olsen, Martin
Omley, Kenneth
Oram, King
Orechio, Carmen
O'Reilly, Tom
Orr, Raheem
Orrizzi, John
Orro, Bobby
Ortiz, Rick
Osinski, Kenneth
Ottley, Howard
Overton, Chalmers
Owen, Arthur
Owens, James
Owens, John
Owens, Maurice
Ozais, Arthur

-**P**-

Pace, George
Pacilio, Errico
Pahls, George
Pahls, Justin
Painter, Dwain
Palumbo, Dave
Pandick, Oakley
Pannucki, Michael
Parigian, Berge
Parisi, Lore Dana (Mgr.)
Parker, J'Vonne
Parker, William
Parkins, Phil
Parsons, Ralph
Parsons, Robert
Pasternack, Fred
Patkochis, Scott
Patterson, William
Pattison, Charles
Paugh, Charles
Paulson, Jon
Pawlik, Tony
Peacock, Richard
Pearch, James
Pease, Fran
Pellington, William
Pellowski, Michael
Pendergrass, Boris
Peneck, Richard
Penn, Robert
Pennucci, Joe
Penyak, Mike
Pergolizzi, Mike
Pernetti, Tim
Perry, Arthur
Perry, Marcus
Perseley, George (Mgr.)
Person, Leonard
Pesce, John
Peterson, Alfred
Petko, Thomas
Petruzzi, Anthony (Film Mgr.)
Pettit, Robert (1)
Pettit, Robert (2)
Pfabe, Dan
Pfeiffer, Richard
Pfirman, Steve
Phelps, Apollos
Phillips, Kemar (Mgr.)
Piccirillo, John
Pickel, Christopher
Pickel, George
Pickel, James
Pickel, William
Picketts, Sam
Piegaro, Dominick
Pierce, Carlton
Pierce, James
Pilch, Ray
Pineiro, Mark
Pitt, Sherman
Pittman, Clarence
Pitts, Tyrone
Plevinsky, Morris
Poad, Ritchie
Polack, J. O. (Mgr.)
Poland, Norman
Poland, Rufus
Policastro, Richard
Polidoro, Joseph
Pollard, Roger
Pollock, John
Poole, Charles
Pooley, David
Porter, Joe
Porter, John (Mgr.)
Ports, George
Post, John, Jr.
Potter, Ellis
Potzer, Emil
Powell, William
Pregnolato, John
Preletz, Joseph
Prescott, Matt
Presley, Bruce
Price, Arthur
Price, Keith
Price, Kim (Film Mgr.)
Price, William

Pridgeon, Michael
Prigger, John
Pringle, Wallace
Prisco, Nicholas
Provillon, Fatimah (Mgr.)
Pruyn, Charles
Pryor, Henry
Puaauli, Iosefa
Puelo, Henry
Pulley, Bill
Pumyea, Isaac
Pyszczymuka, Greg
Pyszczymuka, Marty

-**Q**-

Quaye, Chris

-**R**-

Rabuck, John
Radigan, Joe
Raffaelli, Gregory
Rafferty, Joe
Raftery, Bryan
Randel, Francis
Randolph, Thomas
Ranieri, George
Ranney, William
Ranson, Alonzo
Raphel, Jerome
Rapolje, Ernest
Ratti, Ford
Raub, Howard
Ray, Albert
Ray, Tony
Raymond, Andrew
Rayner, Albert
Razey, Phillip
Read, Earl
Read, Frederick
Rebholz, Jeff
Redman, Robert
Redmond, Herbert
Redmond, Mortimer
Redmond, Phillip
Rees, Athol
Reeser, Douglas
Regan, William
Reid, Eric
Reid, Greg
Reiger, Bela
Reiley, DeWitt
Remy, Nkosi
Rendall, Kenneth
Renkart, Brandon
Renna, Eugene
Renshaw, James
Renshaw, Richard
Resh, Gary (Mgr.)
Resnick, Irving
Rhines, Sidney
Rice, Ray
Rice, Richard
Richardson, Charles
Richardson, Rashied
Richmond, H.
Ricks, Rashawn
Riddick, Tosh
Riesett, Donald
Rigole, Anthony
Rinehimer, Dave
Ring, Rob
Rivas, Luis
Rivers, Paul
Roberson, Derrick
Roberts, Christopher
Roberts, Edwin
Roberts, Marshall
Roberts, Michael
Roberts, Thomas
Robertson, Larry
Robertson, Wesley
Robeson, Paul
Robinson, Arthur
Robinson, George
Robinson, Jermaine
Robinson, Nate
Rockafeller, Claudius
Rockafeller, Eugene
Rockafeller, Harry
Rockwell, Bruce
Rogers, Charles (1)
Rogers, Charles (2)
Rogers, DeWitt
Rogers, Ferdinand
Rogers, Jim
Roll, William
Rollins, Frederick
Rolph, Arthur
Root, Leon
Rosen, Stanley
Rosenberg, Harold
Rosenow, Jason
Ross, Donald
Ross, Edwin
Ross, Gil
Ross, Julian
Rossmango, Nicole (Film Mgr.)
Rowe, John (Mgr.)
Ruch, Kenneth
Rudanovic, Milan
Rudanovic, Mitar
Ruddy, George
Rudinski, Wayne
Ruger, John (Mgr.)
Ruggieri, Tony (Mgr.)
Rumney, Richard
Runyon, Ralph
Ruroede, Glen
Russo, Ralph
Russum, Frank
Rustemeyer, Mike
Rutgers, Henry
Rutkowski, Bron
Rutkowski, Roman
Ryno, Corydon

-**S**-

Sabo, John
Sabo, Ronald
Sacca, Ralph
Sadloch, Michelle (Film Mgr.)
Sadowski, Mike
Safford, Daniel
Sagnella, Anthony
Salau, Ruth Ann (Mgr.)
Salek, Jerrold
Salemi, Jack
Salter, Brian (Mgr.)
Saltsman, G. (Mgr.)
Sandblom, Russell
Sands, Ryan
Sandy, Mike
Santarpio, Mike
Sarna, Guy
Sauter, Nick
Savidge, Peter
Savino, Peter
Savoy, Joseph
Savoye, Richard
Saxe, Ray (Mgr.)
Saxton, Donald
Scaliotta, Joseph
Scarr, Francis
Schaffle, Albert
Schank, Harold
Schedeneck, Jim
Scherr, Tom (Mgr.)
Schlick, John (Mgr.)
Schlick, Volney
Schmid, Alan
Schmidt, John
Schmidt, Ralph
Schmidt, William
Schneider, Lee
Schomp, William
Schoomaker, Oliver
Schottinger, John
Schroeder, Rob
Schuck, John
Schults, Wm. (Mgr.)
Schutte, Bob
Schwartz, Edward
Schwedo, Donald
Schwenk, Chad
Schwenker, Carl
Sclafani, Carmen
Scott, James

Scudder, Charles
Scudder, Clarence
Scudder, Dana
Scudder, Henry
Scudder, Jared
Scudder, Joe (Mgr.)
Scudder, John
Scudder, Myron
Scudder, Walter
Seabrooks, Shawn
Seaman, Lloyd
Searle, Robert
Seddon, Jon
See, William
Seeger, Robert
Segaloff, Mark
Seger, Mark
Segoine, H. Richard
Seiler, Ralph
Sellari, Don
Senft, Les
Senko, Steve
Sertick, Jerry
Sexton, J. R. (Mgr.)
Shak, Neg (Mgr.)
Sharp, Nugent
Shea, Garrett
Shedden, James
Sheremetta, Nick
Sherengos, William
Sheridan, Brian
Sherman, Lee
Sherrerd, John (Mgr.)
Shutte, Bob
Shycko, Ron
Sica, Jason
Siciliano, Dante
Sickles, Harry
Sigler, Herbert
Simek, Steve
Simms, Frederick
Simms, Robert
Simms, Stephen
Simon, Franklin (Mgr.)
Simone, Donald
Simone, Ronald
Simonelli, Tony
Simonson, Robert
Simpkins, Hillyer
Sims, Herndon
Sinclair, Kevin
Singer, Austin
Sipos, Dale
Sivess, Andy
Sivess, Greg
Slee, John
Sliker, Lawrence
Slovan, Jared
Smirnow, Martin
Smith, Albert
Smith, Arthur
Smith, Cyrus
Smith, George
Smith, Howard
Smith, James
Smith, Jerry
Smith, Ken
Smith, L. J.
Smith, Lewis
Smith, Marc (Mgr.)
Smith, Ralph
Smith, Randy
Smith, Richard (Mgr.)
Smith, Rudy
Smith, Russ (Mgr.)
Smith, Shaun
Smith, William
Smolyn, Gary
Smoyer, Thomas
Sneathen, Bob
Snyder, Brett
Snyder, Louis
Sosa, Pedro
Sowick, Fred
Sparks, William
Spaulding, Bruce
Speidel, Robert
Spells, Shane
Spencer, Scott
Speranza, William
Spitzer, Kevin
Spitzer, Mike
Spitzer, Rich
Spizzo, T. J.
Spray, Herbert
Staats, Peter
Stager, Walter
Stalker, William
Stanowicz, Steven
Stanton, Seth
Staples, Parker
Stapleton, Darnell
Startzell, Kennan
Stasiak, Walter
Steele, Charles
Stegeman, W.
Stegmann, Ralf
Steinke, Rudolph
Stephans, Mike
Stephens, Curtis
Stephens, Reggie
Stephenson, Cameron
Stevens, George
Steward, Ed
Steward, Fritz
Stewart, George
Stewart, Jon
Stewart, Wm., Jr.
Stillman, A. L. (Mgr.)
Stites, Robert
Stitik, Paul
Stohrer, Robert
Stoll, Chris
Stonebraker, Robert
Storck, Donald
Stotesbury, Louis
Stout, David
Stowe, Raymond
Stowe, Tyronne
Strang, Clifford
Strasburger, Paul (Mgr.)
Strelick, Paul
Strickland, Douglas
Strickland, William
Stringer, David
Strohmeyer, Dax
Stryker, Edgar
Strys, John
Studivant, Vantrise
Sullivan, Mike
Sullivan, Theresa (Mgr.)
Summerhill, John
Surlis, Timothy
Sutton, John
Swartz, Rusty
Swayne, Harry
Sweel, John
Sweeney, Andrew
Sweeney, John
Sweeney, Tom
Sweetman, Ch. (Mgr.)
Swinger, Rashod
Szot, Alex
Szydiowski, Cathy (Mgr.)

-T-

Taigia, James
Tait, Harold
Tait, John
Talan, Walter
Talbot, Arthur
Talman, Howard
Tango, Tony
Tanribilir, Steve
Tappen, Tom
Tarcher, Leonard
Tardy, Steve
Tarver, Tom
Taylor, Brian
Taylor, Jim (Mgr.)
Taylor, Linwood
Teatom, Jim
Teel, Mike
Tepper, Louis
Terhune, Clarence
Ternyila, Jeff
Terrill, C. Hoyt
Terry, Dawn (Mgr.)
Tharp, Reuben, Jr.

Theokas, Michael
Thomas, Dennis
Thomas, William
Thompson, Art
Thompson, Devraun
Thompson, DeWayne
Thompson, Elias
Thompson, John
Thompson, Peter
Thompson, Wayne
Thompson, William (1)
Thompson, William (2)
Throop, Frank
Throup, Tim
Tierney, Michael
Tighe, Andy
Tillotson, Bob
Tinney, Gary
Titsworth, Arthur
Titus, Charlie
Tobish, Theodore
Todd, Harvey
Todd, Ralph
Tomaini, Darlene (Mgr.)
Tomkins, Steven
Toohey, John
Toran, Nate
Torrey, James
Townley, David
Townsend, James
Tracy, George
Tranavitch, William
Traver, Charles
Tremper, Henry
Tribitt, Curtis
Triggs, Francis
Troup, Harry
Truex, Arnold
Trump, Ted
Tucker, Shawn
Tulloch, Billy
Tully, William
Turner, Sam
Turso, Louis
Tverdov, Pete
Twamley, Steve
Twing, Wainwright
Twitchell, Albert
Twitty, Mark

-**U**-

Udovich, Clement
Udovich, Patrick
Underwood, Tiquan
Updike, Harold
Urbanick, Joseph
Urda, Nicholas
Utz, Vincent

-**V**-

Valentine, Roy
Van Aken, Alexander
Van Brackle, Henry
Van Der Noot, George
Van DeVenter, John
Van Duzer, George
Van Dyck, Francis
Van Dyck, William, Jr.
Van Fleet, Jacob
Van Hee, Isaac
Van Hoevenberg, H.
Van Mater, Daniel
Van Ness, Bruce
Van Neste, John
Van Orden, Percival
Van Sickle, Russell
Van Slyke, Warren
Van Winkle, Isaac
Van Winkle, Stephen
Van Winkle, Theodore
Van Winkle, Thomas
Van Winkle, Winant
Van Zandt, William
Van Zee, Charles
Varju, Joseph
Vaughan, William
Vaughn, Scott
Venezia, Frank
Verbitski, John (1)
Verbitski, John (2)
Verduzco, Perris
Veth, George
Viggiano, Donald
Vigh, William
Vinet, Pierre
Vitolo, Tom
Voelker, Otto
Vogt, Will
Vohden, Raymond
Volker, Frederick
Volpe, Mike
VonBischoffshausen, R.
Von Glahn, Clarence
Voorhees, Charles
Voorhees, Garrett
Voorhees, Ralph
Vorhees, Nathaniel
Vrelland, Stephen

-**W**-

Wackar, Richard
Waggoner, Elon
Wagman, Richard
Wagner, Rich
Waite, Carl
Walbrook, Reynold
Waldron, John
Walker, Ed
Wallace, James
Wallace, John
Wallace, William
Wallach, Howard
Walling, Jon
Walser, H. (Mgr.)
Walser, Oliver
Walsh, Larry
Walter, Andrew
Walters, John
Ward, Chester
Ward, Derek
Ward, William
Ware, Kerry
Warner, Ronald
Washington, Chris
Washington, Elvin
Washington, Ibrihim
Washington, John
Washington, Lionel
Washington, Mark
Washington, Matt
Washington, Sean
Watson, Ripley
Watson, Russell
Watson, William
Watson, William (Mgr.)
Watts, Gary
Weaver, Elmer
Webb, Richard
Weber, Garth
Webster, Bruce
Webster, Elnardo
Weiner, Charles
Weingarten, Milton
Weiss, Steve (Mgr.)
Weller, Samuel
Welsh
Wermuth, Charles
Westcott, Chester
Westerman, Jamaal
Wetherbee, Jeff (Mgr.)
Whalen, Robert
Wheat, Howard
Whitacre, William
White, Dexer
White, Ralph
White, Shabib
Whitehead, William
Whitehill, John
Whitenack, Erastmus
Wilcox, Douglass (Mgr.)
Wiley, Albert
Wiley, Charles
Wilkes, Willie
Williams, Earl
Williams, Ira
Williams, Jerome
Williams, Kareem

Williams, Kevin
Williams, Roger
Williams, Shawn
Williams, Vernon
Williamson, Douwe
Williamson, Mike
Willis, Terrell
Willits, George
Wills, John
Wilson, Bilal
Wilson, Bryan
Wilson, George
Wilusz, Bob
Wingate, Roger
Winika, Walter
Winika, Wilho
Winkelreid, Irwin
Winner, John
Wirth, John (1)
Wirth, John (2)
Witkowski, John
Wittpenn, John
Wittpenn, John (Mgr.)
Woetzel, Keith
Wolff, William
Womack, Jeremy
Wood, Brandon
Woodard, Billy
Woodard, Dan
Woodruff, Graham
Woodward, Kelly
Woolridge, Charles
Wright, Charles
Wright, Richard
Wright, Richard A.
Wright, Tom
Wurtz, William
Wyckoff, Herbert
Wyckoff, John
Wycoff, William
Wygant, Robert
Wyman, Theodore
Wynkoo, Asa

-Y-

Yacaginsky, Joe
Yaksick, Bob
Yancheff, Mike
Yanowitz, Brandon
Yates, Andre
Yates, Keith
Yeager, Bryan
Young, Derek L. (Mgr.)
Young, Eric
Young, Frank (Mgr.)
Young, George
Young, Harold
Young, Kordell

-Z-

Zack, Dee Dee (Mgr.)
Zdobylak, Andy
Zelenky, John
Ziegler, James
Zieniuk, Bob
Zimmerman, Dave
Zimmerman, Peter
Zimmerman, Robert
Zingg, Wherry
Zoller, Anton
Zukas, Frank
Zukaukas, Charles
Zurich, James
Zuttah, Jeremy

List compiled based on Rutgers Athletic Communications' media guides and lettermens' list, in addition to the lettermens' list in Larry Pitt's *Football at Rutgers: A History, 1869–1969*.

BIBLIOGRAPHY

Brown, Gene, editor. *The New York Times Encyclopedia of Sports: Vol. 1, Football*. Connecticut: Grolier Educational Corp./Arno Press, 1979.

ESPN Sports Almanac 2004. New York: Hyperion ESPN Books, 2003.

Herzog, Brad. *The Sports 100*. New York: Simon & Schuster/Macmillan, 1995.

Hickok, Ralph. *Sports Champions*. New York/Boston: Houghton Mifflin, 1995.

Jennison, W. Keith, editor. *The Concise Encyclopedia of Sports*. New York: Franklin Watts, 1970.

Keith, Harold. *Sports and Games*. New York: Thomas Y. Crowell & Sons, 1960.

Maule, Tex. *The Game: The Official Picture History of the NFL and AFL*. New York: Random House, 1968.

Meserole, Mike, editor. *Information Please Sports Almanac*. Boston: Houghton Mifflin, 1996.

Miers, Earl Schenck. *Football*. New York: Grosset & Dunlap, 1972.

Mullin, Willard, editor. *The Junior Illustrated Encyclopedia of Sports*. New York: Bobbs-Merrill, 1966.

Official NFL 1996 Record and Fact Book. New York: Workman, 1996.

Oshin, Louis. *A Handy Football Library*. New York: Blue Ribbon Books, 1949.

Pellowski, Michael J. *Football's Wackiest Moments*. New York: Sterling, 1998.

———. *The Great Football Question and Answer Book*. New York: Moby Books, Waldman, 1982.

———. *Little Giant Book of Football Facts*. New York: Sterling, 2005.

———. *Not So Great Moments in Sports*. New York: Sterling, 1994.

Pitt, Larry. *Football at Rutgers: A History, 1869–1969*. College Football Centennial Committee, 1972.

Sports Illustrated Sports Almanac 2000. New York: Time, 1999.

Terzian, Jim. *New York Giants*. New York: Macmillan, 1973.

Treat, Roger. *The Encyclopedia of Football, 12th Edition*. New York: A. S. Barnes, 1974.

Weyand, Alexander M. *Football Immortals*. New York: Macmillan, 1962.

World Almanac and Book of Facts 1980. New York: Newspaper Enterprise Association, 1980.

INDEX

Note: Page numbers in **boldface** type indicate photographs or other illustrations.

Rutgers football players listed under headings delineating special recognition or awards are also listed alphabetically by last name.

About the Author

Michael J. Pellowski was born in New Brunswick, New Jersey, on January 24, 1949. He won numerous sports awards at Franklin High School in New Jersey and accepted a Barr football scholarship to Rutgers, the State University of New Jersey. As a Scarlet Knight, he won two freshman letters and five varsity letters in football and baseball. Pellowski was defensive captain of the 1970 team and had pro trials in the NFL and CFL after graduating from Rutgers College with a degree in education. His full-time writing career began in 1975, and he has published more than 100 sports, humor, and children's books under the pen names Ski Michaels, Morgan Matthews, and Melanie Morgan. He is married to his former high-school sweetheart, Judy Snyder Pellowski, and the couple has four children, Morgan, Matthew, Melanie, and Martin.